Dedication

To Tom Winnett, who gave me the chance of a lifetime and who has bravely endured the consequences, which include having to expertly edit the resulting manuscripts. Thank you. (Tom Winnett is the Publisher Emeritus of Wilderness Press.)

A hiker savors a refreshing splash in the sun-dappled pool at Manoa Falls (Trip 16)

Oahu Trails

Walks, Strolls and Treks on the Capital Isle

Kathy Morey

WILDERNESS PRESS
BERKELEY

Oahu Trails

1st EDITION January 1993
2nd EDITION March 1999
2nd printing January 2002
3rd printing January 2003
4th printing August 2004

Copyright © 1993, 1999 by Kathy Morey

Front cover photos copyright © 1999 by David Muench
Interior photos by the author, except as noted
Maps: Kathy Morey
Cover design: Larry B. Van Dyke
Book design: Thomas Winnett and Kathy Morey

Library of Congress Card Number 99-24824
ISBN 0-89997-245-4
UPC 7-19609-97245-7

Manufactured in the United States of America

Published by: **Wilderness Press**
1200 5th Street
Berkeley, CA 94710
(800) 443-7227; FAX (510) 558-1696
info@wildernesspress.com
www.wildernesspress.com

Visit our website for a complete listing of our books and ordering information.

Cover photos: Nuuanu Pali, Koolau Range *(large photo)*;
Mokapuu Beach and Rabbit Island *(inset photo)*

SAFETY NOTICE: Although Wilderness Press and the author have made every attempt to ensure that the information in this book is accurate at press time, they are not responsible for any loss, damage, injury, or inconvenience that may occur to anyone while using this book. You are responsible for your own safety and health while in the wilderness. The fact that a trail is described in this book does not mean that it will be safe for you. Be aware that trail conditions can change from day to day. Always check local conditions and know your own limitations.

Library of Congress Cataloging-in-Publication Data
Morey, Kathy.
    Oahu trails : walks, strolls, and treks on the Capital Isle /
Kathy Morey. -- 2nd ed.
        p.   cm.
    Includes bibliographical references (p.) and index.
    ISBN 0-89997-245-4 (alk. paper)
    1. Hiking--Hawaii--Oahu Island Guidebooks. 2. Oahu (Hawaii)
Guidebooks. I. Title.
GV199.42.H320145 1999
919.69'3--dc21   99-24824
                                                        CIP

Contents

View from the Maunawili Demonstration Trail (Trip 29) of Mt. Olomana on windward Oahu

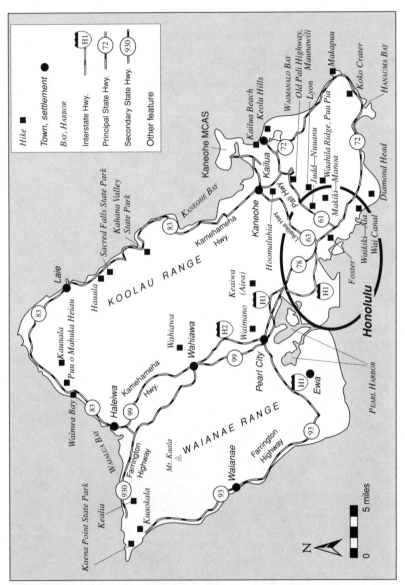

Oahu: Overview of Principal Hiking Areas

Introduction

"The Surprising Isle"—that's what I'd call Oahu. Or perhaps "The Contradictory Isle." Sprawled across the southeast corner of Oahu is Honolulu, a spaghetti-like tangle of traffic-jammed streets reminiscent of any mainland metropolitan downtown area. Honolulu is about commerce, not about pleasure! Its Waikiki district is a maze of crowd-choked streets deep in the canyons formed by one sky-scraping hotel after another. (Yes, there is still a beach in there—see Trip 32.) Almost half the population of the state of Hawaii weighs down this one corner of Oahu.

Yet even in the midst of that urban turmoil, you'll find quiet walks along canals and through gardens. Inland toward the mountains behind the city, within a few blocks of all its busy-ness, there are miles of fine hiking trails that offer pure delight.

And there is much more to Oahu than Honolulu. Driving along the northeast (windward) side of Oahu and its North Shore, you enjoy breathtaking views of knife-edge cliffs inland, their vertical drop thinly disguised by thick green vegetation here, exposed as stark gray stone there. Seaward, one magnificent beach or bay follows another for mile after mile, the sweep of the coast only occasionally interrupted by a tiny commu-

Along a trail high above Honolulu, branches frame Diamond Head and Waikiki's highrises

nity. Some of the world's most famous surfing spots are here: the Banzai
Pipeline, Waimea, Sunset Beach. . . .During the warm season, gray veils of
rain sweep across the land from time to time; this *is* the rainy side. During
the winter, storms pound the North Shore, raising killer waves and even
closing the highway. Except for the towns of Kailua and Kaneohe, this
side of Oahu seems almost empty. Hiking trails beckon you to explore the
inland rainforest. Miles-long stretches of lightly used beaches with sand
as fine as powder invite you to sun, stroll, and swim.

On the west and south (leeward) sides, once you escape Honolulu
and reach the coast near Nanakuli, the panorama of beach and cliff is
just as striking and nearly as empty. The drier climate here leaves the
coast clad not in rainforest but in scrub, soft and gray-green at a distance, scratchy and impenetrable close-up. Few public trails penetrate
this region, but at the westernmost end of it at Kaena Point, you'll find
a rewarding wilderness-hiking experience unlike any other on Oahu.

Resist the temptation to confine your visit to Waikiki. There really are other places to stay on Oahu. No matter where you stay, get out
of your hotel and savor Oahu firsthand. That's where the best of Oahu
is! The island has splendid dayhiking, though no backpacking to speak
of. There are urban walks through gardens with spectacularly strange
plants; trails where you'll find the rare fragrant white hibiscus native
only to Hawaii; trails that lead to cool swimming holes on tropical
streams; trails where the sheer exuberance of tropical growth and the
richly varied music of birds inspire awe; and trails that offer spectacular views—even overbuilt Honolulu is spectacular from such a vantage
point. How do I know? I walked every trail that's used as a trip in this
book at least once, many more often.

The shape of things. Viewed on a map, Oahu is shaped like a
lumpy trapezoid whose "left" (west) side is far shorter than its "right"
(east) side. It's made up of two extinct volcanoes whose original shapes
must have been much more oval than circular. Now, all that's left is
one long wall of each volcano and the plateau that formed between
them. The remnant of the older volcano, looking like a short chain of
mountains, is called the Waianae Range and it defines the shorter west
side of the island. The volcano's crater probably lay where the Lualualei
and Waianae valleys are now. The remnant of the younger volcano,
looking like a long chain of mountains, is called the Koolau Range and
it defines the longer northeast side of the island. Its crater lay near
present-day Kaneohe and Kailua. When they were both younger, material from the Koolau volcano built up against the Waianae volcano to
form the inland plain between them, the Schofield Plateau.

Oahu was never politically dominant in old Hawaii. Hawaii and

Maui were far more important then. Today's Oahu owes its preeminence to a unique feature on its south ("bottom") edge: the three deep lochs of Pearl Harbor, one of the Pacific's finest harbors. The lochs are actually river valleys, gouged out when the sea level was much lower during the last Ice Age. They subsequently drowned when the world warmed, the great ice sheets melted, and sea level rose. Native Hawaiian canoes needed no such harbor, but European ships did. As Europeans and their trade came to dominate Hawaii's everyday life, Hawaii's political and economic life shifted to Oahu and Pearl Harbor.

Take time for Oahu. It's bigger and far more interesting than you may think at first. You can't drive all the way around Oahu on coastal roads because the westernmost point, Kaena Point, is closed to vehicles. Few roads cross the mountain ranges, and those that cross the Waianae Range are closed to the general public. Road conditions and traffic around Honolulu (and even Kaneohe and Kailua during rush hour) will slow you down, too. Plan to spend several days exploring Oahu, either by rental car or by Oahu's excellent public bus system ("TheBus").

Be a good visitor. Hawaii is not Paradise. Paradise is infinite and self-renewing. Hawaii, and particularly Oahu, is a real place of finite space and resources, where real people live real lives with jobs, families, budgets, and bills. Hawaii needs loving care from its visitors as well as from its natives—especially on overdeveloped, overused Oahu. As the number of tourists increases, I think it becomes important that we visitors actively contribute to the *aloha* spirit instead of just passively expecting to receive it. Bring your best manners and your patience with you to Oahu. Be patient with the many traffic obstacles. Be the first to smile and wave. Be the first to pull your car over so that someone else can pass. Be scrupulous in observing the rules of the trail in order to help preserve what's left of Oahu's few open spaces. NO TRESPASSING, KEEP OUT, or KAPU ("forbidden") signs mean, "You stay out." Please respect those signs.

A few words for the second edition. . . .

I've incorporated two new trips and updated a number of existing ones. There are numerous new photos that enliven these pages and better illustrate the beautiful Hawaiian landscape for you.

I've redone all the maps, and I think those of you who've used the first edition will find the maps much improved. On many maps I eliminated needless and distracting detail and focused the map more closely on the area of interest. Maps that were spread across two pages are now on one page. Some maps now have irregular shapes and are tilted at angles to fit on the page, and I think you'll find them easier to use.

Getting Information About Oahu

The search for the perfect trail guide. I wish I could be certain this was a flawless book. However, some things limit an author's ability to produce a perfect, error-free, always up-to-date book. Here are some of the factors, and what you can do to help yourself (and me).

Nature makes constant revisions; so do agencies and landowners. Nature constantly reshapes the landscape across which we plan to trek. It's usually a gradual process, but once in a while she makes drastic changes overnight. A landslide, a volcanic eruption, or a hurricane can erase a trail in seconds. Erosion can undercut a cliff edge and make last year's safe hike an extremely dangerous one, so that the local authorities close a trail you'd hoped to ramble on. And Hawaii's fragile volcanic terrain erodes quite rapidly.

Agencies in charge of hiking areas may close an area because they've realized it's environmentally too sensitive to withstand more human visits. An area once open to overnight camping may become a day-use-only area. Trails become impassable from lack of maintenance. Happily, agencies may open new areas because they've been able to acquire new acreage or complete a trail-building project.

Landowners change; so does land usage. A landowner who has not previously objected to public use of a trail on his land may change his mind or sell to someone else who posts it off-limits. Development may cut off public access to a trail. Or a reexamination of boundaries may reveal that a trail long thought to be on public land is in fact on private property, and the trail may be closed off and abandoned.

Change is the only thing that's constant in this world, so that guidebook authors and publishers always play "catch up" with Nature and with agencies. We want to keep the guidebooks up to date, but we are always at least one step behind the latest changes. The day when you'll have constantly revised books on-line at your wristwatch/computer terminal isn't here yet. So it's possible that a few trail descriptions are becoming obsolete even as this book goes to press.

Get the latest official information. It's a good idea to use this book in conjunction with the latest information from the agency in charge of the areas you plan to hike in. The principal statewide agency in charge of areas that offer hiking opportunities is the Department of Land and Natural Resources (DLNR), particularly two of its subordinate branches: the Division of Forestry and Wildlife and the Division of State Parks. Each of these branches has a subdistrict for each island.

Division of Forestry and Wildlife. The district branches of the Division of Forestry and Wildlife for the other three major Hawaiian islands each offer a pamphlet that summarizes hunting and hiking opportunities in the areas under that district's control. This map lets you know what hiking trails currently exist and where they are, although it lacks the details a hiker needs. Unfortuntately, the Oahu District does not have such a map as of this writing (spring of 1992). One person in their office told me they had been trying to revise the Oahu map for several years, but. . . .They do have a number of maps (Xeroxed copies of marked parts of topographic maps) that they hand out if you come down to their office to pick them up. These maps show the trails and, on the back, tell you about them.

You will need to go in person to get permits for some of the hiking trails (see the individual trips for permit information). The address of the Oahu District of the Division of Forestry and Wildlife is in this book in the chapter "Getting Permits and Permission."

Division of State Parks. In response to a written request, the Division of State Parks sends out a standard state-wide map that summarizes state-park recreational opportunities on all the islands, including hiking. This is a very useful publication, but it has very little map or trail information. The address of the Oahu District of the Division of State Parks is in this book in the chapter "Getting Permits and Permission."

For those reasons, this book gives you a far more complete and detailed picture of Oahu's principal hiking opportunities than the Oahu District's non-existent Division of Forestry and Wildlife recreation map or the Division of State Parks recreation map. And it describes those opportunities from a hiker's perspective.

Prepare yourself with general information, too. A generous source of a wide variety of useful information about Hawaii is the Hawaii Visitors Bureau. Here are the addresses of their offices on the mainland:

Canada: 205-1624 56th St., Delta, B.C. V4L 2B1, Canada

Chicago: 180 North Michigan Avenue, Suite 1031, Chicago, IL 60601

Los Angeles: Central Plaza, 3440 Wilshire Boulevard, Room 502, Los Angeles, CA 90010

New York: 441 Lexington Avenue, Suite 1003, New York, NY 10017

San Francisco: 50 California Street, Suite 450, San Francisco, CA 94111

Washington, D.C.: 1511 K Street N.W., Suite 519, Washington, D.C., 20005

A letter to them will get you a fat packet full of all kinds of handy information.

Check out the following Web sites and their links, too:

Hawaii Visitors Bureau sites: www.visit.hawaii.org, www.gohawaii.com

Hawaii State Government offices: www.hawaii.gov

Department of Land and Natural Resources (DLNR): www.hawaii.gov/dlnr/

DLNR, Division of Forestry: www.hawaii.gov/dlnr/dfw/dfw.html

DLNR, Division of State Parks: www.hawaii.gov/dlnr/dsp/dsp.html

State Tourism Office: www.hawaii.gov/tourism/index.html

Great Outdoors Recreation Pages (GORP): www.gorp.com—lots of info as well as an on-line bookstore

Let me know what you think and what you find. I hope this book helps make your visit to Hawaii even more enjoyable than it would have been. I plan to update it regularly, and you can help me. Let me know what you think of it. Did you find it helpful when you visited Oahu? Was it accurate and complete enough that you enjoyed the walks and hikes you took based on the book? Did you notice any significant discrepancies between this book and what you found when you visited Oahu, discrepancies that you judge are not just the result of two different perceptions of the same thing? What were they? The publisher and I are very concerned about accuracy. We'd appreciate your comments. I'd also like to know about it if you think there are ways in which the book can be improved. Write to me in care of Wilderness Press, 1200 5th Street, Berkeley, CA 94710.

Ready for a break from hiking? Try exploring the tidepools on Oahu's beautiful North Shore

Spoken Hawaiian: An Incomplete and Unauthoritative Guide

What, only 12 letters?! Nineteenth-century American missionaries used only 12 letters to create a written version of the spoken Hawaiian language. Superficially, that might make Hawaiian seem simple. But Hawaiian is a much more complex and subtle language than 12 letters can do justice to. However, we're stuck with those 12 letters—the five English vowels (a, e, i, o, u) and seven of the consonants (h, k, l, m, n, p, w).

Consonants. The consonants have the same sound in Hawaiian as they do in your everyday English except for "w." "W" is sometimes pronounced as "v" when it follows "a," always pronounced as "v" when it follows "e" or "i."

Vowels. The vowels are generally pronounced as they are in Italian, with each vowel sounded separately. Authentic Hawaiian makes further distinctions, but those are of more interest to scholars than to hikers.[1] The following is a simplified system. Vowel sounds in general are:

a   like "ah" in "*Ah!*"
e   like "ay" in "d*ay*."
i   like "ee" as in "wh*ee*!"
o   like "o" in "g*o*."
u   like "oo" in "f*oo*d" (or "u" in "r*u*de").

Notice that that means that when you see two or more of the same letter in a row, you pronounce each of them separately:

"Kaaawa" is Ka-a-a-wa
"Heeia" is He-e-i-a
"Molii" is Mo-li-i
"Hoomaluhia" is Ho-o-ma-lu-hi-a
"Nuuanu" is Nu-u-a-nu.

---

[1] Remember that Hawaiian evolved as a spoken, not a written, language. Authentic *written* Hawaiian uses two special marks to indicate other variations on pronouncing vowels in *spoken* Hawaiian. Those variations change the meaning of a word. One is the glottal stop, indicated by a single quotation mark ('). It indicates that you should make a complete break in your voice before sounding the vowel that follows it. There really isn't an English equivalent, though the break in "uh-oh!" is close. Another is the macron mark, which is a straight line over a vowel. It indicates that you should pronounce a vowel as a long sound instead of a short sound. For example, the Hawaiian long-a sound is "ah," and the Hawaiian short-a sound is "uh." We have the same sounds in English but don't use special marks to distinguish between them except in dictionaries. Topographic maps and this book don't use glottal stops or macron marks. (Unlike their counterparts on the Neighbor Islands, however, many street signs on Oahu use glottal stops and macron marks.)

That seems *too* simple, and it is. If you tried to pronounce every vowel, speaking Hawaiian would turn into a nightmare. You wouldn't live long enough to pronounce some words. Fortunately, several pairs of vowels often—but not always—form merged sounds.

Vowel Pairs Whose Sounds Merge. Like every other language, Hawaiian has vowel pairs whose sounds naturally "smooth" into each other. They're similar to Italian or English diphthongs. The degree to which the two sounds are merged in Hawaiian is officially less than occurs in English, but most Hawaiian people I've talked with merge them fully. Vowel-pair pronunciation is approximately:

ae   often smoothed to "eye" as in "<u>eye</u>ful" or "i" in "<u>i</u>ce"
ai   often smoothed as for "ae," above
ao   often smoothed to sound like "ow" in "c<u>ow</u>
au   often smoothed to "ow" in "c<u>ow</u>", too
ei   sometimes smoothed to "ay" as in "da<u>y</u>
eu   smooth the sounds together a little, like "ayoo"
oi   usually like "oi" in "<u>oil</u>"— just what you're used to
ou   often smoothed to "oh," the long-o sound

Syllables. Every Hawaiian syllable ends in a vowel sound. A Hawaiian syllable never contains more than one consonant. That means every consonant goes with the vowel that *follows* it. Every vowel *not* preceded by a consonant stands alone when you break a *written* word into syllables (you may smooth some of them together when you *speak*). For example:

"Ua" consists of the two syllables u-a (it means "rain")
"Manoa" consists of the three syllables Ma-no-a (a beautiful valley you'll see on your hikes in the mountains behind Honolulu)
"Kaneohe" consists of the four syllables Ka-ne-o-he (a large town on windward Oahu and also Marine Corps Air Station near there)
"Anuenue" consists of the five syllables A-nu-e-nu-e (Hawaiian name for Sand Island, which separates Honolulu Harbor from the rest of Malama Bay)
"Konahuinui" consists of the six syllables Ko-na-hu-i-nu-i (it's the highest peak in the Koolau Range)
"Liliuokalani" consists of the seven syllables Li-li-u-o-ka-la-ni (Hawaii's last monarch and author of the beloved song "Aloha Oe")

Accent. In general, the accent falls on the next-to-last syllable for words with three or more syllables and on the first syllable for words of two syllables. For words of more than three syllables, you put a little stress on every other syllable preceding the accented one. Don't worry about this; it seems to come naturally.

There are common-usage exceptions, such as *makai* (ma-KAI, with the accent on the last syllable). When you see exceptions such as those, chances are that what has happened is that European usage has fully merged two sounds into one. Proper Hawaiian pronunciation of *makai* would be closer to "ma-KA-i," a three-syllable word with the last two syllables almost merging.

Hint for Longer Words: Repetition and Rhythm. Have you noticed the tendency in long Hawaiian words for groups of letters to repeat? That kind of repetition is fairly common. When you see a long Hawaiian word, don't panic. Identify its repeating letter groups, figure out how to pronounce them individually, then put the whole word together. Chances are you'll come pretty close to getting it correct.

For example, *Wiliwilinui* might throw you (it's a ridge leading up into the mountains behind Honolulu and formerly the site of a popular hiking trail). But look at the repeating letter group *wili* (wi-li). See the word as "Wili/wili/nui"—two "wili"s followed by a "nui" (nu-i)—that makes "wi-li/wi-li/nu-i." Once you've identified the repeating groups, the rhythm of the word comes naturally. Try this approach for longer words, including the state fish: *humuhumunukunukuapuaa*: two "hu-mu"s, two "nu-ku"s, and an "a-pu-a-a." Now try it: "hu-mu/hu-mu/nu-ku/nu-ku/a-pu-a-a.". . . .Very good!

Makai **and** *mauka.* In Hawaii, local people often give directions or describe the location of a place as *makai* (merge the *ai*), which means "toward the sea," or *mauka* (merge the *au*), which means "toward the mountains; inland." I had a terrible time remembering which was which until I came up with this mnemonic:

Go *makai*
Where sea meets sky,

and Tom Winnett came up with:

Mauka is toward the MAUntains.

However, I still think in terms of left, right, north, south, east, and west. I don't often use *mauka* and *makai* in this book.

Two other local-style directions you may encounter in Honolulu are "Ewa" (e-va), which means west toward Ewa town, and "Diamond Head," which means east toward Diamond Head. Again, I don't use these directions.

Do your best, with respect. Approach the language with respect, and give it your best shot. Then be prepared to hear local people pronounce it differently. Learn from them. Maybe it's part of our jobs as visitors to inadvertently provide a little comic relief for those living and working here as opposed to just vacationing here.

Instant Hawaiian (see Bibliography) is a useful booklet that's a lot less frivolous than its title implies. It begins, "So you'd like to learn to speak Hawaiian—you should live so long!" I felt I'd come to the right place. Look for it when you get to Hawaii.

Geology and History, Natural and Human

First, the earth

According to the theory of *plate tectonics*, the earth consists of:
A rigid, rocky outer shell, the *lithosphere* ("rocky zone")
Beneath the lithosphere, a hot, semifluid layer, the *asthenosphere* ("weak zone")
A core that doesn't play a part in this oversimplified discussion
The lithosphere is broken into *plates* that move with respect to one another. Hot, fluid material, possibly from the asthenosphere or melted by contact with the asthenosphere, penetrates up through the lithosphere at three kinds of places:
Mid-oceanic ridges, where plates spread apart
Subduction zones, where plates collide and one dives under the other (subducts)
Hot spots, where a plume of molten material appears in the middle of a plate.

Next, the land

It's believed that the Hawaiian Islands exist where the Pacific Plate, on which they ride, is moving northwest across a hot spot. An undersea volcano is built at the place where the plate is over the hot spot. If the volcano gets big enough, it breaks the ocean's surface to become an island. Eventually, the plate's movement carries the island far enough away from the hot spot that volcanism ceases on that island. Erosion, which begins the moment the new island appears above the sea, tears the land down.

The Hawaiian Islands are successively older toward the northwest and younger toward the southeast. Northwestern islands, like Necker, are hardly more than bits of volcanic rock now. Southeastern islands, including the major Hawaiian Islands, are still significant chunks of land. Kauai and Niihau are the oldest and the farthest northwest of the major islands. Oahu is younger, Maui younger yet. The Big Island of Hawaii is the youngest and the farthest southeast of the major islands.

The molten material—lava—characteristic of Hawaiian volcanoes is relatively fluid. The fluidity of the lava allows it to spread widely, and repeated eruptions produce broad-based, rounded volcanoes called shield volcanoes. The volcano expels not only flowing lava but volcanic fragments such as cinder and ash. Alternating layers of these materials build up during periods of volcanic activity.

Erosion has sculpted the exotic landscapes we associate with volcanic tropical islands. Waves pound the volcano's edges, undercutting them and, where the volcano slopes more steeply, forming cliffs. The cliffs at the extreme west and east ends of Oahu are wave-cut cliffs. These wave-cut cliffs grade into the dramatic, fluted stream-cut cliffs (*pali*) and lush valleys. Streams take material from higher on the volcano, cutting valleys into its flanks and depositing the material they carry as alluvium. Alluvial deposits cover the floors of the stream-cut valleys. New episodes of volcanism wholly or partly fill in those landscapes, and erosional forces immediately begin sculpting the new surface as well as the remaining older surface.

Oahu is geologically an infant on an Earth more than four billion years old. Potassium-argon dating of rocks suggests that lava welled forth to build the Waianae volcano between 3 and 4 million years ago. After three major periods of activity, it finally became quiet about 2.5 million years ago. Since then, erosion has carried away most of it, leaving only a crescent-shaped piece of its east rim standing as the Waianae Range. The Koolau volcano burst forth between 2.6 and 1.8 million years ago, building its shield in a single major period of activity and building up the plateau between the two volcanoes. Now, erosion has worn away most of the volcano's eastern rim, leaving its long west rim standing as the Koolau Range.

Then, about 1.1 million years ago, a period of secondary, cone-

Deep valleys surrounded by steep cliffs are typical landforms sculpted by the erosion of Hawaiian volcanoes—here, windward Oahu

building eruptions began on southeast Oahu. By the time it ended some 31,000 years ago, it had left cones that are some of Oahu's most famous landmarks: Diamond Head, Koko Head, Koko Crater, and Hanauma Bay, to name a few. Is it all over now? No one can be sure. There is circumstantial evidence that an undersea eruption may have occurred between Oahu and Kauai in 1956. In the meantime, however, erosion prevails on Oahu, changing the landscape constantly.

Life arrives

Living organisms colonize new land rapidly. In Hawaii, plants established themselves once there was a little soil for them. Seeds arrived on the air currents, or floated in on the sea, or hitched a ride on the feathers or in the guts of birds. Insects and spiders also took advantage of the air currents. Birds were certainly among the first visitors. Living things found little competition and quickly adapted to their new home, evolving into an astonishing variety of species many of which occur naturally only on the Hawaiian Islands ("endemic to Hawaii"). The only mammals to arrive were the bat and the seal. Some birds became flightless—a fairly common adaptation on isolated islands with no ground predators.

People arrive

It's unlikely that the site of the very first human colony in the Hawaiian Islands will ever be found. Too much time has passed; too many destructive forces have been at work. However, recent archaeological work has established that people had settled in Hawaii by 300–400 A.D, earlier than had previously been thought. Linguistic studies and cultural artifacts recovered from sites of early colonization point to the Marquesas Islands as the colonizers' home; the Marquesas themselves seem to have been colonized as early as 200 B.C.

The colonizers of Hawaii had to adapt the Marquesan technology to their new home. For example, the Marquesans made distinctive large, one-piece fishhooks from the large, strong pearl shells that abounded in Marquesan waters. There are no such large shells in Hawaiian waters, so the colonists developed two-piece fishhooks made of the weaker materials that were available in Hawaii (such as bone and wood). Over time, a uniquely Hawaiian material culture developed.

At one time, scholars believed that, as related in Hawaii's oral traditions and genealogies, a later wave of colonizers from Tahiti swept in and conquered the earlier Hawaiians. Research does not support that theory. Instead, research has revealed that before European contact, Hawaiian material culture evolved steadily in patterns that suggest gradual and local, not abrupt and external, influences. The archaeo-

Flourishing taro patch
(Colocasia esculenta)

logical record hints that there may have been some Hawaiian-Tahitian contact in the twelfth century, but its influence was slight.

The Hawaiians profoundly altered the environment of the islands. They had brought with them the plants they had found most useful in the Marquesas Islands: taro, *ti*, the trees from which they made a bark cloth (*tapa* or *kapa*), sugar cane, ginger, gourd plants, yams, bamboo, turmeric, arrowroot, and the breadfruit tree. They also brought the small pigs of Polynesia, dogs, jungle fowl, and, probably as stowaways, rats. They used slash-and-burn techniques to clear the native lowland forests for the crops they had brought. Habitat loss together with competition for food with and predation by the newly introduced animals wrought havoc with the native animals, particularly birds. Many species of birds had already become extinct long before Europeans arrived.

On the eve of the Europeans' accidental stumbling across Hawaii, the major Hawaiian islands held substantial numbers of people of Polynesian descent. They had no written language, but their oral and musical traditions were ancient and rich. Their social system was highly stratified and very rigid. Commoners, or *makaainana*, lived in self-sufficient family groups and villages, farming and fishing for most necessities and trading for necessities they could not otherwise obtain. The land was divided among hereditary chiefs of the noble class (*alii*). Commoners paid part of their crops or catches as taxes to the chief who ruled the land-division they lived on; commoners served their chief as soldiers. Higher chiefs ruled over lower chiefs, receiving from them taxes and also commoners to serve as soldiers. People especially gifted in healing, divination, or important crafts served the populace in those capacities (for example, as priests). There was also a class of untouchables, the *kauwa*. Most people were at death what they had been at birth.

Strict laws defined what was forbidden, or *kapu*, and governed the conduct of *kauwa* toward everyone else, of commoners toward *alii*, of *alii* of a lower rank toward *alii* of higher rank, and of men and women toward each other. Some of the laws seem irrationally harsh. For example, a commoner could be put to death if his shadow fell on an *alii*.

Chiefs frequently made war on one another. If the chiefs of one island were united under a high chief or a king, often that island would make war on the other islands.

The Hawaiians worshipped many gods and goddesses. The principal ones were Ku, Kane, Kanaloa, and Lono. Ku represented the male aspect of the natural world. Ku was also the god of war, and he demanded human sacrifice. Kane was the god of life, a benevolent god who was regarded as the Creator and the ancestor of all Hawaiians. Kanaloa ruled the dead and the dark aspects of life, and he was often linked with Kane in worship.

Lono was another benevolent god; he ruled clouds, rain, and harvests. The annual winter festival in Lono's honor, *Makahiki*, ran from October to February. *Makahiki* was a time of harvest, celebration, fewer *kapu*, and sporting events. Images of Lono were carried around each island atop tall poles with crosspieces from which banners of white *tapa* flew. (Legend said Lono had sailed away from Hawaii long ago and would return in a floating *heiau* (temple) decked with poles flying long white banners from their crosspieces.) Chiefs and chiefesses met the image of Lono with ceremonies and gifts, and commoners came forward to pay their taxes.

Systems like that can last for hundreds and even thousands of years in the absence of compelling internal problems or changes and of external forces, as the Hawaiian system did. But change eventually comes.

The Europeans arrive by accident

Christopher Columbus had sailed from Spain to what he thought was the Orient, hoping to find a sea route to replace the long, hazardous land route. But in fact he discovered an obstacle now called North America. With a direct sea route between Europe and the Orient blocked, people sought other sea routes. The southern routes around the Cape of Good Hope at the tip of Africa and Cape Horn at the tip of South America proved to be very long and very treacherous. Still, the trade was lucrative. The European demand for Oriental goods such as spices, Chinese porcelain, and silk was insatiable. By trading their way around the world, a captain, his crew, and the government or the tradesmen that financed them might become very wealthy in just one voyage.

All over Europe, people came to believe that a good, navigable route *must* exist in northern waters that would allow them to sail west from Europe around the northern end of North America to the Orient. (It doesn't exist.) Captain James Cook sailed from England on July 12, 1776, to try to find the Northwest Passage from the Pacific side.

In December of 1777, Cook left Tahiti sailing northeast, not expecting to see land again until he reached North America. Instead, he sighted land on January 18, 1778, and reached the southeast shore of Kauai on January 19th. In Hawaii, it was the time of *Makahiki*, the festival honoring the god Lono. The Hawaiians mistook the masts and sails of Cook's ships for the poles and tapa banners of the floating *heiau* on which Lono was to return and received Cook as if he were Lono.

Cook was an intelligent and compassionate man who respected the native societies he found and who tried to deal with their people fairly and decently. He tried to keep crewmen who he knew had venereal diseases from infecting the natives, but he failed. Cook did not stay long in Hawaii. He spent most of 1778 searching for the Northwest Passage; unsuccessful, he returned to Hawaii in early 1779 to make repairs and resupply. It was *Makahiki* again. All went well at first, but the Hawaiians stole an auxiliary boat from one of his ships. When he tried to retrieve it, there was a brief skirmish, in which Cook and four of his crew were killed.

Cook's ships survived a second futile search for the Northwest Passage, after which the crew sailed westward for England, stopping in China. There the crew learned the astonishing value of another of the expedition's great discoveries: the furs of the sea otters and seals of the Pacific Northwest. Trade with the Orient suddenly became even more profitable, and Hawaii was to become not an isolated curiosity but an important point on a major world trade route.

The Hawaiian chief Kamehameha began his conquest of the islands in 1790. Kamehameha actively sought Western allies, weapons, and advice; he conquered all the islands but Kauai and Niihau.

Kamehameha's wars, Western diseases, and the sandalwood trade decimated the native Hawaiians. Chiefs indebted themselves to foreign merchants for weapons and other goods. New England merchants discovered that Hawaii had abundant sandalwood, for which the Chinese would pay huge prices. Merchants demanded payment from the chiefs in sandalwood; the chiefs ordered the commoners into the mountains to get the precious wood. The heartwood nearest the roots was the best part; the whole tree had to be destroyed to get it. The mountains were stripped of their sandalwood trees. Many of those ordered into the mountains died of exposure and starvation. Communities that had depended on their labor for food also starved.

Kamehameha I died in 1819, leaving the monarchy to his son Liholiho and a regency in Liholiho's behalf to his favorite wife, Kaahumanu. Liholiho was an amiable, weak-willed alcoholic. Kaahumanu was strong-willed, intelligent, capable, and ambitious. She believed that the old Hawaiian *kapu* system was obsolete: no gods struck down the Westerners, who daily did things that were *kapu* for Hawaiians. Six months after Kamehameha I's death, she persuaded Liholiho to join her in breaking several ancient *kapu*. The *kapu* system, having been discredited, crumbled; the old order was dead.

The missionaries arrive

Congregationalist missionaries from New England reached Hawaii in 1820; Liholiho grudgingly gave them a year's trial. The end of the *kapu* system had left a religious vacuum into which the missionaries moved remarkably easily. To their credit, they came with a sincere desire to commit their lives to bettering those of the people of Hawaii. Liholiho's mother converted to Christianity and made it acceptable for other *alii* to follow her example. Kaahumanu became a convert, too, and set about remodeling Hawaii socially and politically, based on the Ten Commandments.

An ecosystem passes

Cook and those who came after him gave cattle, goats, and large European pigs as gifts to the Hawaiian chiefs, and the animals overran the islands. They ate everything. Rainwater sluiced off the now-bare hillsides without replenishing the aquifers. Areas that had been blessed with an abundance of water suffered drought now. Native plants could not reestablish themselves because the unrestrained animals ate them as soon as they sent up a shoot. People wrongly concluded that native plants were inherently

unable to reestablish themselves, and they imported non-native trees like the eucalyptuses and ironwoods that you see so often today.

The native habitat area and diversity shrank still more before the new sugar plantations. Planters drained wetlands for the commercially valuable crop and erected dams, ditches, and sluices to divert the natural water supply into a controllable water supply. What they did was not so very dif-

Native beach naupaka *(Scaevola sericea, foreground) and* hala *(Pandanus odoratissima, middle ground) arrived on oceanic currents*

ferent from what the Polynesians had done when they had cleared the native lowland forests in order to plant their taro, but the scale was far vaster. In one particularly terrible mistake, growers imported the mongoose to prey on the rats that damaged their crops. But the rat forages at night, while the mongoose hunts by day: they seldom met. What the mongooses preyed on instead were the eggs of native ground-nesting birds.

Few of Hawaii's native plants put forth showy flowers or set palatable fruit, so the new settlers imported ornamental and fruiting plants to brighten their gardens and tables. Many shrubs and trees did so well in Hawaii's favorable climate that they escaped into the wild to become pest plants, crowding out native species and interrupting the food chain.

Birds brought over as pets escaped to compete with native species. More species of native birds have become extinct in Hawaii than anywhere else in the world, and most of the birds you see will be introduced species like the zebra dove and the myna.

It is tragic but true that when you visit Hawaii, you will probably see very few of its native plants and animals. But don't give up: your chances of seeing native plants and animals are better on the trail than elsewhere on Oahu!

A culture passes

Literacy replaced the rich Hawaiian oral tradition, and many legends and stories were forgotten before someone thought to write them down. The significance of many place names, apart from their literal meaning, has been lost forever. Zealous missionaries and converts believed that the native traditions were evil, and they nearly succeeded in eradicating all traces of the native culture.

A nation passes

Hawaiians saw that their only hope of surviving as an independent nation in the modern world was to secure the protection and guarantees of freedom of one of the major powers. The Hawaiian monarchs would have preferred the British, but British influence was ultimately inadequate to withstand American influence. American missionaries doled out God's grace. American entrepreneurs established plantations and businesses. American ships filled the harbors. Economic and cultural domination of Hawaii eventually passed into American hands, particularly after the new land laws of 1850 made it possible for foreigners to own land in Hawaii. The Hawaiian monarchy lasted until 1893, but most of its economic and therefore its political power was gone. Hawaii as an independent nation disappeared soon after.

A race passes

The native Hawaiian people lost much of their importance in the

changing, Westernized economy early in the nineteenth century. The bur-
geoning sugar and pineapple plantations needed laborers, and the Hawaiians were diligent, capable hired hands when they wanted to be. But they
did not comprehend the idea of hiring themselves out as day laborers for
wages. Planters began to import laborers from other parts of the world:
China, Japan, the Philippines, Portugal. Many imported laborers stayed,
married, raised families, and went on to establish their own successful
businesses. The Hawaiians were soon a minority in their own land.

The numbers of full-blooded Hawaiians declined precipitously
throughout the nineteenth century. Beginning with the tragic introduction of venereal disease by Cook's men, venereal diseases swept
through the native population who, particularly at *Makahiki*, exchanged
partners freely. Venereal disease often leaves its victims sterile, and many
who had survived Western diseases, wars, and the sandalwood trade
were unable to reproduce. Others married foreigners, so their children
were only part Hawaiian. Today most authorities believe that there are
no full-blooded Hawaiians left, not even on Niihau, the only island
where Hawaiian is still the language of everyday life.

Hawaii becomes American

In the late nineteenth century, the Hawaiian monarchy seemed
to some powerful businessmen and civic leaders of American descent
to get in the way of the smooth conduct of business. They thought
Hawaii would be better off as an American territory. Queen Liliuokalani
did not agree. She wanted to assert Hawaii's independence and the authority of its monarchs. The business community plotted a coup, de-
posed Liliuokalani in 1893, formed a new government, and petitioned
the United States for territorial status. The United States formally annexed Hawaii in 1898.

Military projects and mass travel brought mainland Americans
flooding into Hawaii. Many stayed, and so the majority of people in
Hawaii came to see themselves as Americans, though a minority dis-
agreed (some still do). After many years as a territory, Hawaii became
the fiftieth state in 1959.

Things to come

The huge tourist industry is both a blessing and a curse. Massive
development pushes the Hawaii-born off the land to make way for hotels
and golf courses. Displaced Hawaiians, whatever their ethnic background, find themselves having to survive as waiters, chambermaids,
clerks—in essence, as the servants of those who have displaced them.
Many also fear that tourism will result in the Hawaiian paradise being
paved over and lost forever; others feel that it already has been.

The hundredth anniversary of the overthrow of the Hawaiian monarchy was January 17, 1993. On November 23, 1993, the U.S. belatedly offered a formal apology. Today, a growing movement seeks to return to people of native Hawaiian ancestry some of the lands they lost as well as some degree of autonomy, ranging from that granted Native Americans to full independence for a new Hawaiian nation. The idea is just, but implementing it is controversial. Hawaii's evolution is far from over.

> Life is complicated and not for the timid. It's an experience that when it's done, it will take us a while to get over it. We'll look back on all the good things we surrendered in favor of deadly trash and wish we had returned and reclaimed them.
> ——From *Leaving Home* by Garrison Keillor

Bishop Museum

The Bernice Pauahi Bishop Museum in Honolulu houses what is considered to be the finest collection of Hawaiiana available for public viewing anywhere. The museum is located at 1525 Bernice St., and it's open seven days a week from 9 AM to 5 PM. Admission may seem a bit steep, but the museum complex offers far more than Hawaiian artifacts: a planetarium, hula exhibits, crafts demonstrations, and a special exhibit that changes from time to time.

Head for the Hawaiian exhibits. The museum's collection of Hawaiian featherwork (capes, helmets, and the feathered standards called *kahili*) and of tapa (the native barkcloth, also called *kapa*) is unmatched and irreplaceable. Hawaii produced the finest featherwork and tapa in all of Polynesia. Particularly interesting is a series of cases comparing the material cultures of the different Polynesian societies: for example, the uses to which various societies had put coconut shells and fibers.

Bernice Pauahi Bishop (1831–1884) was a high chiefess and the last direct descendant of Kamehameha I. She was offered the crown of Hawaii twice and both times declined it. She had been raised in missionary ways and believed her place was in the home with her American-born husband, Charles R. Bishop, who had become a citizen of Hawaii. She dedicated herself to helping her fellow Hawaiians adjust to the changes that had overwhelmed their homeland. She saw that her people were falling into political insignificance and dire poverty in the new Hawaii and believed that education would help elevate them to their rightful place. She inherited a great deal of wealth in the form of land, and she used her wealth to found the Kamehameha Schools, which accept as pupils only children who are of Hawaiian or part-Hawaiian ancestry. The Bishop Estate continues to be a powerful force in Hawaii.

Bernice Bishop's husband founded the Bishop Museum in her memory entirely from his own funds; it is independent of Bishop Estate.

Getting Around on Oahu and Finding Maps to Help You

Driving

On the other islands, visitors find that a rental car is almost a necessity. On Oahu, it can be more of a curse than a blessing. While the new H3 freeway has considerably improved driving on Oahu, visitors are increasingly staying outside Waikiki and Honolulu where traffic is less dense. If you are not staying in Waikiki, consider asking your host/hostess the best way to get to the area or town nearest the trailhead. Otherwise, ponder the following before you waste time and money renting a car on Oahu:

Getting around in Honolulu: the driving conditions from hell. No Pacific coast city I've been in has worse driving conditions for visitors than than Honolulu (which includes Waikiki). Here are some of the reasons:

• *The street system is laid out like the aftermath of a spaghetti fight in a school cafeteria.* Honolulu sprawls over a wide area, including some very steep hills. Streets wander first this way, then that; change names for no apparent reason; crisscross one another randomly; dump you onto freeways, lead you into dead ends, or abruptly become one-way (probably the wrong way for you) with little or no warning. . . .Count on it: you'll get lost almost every time you try to drive somewhere, in spite of the help of the best street maps.

• *On weekdays, the direction of traffic on major streets is altered by police to accommodate commuter traffic.* The street system, which makes no sense to start with, gets even more confusing when this happens. Hapless visitors may find themselves anywhere—or nowhere.

• *You can't return the way you came.* It is usually impossible for you to simply retrace the route you took to the trailhead in order to return to your hotel. You will have to figure out two different routes, one out, one back. One-way streets are particularly responsible for this problem.

• *You can't get back on the freeway where you got off it.* Freeway on- and off-ramps are almost never logically paired. The freeways do not link parts of the city; rather, they slice the city apart. The freeways' purpose is to link major military installations (Hawaii, particularly Oahu, is full of military sites). This is why an island-state over 2,000 watery

20

miles from the nearest other state nevertheless has federally-funded *interstate* highways.

- *Commuter traffic is extremely heavy.* It's as bad as downtown L.A. at times.

All these problems are magnified when you try to drive in downtown Honolulu, where parking is yet another nightmare. See Appendix D for some suggestions about driving routes out of and into Waikiki.

Avoiding the drive from hell. Here are some suggestions for driving in Honolulu:

- *Don't.* You can reduce your need to drive in Honolulu (which includes Waikiki) by staying somewhere else. There *are* accommodations elsewhere on Oahu; check the "Accommodations" brochure from the Hawaii Visitors Bureau, for example.

Nevertheless, you will probably find yourself booked into the high-rise canyons of Waikiki. It's where most tourists wind up. In that case, you should—

- *Take TheBus.* Oahu has a fine public transportation system called simply TheBus. Many trailheads can be reached by TheBus. You can even go nearly around the island on TheBus—to the extent that the routes permit. (TheBus does not circle the westernmost part of Oahu.) You can get the latest route and schedule information on TheBus by writing to the following address and enclosing a stamped, self-addressed envelope in which the information will be sent to you:

    TheBus
    811 Middle Street
    Honolulu, HI 96819

Note that TheBus allows you to carry a pack no larger than you can hold on your lap—practically, no larger than a big daypack. As there are no backpacking opportunities to speak of for visitors to Oahu, you shouldn't find this limitation to be a problem. Also, TheBus stops running late at night—don't let yourself get stranded.

- *Drive it one day at a time.* A few prime hiking areas, like the Tantalus-Roundtop area and the extreme west end of Oahu, are not served by TheBus. For these, you may wish to rent a car for a day, or arrange for a pickup and a ride as part of taking the hike with an organized group, or—if it's practical—add to your foot miles the walk from and to the nearest TheBus stop.

I drove in Honolulu and all around Oahu. I took TheBus only once and wished I had had the luxury of taking TheBus more often.

If you must drive, have a good road map. It's a good idea to get a road map of Oahu and a street map of Honolulu well in advance of your visit so that you can study them. Some of the free tourist maps you'll be handed on Oahu are so cute they're useless. National automobile clubs may offer free maps to their members. The excellent *Full Color Topographic Map of Oahu* from the University of Hawaii Press includes street maps of Honolulu, Kailua, and Kaneohe. The latter is usually available at travel stores on the mainland and just about everywhere on Oahu.

What to leave in the car. Nothing. Never leave valuables in your car, even in a locked trunk. "Valuables" include not only jewelry, money, checks, and credit cards but things you can't readily replace: glasses, prescription medication, identification, keys, snapshots of loved ones, etc.

Hiking. Road maps are useless for hiking trails. For trail maps, I recommend the maps in this book and the United States Geological Survey (USGS) $7^{1}/2'$ series of topographic ("topo") maps for Oahu. Topos show elevation details as well as roads and trails. However, topos are not updated as often as you'd like. That's why you should use them in conjunction with the maps in this book and information from the agencies in charge of the island's hiking areas—under the Department of Land and Natural Resources (DLNR), the Division of State Parks, Oahu District, and the Division of Forestry and Wildlife, Oahu District. It is worth your while to write to them in advance, but you may not get a reply from them even if you enclose a stamped, self-addressed envelope. Oahu is the only one of the four major islands from whose Division of Forestry and Wildlife I could not get any information by mail; I don't know if that was the result of their policies or just a fluke. Still, it is worth a try, because otherwise you will have to go into downtown Honolulu (horrors!) to get the Division of Forestry and Wildlife's maps. See these agencies' addresses in "Getting Permits or Permission" in this book.

If you've written ahead for recreation information about one of the other major islands, you've probably received a copy of that island's DLNR recreation map. These maps give you an island-wide overview map and brief text descriptions of hiking and hunting opportunities. When up-to-date they're valuable for showing where the public recreation opportunities are. Oahu, unlike the other major islands, lacks a DLNR recreation map.

Oahu is covered by 15 USGS $7^{1}/2'$ topos, as shown in the illustration at right. (You won't need them all.) It's best to get the topos you want in advance so you can study them.

If your mainland backpacking store does not carry the Hawaii topos, you can get them directly from the USGS. Their Web site has an excellent interactive topo-purchasing feature, so log onto http://mapping.usgs.gov/esic/to_order.html. You can search for the topos you want by populated area, by zip code (Hawaii's zip codes start with "968," so make up one and go for it), and by clicking on maps. The site may claim that it works only for the contiguous 48 states, but in fact, it works for Hawaii, too. And there are some odd omissions, such as the *Honolulu* topo on Oahu, but otherwise, the site is a wonderful resource. It also allows you to buy topos on-line.

The site includes listings of retailers that sell USGS topos, with additional links to those retailers' Web sites, if any.

If shopping on the Internet doesn't appeal to you, you can reach the USGS at 1-800-HELP-MAP, contact any USGS Earth Science Information Center (ESIC), or write:

USGS Information Services
Box 25286
Denver, CO 80225

Or there may be a store near you that specializes in maps, though most retailers carry only maps for their local area. Look in your local Yellow Pages under "Maps." (For example, the store where I get Hawaii topos isn't a backpacking store; it's a mining-supplies store, Allied Services, 966 N. Main St., Orange, CA 92867, 714-532-4337. They have every available topo for the U.S. and then some, take credit-card orders by phone, and will ship promptly and reliably. You need to know which maps you want when you visit or order, because Allied's policy is that if they pull out a map for you, you've bought it: their stock is so huge that they won't put it back. They also carry the USGS booklets or sheets showing all the topos for, for example, a particular state. If you're uncertain which topos you want, request the appropriate booklet/sheet first.)

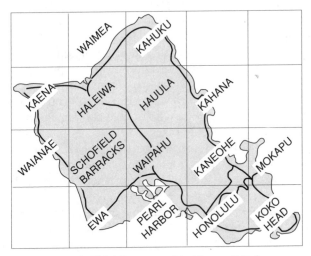

U.S.G.S. 7¹/2' Topographic Maps of Oahu

Getting Permits or Permission

Dayhiking permits. The trip descriptions in this book include information about what permits you need (if any) and to whom you should apply for them.

There is no backpacking to speak of on Oahu for the visitor from the mainland (and not much for anyone else, either—see below). You don't need to worry about or plan for backpacking and backcountry camping permits on Oahu.

Several dayhikes do require permits from the Division of Forestry and Wildlife. You must go into downtown Honolulu to the Division of Forestry and Wildlife to get those permits. Depending on the trail, the Division of Forestry and Wildlife is acting as the agent for hiking trails under its own control or it may be acting on behalf of another property owner or owners.

Any hike on private or military property is subject to the owner's wishes, and an owner may decide at any time to require permits or even to deny access altogether. To be absolutely sure your hiking plans won't be foiled by such a change of heart, call ahead if possible. Check the trip descriptions for whom to call, if anyone. (And if you find a route closed, please let me know, too.)

A few dayhikes require permission from several owners. Your vacation time is too valuable to waste running around trying to get multiple permits from different landowners, so I've left these hikes out. See Appendix B for more details. Note that you may be able to take these dayhikes with organized groups whose leaders will coordinate the getting of permits, thus saving you the trouble. See Appendix D for a list of organized groups that offer hikes.

Camping permits. Car and cabin camping are the only kinds of camping available to visitors, for all practical purposes. Appendix A in this book gives you detailed information about camping, including permit requirements, fees, etc.

Why no backpacks? Trail camping doesn't exist in Oahu's state parks. That leaves the Division of Forestry and Wildlife trails. Nearly all Division of Forestry and Wildlife trails are in hunting areas. Camping is permitted along some trails provided you have a permit from the Division of Forestry and Wildlife. In my judgment, this is to accommodate hunters rather than backpackers. There are also a very few trail shelters intended for use by hunters. These areas may be attractive for dayhiking, but I saw nothing to recommend them for backpacking, especially to visitors, who have the extra hassle of bringing their backpacking equipment, too.

Let's face it: while Oahu's dayhiking opportunities are second to none, for high-quality Hawaiian backpacking opportunities, Oahu has nothing to offer compared to the other major islands: Maui, Hawaii (the Big Island), and Kauai.

Division of State Parks

Dayhiking in Oahu's state parks does not require permits as of this writing. Car camping or use of the cabins in a state park does require a permit and sometimes a fee. See Appendix A in this book. For more information, write or call:

Department of Land and Natural Resources
Division of State Parks, Oahu District
1151 Punchbowl Street, Room 310
Honolulu, Hawai`i 96813
Phone 808-587-0300, FAX 808-587-0311

Division of Forestry and Wildlife

As noted above, hiking some trails requires permits from the Division of Forestry and Wildlife. For *information* from this agency, write or call:

Department of Land and Natural Resources
Division of Forestry and Wildlife
1151 Punchbowl Street, Room 325
Honolulu, Hawai`i 96813
Phone 808-587-0166, FAX 808-587-0160

If you need to see the division in person—*and you must if you want to obtain hiking permits*—double-check the lobby directory for their current office number.

Useful Web sites

See the chapter on "Getting Information About Oahu," beginning on page 4, for a list of useful Web sites. In particular, see the Web site for the Department of Land and Natural Resources, www.hawaii.gov/dlnr/divisions.html, to double-check on the latest addresses and voice/FAX numbers.

Weather

The short of it. Oahu is:

- Rainiest on its windward side, which boasts rainforests. Kahana Valley and Sacred Falls state parks are in rainforests.
- Driest and hottest on the south and west sides. These areas lie in the rain shadows of the island's mountains. Waikiki is one such hot, dry area, as is the rest of Honolulu. Honolulu lies in the rain shadow of the Koolau Range, which defines northeast Oahu. The hot, dry southwest coastal plains, home to famous surfing areas like Makaha, lie in the rain shadow of the Waianae Range, which defines southwest Oahu. Between the ranges lies the Schofield Plateau, shielded by the Koolaus and also warm and dry.
- Rainier in the mountains, particularly the Koolaus. The Koolaus, though barely over 3,000 feet high at most, harbor rainforests not only on their windward slopes but on the upper reaches of their leeward slopes. The Waianaes are largely shielded by the Koolaus, however; only the highest points, like Mt. Kaala, have rainforests and swamps.

The dry Honolulu area, particularly Waikiki, has the greatest concentration of visitors, hotels, and resorts. The figure on the next page summarizes the situation.

The long of it. Hawaii's coastal weather is temperate to a degree that puts the so-called "temperate" zones of the world to shame. The humidity is moderate, too: 50 to 60%, not the sweltering horror of some other tropical lands. It is warmer in the summer and cooler in the winter, but the "extremes" are only a few degrees apart—nothing like those on the mainland.

Hawaii's mild climate is determined largely by its tropical location and also by the northeast trade winds that sweep across it. The northeast *trade* winds—so-called because sea captains took advantage of them on their trade routes—are dependable, steady winds that blow from the northeast across the thousands of miles of open sea that separate the Hawaiian Islands from the continents. They are responsible for keeping the temperature and the humidity moderate. Since they are the prevailing winds in this area, the side of the island that faces them is called the "windward" side. The opposite side of the island is the opposite of windward; in nautical terms, "leeward."

Sometimes the trade winds fail and are replaced by "kona" winds coming from the south. "Kona" means "leeward," because it's the leeward side of the island that more or less faces these occasional winds. Kona winds bring hot, sticky air. Fortunately, they are rare in summer, when they would be really unpleasant, and occur mostly in winter, when the lower overall temperatures moderate their effect. Kona storms are subtropical low-pressure systems that occur in winter, move in from the south, and can cause serious damage. There is apparently no pattern to them; in some years, they do not occur at all, but in others they occur every few weeks.

On Oahu, average temperatures in Honolulu (leeward) range from highs of 80–85° F to lows of 70–75° F. In Kaneohe (windward), temperatures range from highs of 80–82° F to lows of 62–70° F. The "cooler" ones are winter temperatures, the warmer ones summer. It's rainier from November through March than it is the rest of the year. Expect cooler temperatures, more wind, and considerably more rain if you are in a mountainous region.

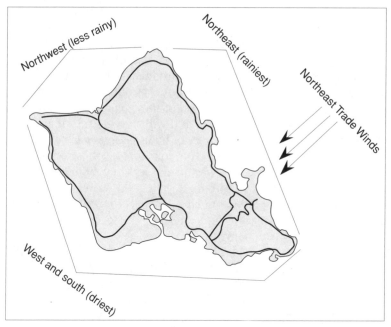

Equipment Suggestions
and Miscellaneous Hints

This book isn't intended to teach you *how* to hike. If you can walk, you can hike, especially the "very easy" hikes. Don't forget that you can cut almost any hike down to your ability by walking only part of it. Just be sure the trips you pick are within *your* hiking limits.

This book is intended specifically to let you know *where* you can hike on Oahu, *what* to expect when you hike there, and *how* to get to the trailhead for each hike. And that, I hope, will help you decide *which* hikes to take.

This section contains suggestions which I hope will make your hikes even more pleasant, and perhaps better protect you and the environment. Of course, you're the only person who lives in your body, so you'll have to judge what's really appropriate for you. But there are a few things you might want to know before you go—things that may be very different from the hiking you've done at home on the mainland. (Maybe you already know them, but it's hard to shut me up when I think I have some good advice.)

It's up to you. No book can substitute for, or give you, five things only you can supply: physical fitness, preparation, experience, caution, and common sense. Don't leave the trailhead without them.

Don't spread pest plants. As I mentioned in the chapter on geology and history, Hawaii has been overrun by introduced plants. It's important to try to control the spread of these plants. One thing you can do to help is to wash the soil, and with it the seeds of any pest plants—you hope—off of your shoes or boots *before you leave* a hiking area. Or pick up a stick and scrape off your soles. Note also that you, like any other animal, can carry pest-plant seeds in your digestive tract and deposit them, ready to sprout, in your solid wastes. (Pest plants include all the guavas.) Either hold it till you get to a toilet or dig your hole deep enough to make it impossible for the seeds to sprout (one foot deep, according to a pamphlet on the subject. I'm just passing this information on. I have no idea how to carry enough equipment to dig a hole that deep when hiking). For more information, call the Hawaii State Department of Agriculture, Weed Control Section, 808-548-7119.

Equipment for strolls and easy hikes. You don't need to make extensive preparations for a stroll along a beach or a half-mile nature trail as long as there's food, water, and shelter nearby—perhaps in your car. The things you *must not* go without are:

> Sunglasses
> Appropriate footwear
> Mosquito repellent
> Strong sunblock applied *before* you set out.

Your mosquito repellent should be "jungle juice" — that is, have a high percentage of DEET (diethyltoluamide). DEET is vile stuff, but it works.

Equipment for moderate and strenuous hikes. Carry at least the Ten Essentials Plus One as I've adapted them from the Sierra Club. They are:

> Pack (to put these good things in; could be a large fanny pack)
> Food and water (assume that all open water sources are unsafe to drink)
> Extra clothing (always take rain gear, as it can rain at any time in Hawaii
> Map (and compass if you can use it)
> Flashlight with extra bulb and batteries
> Sunglasses and strong sunblock
> Means to dig a hole 6–8 inches deep and at least 200 feet from water, in order to bury solid body wastes; tissue that you will also bury (or pack out)
> Pocket knife
> First-aid kit
> Waterproof matches and something you can keep a flame going with (such as a candle) only when necessary to start a fire *in order to save a life*
> Mosquito repellent

Tennis shoes? I've noted in the hike descriptions whether tennis shoes are okay or whether I think you should wear boots. I base that recommendation on the length of the hike and the difficulty of the terrain. What tennis shoes may lack that boots can provide are ankle support and soles that grip. Only you can decide how important those are to you.

A daypack is just the thing for strolling Waikiki's Ala Wai Canal (Trip 31)

Boot care. If you're going to hike a lot, be sure your boot seams are freshly sealed and you've freshly waterproofed the entire boot, including the cloth part, if any. Use a heavy-duty waterproofing compound like a wax, and bring some of it along in order to renew the coating if necessary. Chances are your boots will get wet, especially in the winter. And they'll stay wet, because things dry slowly in the tropical humidity. It's pretty tough on the boots and, together with the abrasion of mud particles, could cause boot seams to fail.

Hiking stick. Take your hiking stick if you usually hike with one. The flight attendants can put it in the closet where they hang the carry-on suits and dresses or in the overhead compartments. Hawaii's terrain can be very slippery when wet, and a hiking stick can be a big help in maintaining your footing. And it can double as a spider stick (see below).

Spider stick. There are a very few overgrown trails where you and some orb spiders may meet unexpectedly, head-on. You probably don't like collecting spiders with your face, but these critters make it hard not to do so. Here's one way to avoid them without killing them. Pick up and use a "spider stick"—a long, strong stick that you carefully wave up and down in front of you as you hike. You can feel the tug when the stick connects with a web. Detach the anchor strands that hold the web in your way, and lay them aside on the adjacent shrubbery. An orb spider normally rebuilds most or all of its web daily, so you've caused it only minor inconvenience. Your hiking stick can probably double as a spider stick.

Hypothermia? On Hawaii? It's possible if you go into the mountains. Remember that going higher is equivalent to going north into colder climates, and mountains are often very windy. Please be prepared as you would be for going into any mountainous region.

Biodegradable? Ha, ha, ha! The following things are popularly supposed to be biodegradable if you bury them: toilet tissue; facial tissue; sanitary napkins; tampons; disposable diapers. That must be a joke. They often last long enough for either running water to exhume them or animals to dig them up. It's actually pretty easy (and much better for the environment and the scenery) to carry them out if you put them in a heavy-duty self-sealing bag like a Ziploc bag.

Companions. The standard advice is: never hike alone and never camp alone.

Water. Take your own drinking water for the day. No open source of water anywhere in the U.S. is safe to drink untreated. If you must drink water from a stream or spring along the trail, treat it chemically with iodine or chlorine preparations designed for the purpose. Look for such preparations in camping stores and drugstores. It now seems that filtering may be ineffective against the bacterium that causes leptospirosis (below). (Boiling water one to five minutes to kill the germs is very effective but is inappropriate for dayhiking, as dayhikers will lack the equipment—stove and pan—for boiling.)

Avoiding leptospirosis. Fresh water on Hawaii may be contaminated with the bacterium that causes leptospirosis. A pamphlet about leptospirosis is available from the Epidemiology Branch of the Hawaii State Department of Health (on Hawaii, call 808-244-4288). The following summarizes some of its contents: Muddy and clear water are both suspect. The bacterium invades through broken skin or the nose, mouth, or eyes. It enters the bloodstream and infects different organs, particularly the kidneys. Precautions that would especially apply to you here are not to go into streams if you have open cuts or abrasions and not to drink (untreated) stream water. Treat water chemically or by boiling it.

The incubation period of leptospirosis is 2–20 days. The onset is sudden, and the symptoms may resemble those of flu: fever, chills, sweating, severe headache, conjunctivitis (red eyes), muscle pains, weakness, vomiting, and diarrhea. *See a physician immediately if you suspect leptospirosis!* Most cases are mild, and people with mild cases usually recover in a week or two without treatment. However, severe infections may damage kidneys, liver, or heart or even cause death.

Cloudy skies over Honolulu, seen from its trail system, threaten afternoon showers. Don't forget that rain gear!

How This Book Organizes the Trips

Imagine the hour hand of a clock pinned to a point near the center of Oahu. Think of it sweeping around clockwise from a 12-o'clock position that's due north. It's easy to envision the hour hand pointing to 3 o'clock (due east), 6 o'clock (due south), and 9 o'clock (due west) as it moves around.

You can think of Oahu as a clock with its hour hand pinned to its approximate middle, a spot on the Schofield Plateau a little east of the H2 freeway and Miilani town. At twelve o'clock, the hour hand points to Kahuku Point at the north tip of Oahu. Around three o'clock, it points to Mokapu Peninsula, site of Kaneohe Marine Corps Air Station. At six o'clock, it points to Pearl Harbor. At nine o'clock, it points to Waianae, a major town on the leeward side of Oahu.

The trips start between twelve and one o'clock, near Hauula on the windward shore (Trips 1 through 3) and move clockwise around the island, ending a little before twelve o'clock near Waimea Bay (Trips 43 through 45). Here's the Oahu clock pointing to Trip 1, the Hauula Loop:

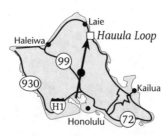

All the clocks are oriented so that their vertical axes ("up") are aligned with true north (also "up"), so I haven't shown north arrows with them.

How to Read the Trip Descriptions

The trip descriptions are in the following format, and here is what the information in each description means. Items marked "(icon)" are shown in the trips by icons (small pictures) arranged in a box at the beginning of each trip and defined below.

Title (pretty self-explanatory)

Type (icon): There are four types of trips described:

G   *Loop trips:* You follow trails that form a closed loop. You don't retrace your steps, or retrace them only for a relatively short distance.

G   *Semiloop trips:* The trip consists of a loop part and an out-and-back part.

    Out-and-back trips: This is by far the most common type of trip in this book. You follow the trail to a destination and then retrace your steps to your starting point.

    Shuttle trips: You start at one trailhead and finish at another, "destination" trailhead. The trailheads are far enough apart, or walking between them is sufficiently impractical, that you need to have a car or a ride waiting for you at the destination trailhead.

Difficulty (icon): A trip's difficulty is based first on total distance and second on cumulative elevation gain and rate of gain. Let's say that the elevation gain is negligible to moderate (it's never steeper than about 500 feet/mile for any significant distance). In that case:

V   A *very easy* trip is 1 mile or less with negligible elevation gain/loss.

E   An *easy* trip is 1–2 miles with little elevation gain/loss.

M   A *moderate* trip is 2–5 miles and has some noticeable elevation gain/loss.

S   A *strenuous* trip is more than 5 miles and has significant elevation gain/loss.

If the trip has a section of, say, a half-mile or more where it's steeper than 500 feet/mile, or if the trail is especially rough or hard to follow, I've given it the next higher difficulty rating.

Shoes (icon): Some trips just aren't safe if you're not wearing boots which have soles that grip and which will give you some ankle support. However, only you live in your body, so you will have to be the final judge of what you can safely wear.

       Tennis shoes are okay.

       Boots are recommended.

       Boots are necessary, as the terrain is rough.

Coastal or inland (icon): General type of area this hike is in. For those hikes that include both coastal and inland segments, this is a judgment call.

 Hike is along the *coast*, on a *beach*, or on cliffs above the ocean. (The icon suggests waves.)

Hike is *inland*, possibly in the hills or mountains. (The icon suggests hills.)

Distance: The distance is the total distance you have to walk.

Elevation gain: This figure is the approximate cumulative elevation gain; it counts all the significant "ups" you have to walk, not just the simple elevation difference between the trailhead and the destination. It's the cumulative gain that your muscles will complain about. Some trips are *upside-down:* you go downhill on your way out to the destination, uphill on your return. Budget your energy accordingly!

Average hiking time: This is based on my normal hiking speed, which is a blazing 2 miles/hour.

Location (icon defined in previous section): The Oahu clock shows the hike's approximate location relative to the rest of Oahu.

Topos: The topo or topos listed here are the ones that cover the area you'll be hiking in on this particular trip. Topos are strictly optional for the very easy and easy trips, but are strongly recommended for the other trips. All listed topos are U.S.G.S. $7^1/2'$ unless otherwise noted.

Trail map: This tells you where this book's trail map for this trip is (usually at the end of the trip or of another trip in the same area). As explained in Appendix E, the trail maps are based on the topos wherever possible. Some Oahu trails do not appear on any official agency map or on the topos. I have approximated their routes based on field notes and sketches and have labeled them "(route approximated)." Some maps are too big for one page and are continued on another page, sometimes at the end of another trip, as noted on the edges of those maps. I've allowed a little overlap between those maps to help you follow them from one page to another.

The following figure shows the trail map legend:

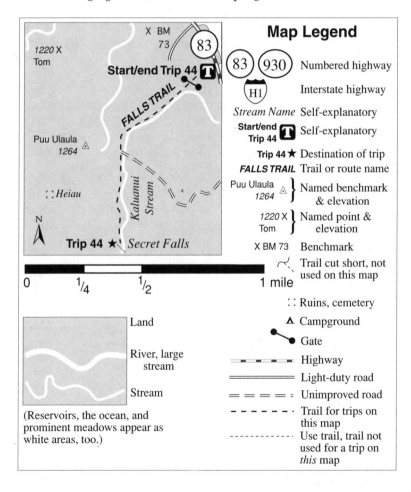

Highlights: This gives you an idea of what I think the best features of the trip are. Usually, it's the scenery—that's one of the principal things you came to Hawaii for!

Driving instructions: This gives you instructions for driving to the trailhead, usually in terms of driving from Waikiki, where most of Oahu's visitors stay. If you can't take TheBus, these may help you. Most directions are given in terms of what I've called the "basic escape route from Waikiki," which starts where McCully Street has just crossed the Ala Wai Canal and intersected Kapiolani Boulevard. (Appendix D offers one visitor's suggestions—mine—for navigating in and out of Waikiki.)

Traffic flow changes. Note that the authorities can and do reverse the flow of traffic on selected streets to accommodate weekday commuter traffic. Note also that it is within their power to declare what are now two-way streets to be one-way streets, to "permanently" reverse the flow of traffic on a one-way street, and so on. So take the driving instructions with a grain of salt, and be sure you have a good road map of Oahu to supplement them. It's worth the trouble!

Mileage markers. On the other major islands, highways have mileage markers at one-mile intervals—very useful for giving directions. However, I found Oahu's mileage markers largely useless: missing, overgrown, or so defaced as to be illegible. I haven't used them in the driving instructions.

TheBus routes. As explained in the earlier chapter on "Getting Around on Oahu...," Oahu's excellent public transportation system, TheBus, is a more reasonable alternative to driving to many trailheads. This section tells you which TheBus routes serve the trailhead (or don't). TheBus stops running late at night, so be sure your plans and timing allow for your return by evening. Routes and schedules may change without notice, so it's a good idea to check with TheBus in advance (808-848-555) and/or with your driver.

Permit/permission required: You need permission to hike some trails. This section will tell you what you need permission for, if anything, and whom to apply to. See "Getting Permits or Permission" and Appendix A in this book for addresses and telephone numbers.

Description. This is the detailed description of the trip as I perceived it. I've tried to give you an idea of the more obvious plants and other features you'll find, where the rough spots are, when you'll be ascending and when descending, where viewpoints are, and what you'll see from those viewpoints.

On a few trips, the trail is faint to nonexistent, and the agency in charge has attempted to mark the route by tying tags of colored plastic ribbon to plants along the route. On Oahu, you may also find metal tags with arrows painted on them or bright paint "tags" splashed on boulders. You navigate by moving from tag to tag. Don't count on tags to get you in and out of an area. Always keep track of where you've been by map and compass or by landmarks, as the tags may just peter out. There's a lot of deadfall in a rainforest, for example, and the tags are lost when the plants they're tied to fall.

Supplemental information.... At the end of most of the trips there's some extra information about the historical significance of places you'll see along the route. Or maybe there's a story—a myth, for example—related to the trip which I hope will add to your enjoyment of the trip. Perhaps there'll be a bit more information about the plants in or the geology of the area. I put most of the supplemental information at the end so that it doesn't interfere too much with the description of the trip itself. I think safety dictates that you give your attention first to the trip and only secondarily to the supplemental information. That is not a problem with easy and very easy hikes, so in those hikes the supplemental information is often part of the main description.

Hiking table. The following hiking table summarizes all the trips in this book. It will help you quickly decide which trips interest you and which are within your party's abilities.

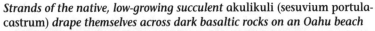

Strands of the native, low-growing succulent akulikuli (sesuvium portula-castrum) *drape themselves across dark basaltic rocks on an Oahu beach*

Trip Number and Name	Type	Difficulty	Miles
1 Hauula Loop	Loop	Moderate	2 1/2
2 Maakua Ridge	Loop	Moderate	3
3 Maakua Gulch	Out & back	Moderate	4
4 Sacred Falls	Out & back	Moderate	4
5 Kapaeleele Loop	Loop	Easy	1
6 Kahana Valley	Semiloop	Strenuous	4
7 Hoomaluhia	Semiloop	Easy	2
8 Kailua Beach Stroll	Out & back	Moderate	5
9 Keolu Hills	Out & back	Moderate	2 3/4
10 Makapuu	Out & back	Moderate	2
11 Koko Crater	Out & back	Very easy	≤ 1/3
12 Waahila Ridge	Out & back	Moderate	3 1/2
13 Puu Pia	Out & back	Easy	1
14 Lyon—Inspiration Point	Out & back	Very easy	1/2
15 Lyon—Cascade	Out & back	Easy	1
16 Manoa Falls	Out & back	Easy	2
17 Aihualama	Out & back	Strenuous	6
18 Kanealole	Out & back	Moderate	1 1/2
19 Maunalaha	Out & back	Moderate	2
20 Makiki Valley Loop	Loop	Moderate	3
21 Manoa Cliffs	Shuttle	Moderate	2 1/2
22 Makiki-Manoa Adventure	Loop	Strenuous	6
23 Ualakaa Loop	Loop	Easy	1
24 Puu Ohia-Nuuanu View	Out & back	Moderate	3 1/2
25 Puu Ohia-Nuuanu Trails	Out & back	Moderate	4
26 Judd Memorial Trail	Loop	Easy	1
27 Judd-Nuuanu Trail	Semiloop	Strenuous	3 3/4
28 Old Pali Highway	Out & back	Easy	1 1/3
29 Maunawili Trail	Shuttle	Strenuous	9+
30 Diamond Head	Out & back	Moderate	1 3/4
31 Ala Wai Canal Stroll	Semiloop	Moderate	3 3/4
32 Rabbit Kekai's Waikiki Stroll	Out & back	Easy	1 3/4
33 Foster Botanical Garden	Loop	Very easy	*

Trip Number and Name	Type	Difficulty	Miles
34 Aiea Loop	Loop	Moderate	$4^3/4$
35 Upper-Lower Waimano	Loop	Moderate	2
36 Upper Waimano Trail	Out & back	Strenuous	14
37 Kuaokala Trail	Loop	Strenuous	5
38 Kaena Point—South	Out & back	Moderate	$4^3/4$
✗ 39 Kaena Point—North	Out & back	Strenuous	$5^1/2$
40 Kaena—Both Sides	Out & back	Strenuous	$9^3/4$
41 Kealia Trail	Out & back	Strenuous	$6^2/3$
42 Wahiawa	Loop	Very easy	*
43 Waimea Bay Loop	Loop	Very easy	1
44 Puu o Mahuka *Heiau*	Loop	Very easy	$1/4$
45 Kaunala Loop	Loop	Moderate	$4^1/2$

*How far you walk is up to you.

Read This

Hiking in the backcountry entails unavoidable risk that every hiker assumes and must be aware of and respect. The fact that a trail is described in this book is not a representation that it will be safe for you. Trails vary greatly in difficulty and in the degree of conditioning and agility one needs to enjoy them safely. On some hikes routes may have changed or conditions may have deteriorated since the descriptions were written. Also trail conditions can change even from day to day, owing to weather and other factors. A trail that is safe on a dry day or for a highly conditioned, agile, properly equipped hiker may be completely unsafe for someone else or unsafe under adverse weather conditions.

You can minimize you risks on the trail by being knowledgeable, prepared, and alert. There is not space in this book for a general treatise on safety in the mountains, but there are a number of good books and public courses on the subject, and you should take advantage of them to increase your knowledge. Just as important, you should always be aware of your own limitations and of conditions existing when and where you are hiking. If conditions are dangerous, or if you are not prepared to deal with them safely, choose a different hike! It's better to have wasted a drive than to be the subject of a mountain rescue.

These warnings are not intended to scare you off the trails. Millions of people have safe and enjoyable hikes every year. However, one element of the beauty, freedom, and excitement of the wilderness is the presence of risks that do not confront us at home. When you hike you assume these risks. They can be met safely, but only if you exercise your own independent judgment and common sense.

On the trail in Maakua Gulch (Trip 3)

Thomas Winnett

The Trips

Trip 1. Hauula Loop

Distance: 2¹/₂ miles

Elevation gain: 700'

Hiking time: 1¹/₄ hours

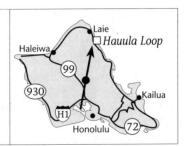

Topos: *Hauula*
Trail map: At the end of this trip.
Highlights: Views over the North Shore and the valleys behind it, interesting plants, colorful volcanic soil, and marvelous songs of the white-rumped shama (also called the shama thrush) make this trip a delight.
Driving instructions: From the intersection of McCully Street and Kapiolani Boulevard just outside Waikiki, continue northeast on McCully, crossing over the Lunalilo Freeway (H1) on a narrow bridge. Just across the bridge, follow the signs to get on H1 westbound (a quick left turn onto Metcalfe Street that leads to a westbound freeway on-ramp). Take H1 westbound past the intersections with the Pali and Likelike highways to its junction with Highway 78. On Highway 78, go west-northwest to the junction with H2 and get on H2 going generally north. Follow H2 northward to Wahiawa, where it becomes Highway 80 (and Highway 99, the Kamehameha Highway, bears away west). Follow Highway 80 north through Whitmore Village, beyond which it merges with Highway 99. Your route is now Highway 99, the Kamehameha Highway, until you reach a junction with Highway 930 shortly before Haleiwa. Turn right here, toward Haleiwa, still on the Kamehameha Highway, which is now renumbered as Highway 83. Follow Highway 83 north-northeast through Haleiwa, past Waimea Bay, around the north tip of Oahu, and then south-southeast through Kahuku and Laie. Keep your eyes peeled for the Polynesian Cultural Center on the inland side of the road in Laie. Two and a quarter miles past the Polynesian Cultural Center, turn right (inland) on unmarked

Maakua Homestead Road. In 1/4 mile, Maakua Homestead Road curves left; you proceed a short distance ahead (right) on a spur road to park either off the road or in a makeshift parking lot on the right side of the road as you face inland, 543/4 miles.

If you miss the first turnoff to Maakua Homestead Road, it curves around to meet Highway 83 again a short distance farther south, and here it *is* marked. Turn right on it and follow it back to the spur road described above.

(H1 and Highway 78, and then H2 and Highway 99, crisscross each other more than once, and it is possible to get to this trailhead by a number of different routes.)

You may also wish to cross the mountains behind Honolulu (the famous Pali) on the Likelike Highway (Highway 63) to Kaneohe and then work your way north-northwest up the windward side on Highway 83 (the Kamehameha Highway). This route is shorter in miles than the route given above but longer in time because it's slower. It's also far more scenic. See Trip 5's driving instructions to get started and then continue past Kahana Valley and Sacred Falls state parks to Hauula.

TheBus routes: Not directly served by TheBus. From Waikiki, take either Route 19 or 20 into downtown Honolulu and transfer to Route 55, which goes north to Kaneohe and then north-northwest up the windward side toward the Polynesian Cultural Center. Get off at the stop nearest the northern intersection of Maakua Homestead Road and Highway 83 in Hauula (ask the driver) and walk up Maakua Homestead Road from there.

Permit/permission required: None.

Description. Walk up the spur road, heading inland (southwest) and uphill, soon turning left into an old driveway at a trail sign. You shortly arrive at a hunters-and-hikers check-in station; please sign in here (and sign out on your return). Now you cross a dry channel on a raised roadbed under *hau* and *kukui*, keeping your eyes peeled for a lone mango tree at an unmarked junction where a grassy but distinct trail branches right, away from the old road.

Turn right onto this trail, which is the Hauula Loop Trail. It's not long before you make a slippery crossing of a damp gully and emerge, going southwest, on a grassy track on the right (west) side of the gully. Ironwood trees, the ones with the long, droopy, pine-like needles, and vines turn the steep left side of the gully into a romantic cascade of tropical greenery. Ahead and above, symmetrical Norfolk pines bristle on a slope, while the shrubby, native, white-flowered *ulei* makes hedges on your right. Spiky palms, the strange octopus tree, with its red "flowers" like beads strung on wires, strawberry guavas, and Christmas berry trees make up the forest along the trail.

You presently begin making gentle switchbacks as the forest closes in and you cross a little gully. Ironwoods now line the trail, their needles thickly carpeting the path. Rocks and exposed ironwood roots protrude through the warm brown carpet, making interesting patterns and minor hazards.

The loop portion begins in this ironwood forest. You can go left or right; arbitrarily, this trip goes left, where the ironwoods temporarily give way to vines. You pass through tunnels hacked through dense Christmas berry thickets, which support their share of these vines—a passionflower whose leaf is lanceolate, not the more common three-lobed passionflower leaf. Coarse ferns dominate the understory until you break out into ironwoods again and notice the occasional silk oak daring to poke its silvery leaves and (in season) large bracts of showy golden-orange flowers through the dominant green of these slopes.

Near a switchback turn around 2/3 mile from your start, you have sweeping views inland over the lush green gulch and up the slopes to the distant, misty mountains and seaward over Hauula town. A couple of turns farther, you'll come across one of the few native plants on this trail: the stiff-leafed, red-berried *pukiawe*. Paperbark eucalyptuses greet you at the next turn, where you cross over a ridge and begin a descent toward—what are those, traffic cones?! No, if something that's a brilliant orange arrests your gaze here, the chances are it's a fiery blossom of the African tulip tree. The African tulip tree is generally welcome in Hawaii for its handsome form and spectacular flowers. Another non-

native here, this one dominating the understory, is a serious threat to the few remaining native ecosystems: Koster's curse, a shrub with insignificant white flowers and bristly black berries, as unattractive as its name suggests.

Non-native paperbarks, guavas, and strawberry guavas begin to dominate the forest now, while the many-branched *uluhe* fern and the red-flowered *ohia* tree represent

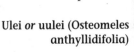

Ulei *or* uulei (Osteomeles anthyllidifolia)

Hawaii's native plants. You cross Waipilopilo Gulch below a pool and switchback steeply up to the next ridge, where you'll find dramatic views across the valley of Kaipapau Stream. Strolling along the ridge, you glimpse the sea as you pass an eroded little knob by some struggling *ohia* trees.

Now you begin an intriguing section of the trail where you sometimes walk right on the narrow ridgetop, sometimes just below it, dipping a little and then climbing a little. To your right there are bare patches of eroded soil where the dominant red of the earth mixes with tints of lavender, gray, and brown.

Suddenly you find you've twined down into a stand of Norfolk pines, huge trees whose massive trunks and branches shut out the light and shelter great numbers of their own light-green young, so fine and delicate that they are easily mistaken for ferns at first glance. Ironwoods droop back into the forest here and there as you at last make a switchback turn, cross Waipilopilo Gulch again, and ascend gradually between swamp mahogany trees (downslope) and Norfolk pines (upslope). The ironwoods come to dominate the forest again as you descend through an understory dotted with white-blossomed Chinese violets to close the loop.

Retrace your steps to the trailhead from here.

The tenacious *ohia* tree....It's almost impossible today to be ignorant of the enormous ecological problems facing Hawaii. Everywhere her native plants and animals retreat before development, agriculture, and encroaching non-native plants. Especially on Oahu, very few naturally occurring pockets of native plants still exist.

So it's a great pleasure to encounter those tenacious natives who persist in surviving these invasions, like the charming *ohia lehua* tree, a member of the myrtle family. A key to the *ohia's* survival is its adaptability. You'll find *ohia* growing, stunted to a few inches high, in mountain bogs; reaching proudly skyward as 80-foot giants; forming thickets along a volcano's edge and bravely colonizing the Big Island's new lava landscapes; and even shading motel parking lots. There seem to be few Hawaiian ecological niches where the *ohia* cannot eke out a living and nourish other native species.

And nourish it does. Its handsome red—rarely, yellow—powderpuff flowers are really dense clusters of red stamens billowing from shallow green cups of nectar beloved by Hawaii's native *apapane* and *iiwi* birds. Standing in a rainforest, its branches may cradle epiphytes and hold vines. Fallen and decaying in that same rainforest, it is a source of support and food for mosses, ferns, and fungi.

Ohia lehua groves are sacred to the volcano goddess, Pele. The goddess Hina was worshipped in several forms, one being that of an *ohia lehua* tree, Hina-ule-ohia. The red blossoms are prized for *lei*. Hawaiians say that if you pick one of them on your way into the mountains, it will rain; *lei*-makers must wait to pluck them on the way out of the mountains. Better yet, don't pick the blossoms at all. Out of respect for their stubbornness and adaptability, leave them to brighten Hawaii's slopes and delight your eye, to feed her native birds, and (best of all) to make more *ohia* trees.

Another myrtle-family member, the Australian bottlebrush, is widely used in landscaping in warm, dry mainland areas. Mainlanders from those areas will recognize the kinship between the *ohia* and the bottlebrush, especially in the red, brushlike flowers. Wouldn't it be interesting to see how the adaptable *ohia* would do on the mainland where the bottlebrush flourishes?

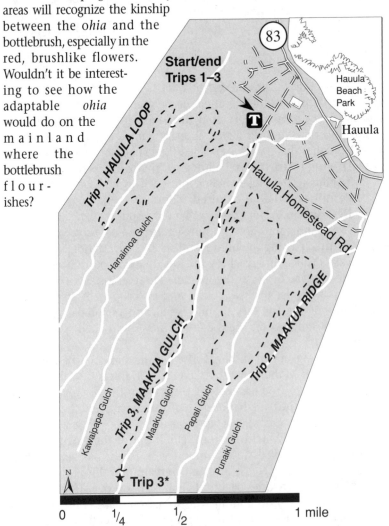

*Not recommended beyond the point where the path ends and you must boulder-hop in the streambed

Trip 2. Maakua Ridge Loop

Distance: 3 miles

Elevation gain: 720'

Hiking time: 1 1/2 hours

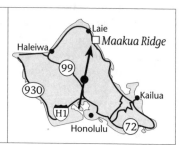

Topos: *Hauula*

Trail map: At the end of Trip 1.

Highlights: Tunneling under dense vegetation and enjoying far-reaching views are real treats along this loop. Tiptoeing across a narrow saddle and thrashing through a slippery gully add a touch of adventure. Note that this trail is also called the Papali/Maakua Ridge Trail.

Driving instructions: Follow the driving instructions of Trip 1.

TheBus routes: Take TheBus route of Trip 1.

Permit/permission required: None.

Description. As for Trip 1, walk up the spur road, heading inland (southwest) and uphill, soon turning left into an old driveway at a trail sign and then passing the hunters-hikers check-in station. After crossing Maakua Gulch and reaching the lone mango tree, don't turn right onto the unmarked trail at the lone mango tree. Instead, continue on the old road under papaya, guava, and avocado trees and along an understory of cayenne vervain, mare's-tail, and a small daisylike plant. Deep in the thickets off the road, you may spot lichen-spattered old stone walls.

You soon come to another fork, this one marked, where you take the left branch to the Papali/Maakua Ridge Trail (as it's called on the present trail sign). You teeter along the bank of the gulch, looking out for holes where the bank has been totally undercut, and then cross the gulch to head off under guava and *hau*.

You make a switchback turn, climb out of the gulch, and find yourself on a *hau*-clad slope. Around you, Christmas berry, swamp mahogany, pink-flowered clover, and vervain crowd in, too. The next switchback turn provides beautiful views seaward over Hauula town.

A little over 1/2 mile from your start, you make another seaward switchback turn and reach the beginning of the loop portion of this trip. Arbitrarily, this trip turns right (inland) and climbs past non-native octopus trees and ti plants (the latter brought by the Polynesians) and native *ulei* and *lauae* (the anise-scented sweet fern). On another ridge, Norfolk pines stand stiffly at attention.

As you curve inland, huge *hala* trees appear, and you may have to scramble over or under *hala* deadfalls. The trail is littered here and there with *hala* leaves and fruits. It's easy to see how the Hawaiians could use the brushy-tipped *hala* fruits as paintbrushes. Purple Philippine orchids peep out of the understory; through the occasional openings in the vegetation, there are fine views over Maakua Gulch.

It's quite a change when you abruptly find yourself southbound on a narrow ridge in a tunnel of non-native acacia. There are glimpses of the ocean on one side and of Maakua Gulch on the other. The trail presently forsakes the ridgetop and begins a gentle descent southward, then curves across *kukui*-filled Papali Gulch. You cross a streambed under *ti* and mountain apple (distinguished by its feathery, shocking-pink flowers) and along ferny slopes.

After you pick your way across an extremely narrow saddle, you swing away from Papali Gulch and traverse above Punaiki Gulch on slopes heavily overgrown and shaded by acacia. Watch out you don't bonk your head on those overhanging branches!

At last you negotiate a switchback turn, descending through much of the same vegetation you've been in, in sound but not sight—except very briefly—of the ocean. As the altitude decreases and the exposure to sea breezes increases, Christmas berry replaces the acacia, and *ulei* appears, too.

The trail gets steeper as you dip into a gully on whose opposite side black cliff faces make you wonder where on earth the trail will be when you get over there. Down in the gully, you pick your way over slippery tangles of boulders and branches. Now you zigzag steeply to moderately out of the gully, passing a huge black

View over Hauula town

outcrop, and trace your way along a blunt ridge nose, enjoying good coastal views. At last you curve inland again, soon closing the loop.

Retrace your steps from here.

Rainforest puzzles.... You've been hiking through an area that includes patches of Hawaiian rainforest, though much altered by the invasion of non-native plants. Recently, many fine television programs have discussed our disappearing rainforests, so you are likely to have heard that cleared rainforests make poor pastures for cattle and poor soil for crops. Agriculture depletes the nutrient-poor soil in as little as three to five years, leaving it incapable of sustaining ranching and farming. Why does so rich an ecosystem—the most varied of all, we are told—yield so poor a soil? The reason seems to be that the nutrients in dead vegetation and animals don't return to the soil. They never form a classic layer of humus, leading to rich soil, as found in temperate forests. Instead, things that have died are consumed, almost on the spot, by the voracious living things of the rainforest—mosses, ferns, lichens, fungi, insects, even young trees—before they can enrich the soil. And that, perversely, leaves rainforest soils remarkably poor.

Here's something else that may not have occurred to you, as it had not occurred to me. Look at some of the huge trees in a tropical rainforest—maybe not this one, but other Hawaiian rainforests. How old are these trees? *Surely,* you may think, *if this great* ohia *were cut down, its annual rings would prove it to be a hundred or more years old.* Alas, its annual rings would prove nothing, because there are no such rings to count. In the steady temperatures of the tropics, trees do not

form the distinct bands of warm-season fast growth/cold-season slow growth that trees in temperate regions form. So no one really knows how old the oldest giants of the Hawaiian rainforest are—and perhaps no one ever will.

Luscious golden-peach blossoms of the native wiliwili *(Erythrina sandwicensis), now largely replaced in populated areas by its non-native cousin the coral tree (Erythrina indica)*

Trip 3. Maakua Gulch

M

Distance: Less than 4 miles (depends on where footpath currently ends)

Elevation gain: 520'

Hiking time: Less than 2 hours

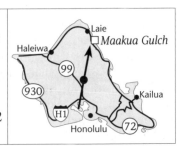

Topos: *Hauula*
Trail map: At the end of Trip 1.
Highlights: The ramble up Maakua Gulch is pretty and enjoyable provided you do not go beyond the point where the footpath ~~point that could vary from year to year and even from~~ Note that it is also extremely mosquito-y, so ~~put~~ Beyond the end of the footpath, you're ~~for~~ ...mbed. It's a miserable, slow, knee- and ankl~~e~~ ... narrow channel on slimy boulders—mo~~re~~ ... or wet soapballs than hiking. Supposedly ~~th~~ ... way up the gulch. You don't need it—espe~~cially~~ ... falls (Trip 4) just down the road.

~~D~~ ... follow the driving instructions of Trip 1.
... ~~t~~ake TheBus route of Trip 1.
Permission required: None.

~~De~~scription. As for Trip 1, walk up the spur road, heading inland (southwest) and uphill, soon turning left into an old driveway at a trail sign and then passing the hunters-hikers check-in station. After crossing Maakua Gulch and reaching the lone mango tree, don't turn right onto the unmarked trail at the lone mango tree. Instead, continue on the old road. You soon come to another fork, this one marked, where you take the right branch south into Maakua Gulch.

The roadside scrub is brightened by the blue spikes of vervain and the white heads of a little daisy. Soon the forest closes in, dominated by strawberry guava and *hala* trees, draped with passionflower vines, and filled with the songs of the white-rumped shama and the constant nattering of the Japanese white-eye. Long, flat, brown mongooses rustle secretively through the understory. Ahead and to the right, you have glimpses of the Norfolk pines on the ridge that the Hauula Loop Trail (Trip 1) climbs.

The trail presently climbs to a large open space affording fine views up and down the gulch, then dips into the greenery again. With *hau* thickets downslope and ironwoods upslope, you cross a trickling stream above a little cascade where, if there is enough water, there are tiny pools up and down the stream. Clumps of *ape*, the giant-leafed relative of *taro*, and tangles of fern make an appropriately tropical understory.

You soon cross the gulch. From here on, tags of colored plastic ribbon tied to the vegetation, tags of metal with arrows painted on them, and splashes of neon-bright paint on the boulders help you stay on the footpath, which may become faint and hard to follow at times. Following them, you work your way upstream, occasionally in the gulch but more often on the footpath along it. In this humid area, even rocks that look perfectly dry and safe prove to be covered with an invisible coating of slime resistant to the grip of boot soles. It pays to search out the next tag in order to keep on the footpath and to stay out of the gulch as much as you can!

The walls of the gulch close in, and you find yourself scrambling along the footpath in the twilight of dense *hau* thickets broken by the occasional strawberry guavas, *hala* trees, and Christmas berry. You soon make a couple of streambed crossings one right after the other.

The *hau* thickets draw back as you gain the footpath again under a tall canopy of *kukui* trees. The path is lined here with mountain apple trees, which in spring leave the track thickly strewn with the brilliant cerise stamens of their powder-puff flowers, sprouting from trunks as well as from branches. In summer they provide edible fruit greatly prized by the old Hawaiians. Alas, mosquitoes swarm so thickly here that you could make a mosquito sandwich by waving a couple of slices of buttered bread around for a few minutes, then slapping them together.

You are increasingly forced into the streambed, stumbling between walls of black rock thickly covered with mosses and ferns, where you must work your way not only over the slippery boulders but over and around numerous tangles of deadfalls. I recommend that you not continue farther up the gulch. Instead, pick a spot to rest, enjoy a snack, and savor the rainforest setting.

Retrace your steps from here.

Flash floods.....Sudden, heavy tropical rains can quickly swell a stream to a deep, swift, cold flood or fill a dry gulch with a flash flood. Even if it isn't raining where you're hiking, beware of rain in the mountains from which the stream springs. Hikers have been caught by these flash floods, swept out to sea, and drowned here at Maakua Gulch, at Sacred Falls, and at similar canyon-bound streams throughout Hawaii. So keep an eye out: if the water begins to rise or if it begins to rain, turn around and get out of the gulch as fast as you safely can. Of course, if it's raining when you get to the trailhead, don't even start out: take a different, drier hike!

Trip 4. Sacred Falls

Distance: 4 miles

Elevation gain: 530'

Hiking time: 2 hours

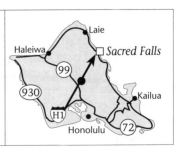

Topos: *Hauula*

Trail map: At the end of this trip.

Highlights: A stroll through dry fields leads abruptly to a rainforest valley and a beautiful waterfall with a pool at its base plenty big ~~~ for swimming, though the water is quite cold. Sacred Falls i~ and even crowded on the weekend; a weekday ~~ better chance to savor the area. **Note:** The ~~~~~~~ ~~osed when it rains, as several tragic flash ~~~~~~~ ~~urred here.

Driving instructions: ~~~~~~~~~ ~~uctions of Trip 1, but do not turn right ~~~~~~~~~~~ ~~d Road. Instead, continue on Highway 8? ~~~~~~~~~~~~~, for a total of just over 56 miles. Sometim~~ ~~~~~ ~~ark is not marked by highway signs like ~~~ ~~~~waii Visitors Bureau (HVB) warrior, so it may be ~~~ ~~ok for a large parking lot inland, backed by a wide ~~ ~~ dotted with palms, ironwoods, and tropical almond trees; ~~~~ in and park here. (If you are coming from the north, as you would be following these directions, and you pass an HVB-marked OLD HAWAIIAN CHURCH, you have gone too far.)

You may also wish to cross the mountains behind Honolulu (the famous Pali) on the Likelike Highway (Highway 63) to Kaneohe and then work your way north-northwest up the windward side on Highway 83 (the Kamehameha Highway). This route is shorter in miles than the route given above but longer in time because it's slower. It's also far more scenic. See Trip 5's driving instructions to get started and then continue past Kahana Valley to Sacred Falls.

TheBus routes: Take TheBus route of Trip 1 but get off sooner, at the stop nearest Sacred Falls State Park (ask the driver).

Permit/permission required: None.

Description. Cross the lawn toward a chain link fence in which there is a gate overshadowed by what's supposed to be an automated flash-flood warning station—but the system may be defunct, so don't depend on it. (See the flash-flood caution at the end of Trip 3.) Go through the gate if it's open and follow a dirt road south-southwestward between uninteresting, dry fields toward the mountains. A little beyond the 1/2-mile point, you reach a **Y** junction (not shown on the map). Take the left fork southward here.

You shortly cross a cattle guard. On your left, you can hear a stream running noisily under a cover of Christmas berry and *hala. Koa haole,* Christmas berry, swamp mahogany, and tropical almond trees line the old road here. Nearby, a bench under a tropical almond tree near the stream offers welcome shade and rest on a hot day.

The road ends suddenly at another flash-flood warning station, and your trail plunges into Christmas berry thickets and becomes a narrow, rocky footpath on the west side of the stream. What a change it is from the openness of the road! From here on, the stream is sometimes out of sight but never out of hearing.

The trail wriggles through some huge, mossy boulders, ascends a little rise, and descends briefly, passing an occasional octopus tree. In a few more steps, you make your way across the stream to its east bank at a broad, slippery ford. Sharp-eyed hikers may spot large freshwater shrimp in the stream here.

Now the narrow trail bobs up and down, sometimes high above the stream, but generally climbing under an exotic cover of *kukui,* mountain apple, guava, and tall *ti* plants and through an understory of bracken fern and ginger. In season, the rocky track is often half-buried under a shocking-pink carpet of the fallen stamens of mountain apple blossoms—a sight all the more dazzling for the dark rainforest that presses in around you. The trail may also be very slippery because of the constant dampness. Where the trail runs near the stream, occasional pools may provide an opportunity for a quieter splash than you're likely to find at the falls.

You pass a deep recess in the high canyon walls on your left, probably the now-dry channel of another waterfall. Because Sacred Falls itself is not yet in sight, you may think you've come all this way and been cheated of your waterfall. No, it's a short distance ahead and soon comes into view. You negotiate another slippery stream crossing and climb past yet another automated flash-flood warning station.

Just beyond here, you find yourself on the shattered rock surrounding the pool at the base of Sacred Falls, which splashes some 80 white, foaming feet down a moss- and fern-filled grotto into a large pool. Falling rock is always a hazard this close to a waterfall (see below). Nevertheless, there's usually a light-hearted atmosphere here as laughter and the shrieks of swimmers startled at the chilliness of the

Sacred Falls

water echo off the grotto walls. You may want to join them or to find a comfortable rock on which to enjoy your lunch as you take in your surroundings.

Too soon, you must retrace your steps to the dirt road and then to your car.

Demigods of the valley.... Although the present name of the park suggests that only the falls were sacred, the entire area was in fact sacred to the old Hawaiians. Hawaiian legend says that the demigod Kamapuaa, who was half-pig and half-man, was born in this lovely valley and made his home here for a while. Remember the channel you passed just before you got to Sacred Falls? When Kamapuaa found himself besieged by enemies here, he pressed his body against the valley wall and stretched himself up over the cliff so that his family could climb up his body and escape from the besiegers. Then he, too, escaped. The channel is the place where he pressed himself against the valley wall.

Waterfalls at work.... In Hawaii, the terrain tends to consist of alternating layers of resistant lava and less-resistant material such as consolidated ash or clinker. A stream wears down through the softer layer and cascades over the harder layer. The force of the falling water wears away the rock at the base of the falls, forming a lovely pool. Undercut by that process, the rock above the pool succumbs to gravity and falls away, shattering at the base of the falls. This process erodes the stream's channel farther and farther back into the slope. Over eons, the stream cuts its gorge back toward its headwaters. Because harder and softer layers alternate, streams often form a chain of waterfalls on their long descent to the sea. A close look at the topo shows you that this is indeed the case with Kaluanui Stream, whose final, dramatic plunge we call Sacred Falls.

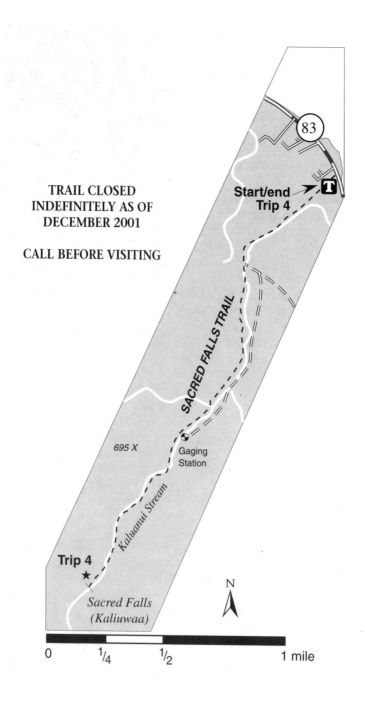

TRAIL CLOSED
INDEFINITELY AS OF
DECEMBER 2001

CALL BEFORE VISITING

Start/end
Trip 4

SACRED FALLS TRAIL

695 X

Gaging
Station

Kaluanui Stream

Trip 4
★

Sacred Falls
(Kaliuwaa)

N

0   ¹⁄₄   ¹⁄₂   1 mile

Trip 5. Kahana Valley State Park—Kapaeleele Loop Trail

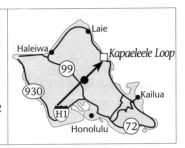

Distance: Just over 1 mile

Elevation gain: 140'

Hiking time: Just over 1/2 hour

Topos: *Kahana*

Trail map (route approximated): At the end of this trip.

Highlights: This short loop offers you fine views over beautiful Kahana Bay from historically significant points. Cheers for the local Boy Scouts for clearing and maintaining this pleasant trail! I've recommended boots rather than tennies because some of the slopes the trail crosses have very loose soil.

Driving instructions: You *could* extend the driving instructions of Trip 1 to continue down the windward side to Kahana Bay State Park, some 60 miles. But the drive northwestward *up* the windward coast of Oahu, especially between Kaneohe and Kahana, is so scenic I can't let you miss it. If the sweeping view of Kahana Bay and Kahana Valley, rimmed by sharp, green peaks, doesn't knock your socks off as you come around Mahie Point, I don't know what will.

From the intersection of McCully Street and Kapiolani Boulevard just outside Waikiki, continue northeast on McCully, crossing over the Lunalilo Freeway (H1) on a narrow bridge. Just across the bridge, follow the signs to get on H1 westbound (a quick left turn onto Metcalfe Street that leads to a westbound freeway on-ramp). Take H1 westbound past the intersection with the Pali Highway to the intersection with the Likelike Highway (Highway 63). Take the Likelike Highway northeast across the Pali to Kaneohe to its intersection with the Kahekili Highway (Highway 83) or, longer and slower but more scenic, to its intersection in another half mile with the Kamehameha Highway (here, Highway 836). Turn left on the highway of your choice and drive northwest up the windward coast. The highways rejoin near Kahaluu to become the Kamehameha Highway (here, it's Highway 83) at an obscure junction currently distinguished by the presence of an organic-foods store. You continue northwest along huge Kaneohe Bay, pass Mokolii Island (aptly nicknamed "Chinaman's Hat"), and then curve out along a cliffbound coast deeply gashed by Kaaawa Stream's valley. The highway abruptly swings south as it rounds Mahie Point, offering you that magnificent view of Kahana Bay and Kahana Valley. As you cross the base of the bay, you spot the sign for Kahana Valley State Park on the inland side. Turn left into the park and continue past a parking lot on your right to the lot at park headquarters, 26 1/2 miles if you take the Kahekili Highway, farther if you take the Kamehameha Highway all the way. If the headquarters lot is full, park back up the road in the lot you passed earlier.

TheBus routes: From Waikiki, take either Route 19 or 20 into downtown Honolulu and transfer to Route 55, which goes north to Kaneohe and then north-northwest up the windward side toward Laie. Or transfer downtown to Route 56 and then transfer again to Route 55 at Kaneohe. Get off at Kahana Bay State Park.

Permit/permission required: None.

Description. Kahana Valley State Park is dedicated to nurturing and fostering native Hawaiian culture and spreading knowledge of its values and ways. Within the park is a living community of some 31 Hawaiian families whose members are part of this effort. You'll pass some of their homes as you explore the park—no intruding or trespassing, please. Be sure to stop at the park headquarters for the latest trail maps and any advice they may have. If the office is not open, you will probably find maps available outside in a self-service rack.

Starting your hike at headquarters, walk northwest along the lane that runs just seaward of the restrooms, putting the restrooms on your left and the ocean on your right. The lane is lined with anise-scented sweet fern, ginger, banana, *ti*, and tall mango and swamp mahogany trees. You pass between a couple of cement pylons, passing to the right of a large boulder, between palms and bananas, and through full, round-leafed shrubs bearing clusters of white to pale pink, double, fragrant flowers. Morning glories twine through the shrubs and trees, which now include *hau*.

Avoid a road that comes in from the left for now. Instead, veer left into the forest on a tagged footpath, then almost immediately veer right under *hau*, octopus tree, and more of the pink-flowered shrubs. The going is level at first and then begins a climb along a beaten and tagged track. A little past the 1/3-mile point, you reach an apparent junction where a trail-of-use comes in from the left; continue ahead on the "main" trail, which may look more like a trail-of-use itself here. Fine views of Kanaha Bay open up as you continue; then you dip down into a gully filled with the mottled gray trunks of octopus trees, cross a rocky little watercourse, and emerge on the open spot called Kapaeleele Koa, again overlooking the bay. There's a shrine here; please *don't* disturb anything, *don't* leave an offering, and *do* show respect. "Kapaeleele" means "black *kapa*," *kapa* being the bark cloth of Polynesia, and may refer to Lono's black *kapa* cape, reported to figure in Hawaiian mythology. The shrine was (and perhaps still is) a place where fishermen came to pray for a good *akule* (shad) catch.

Bear uphill past the shrine and then contour along this breezy, grassy slope dotted with young octopus trees. It may seem that trail tags beckon you straight up or down the hill, but the route actually contours for now. At a **T** junction near the 2/3-mile point, look to your left (uphill) to see a long black boulder about five yards upslope. Follow the track that leads steeply but briefly uphill past the boulder to a fenced area under ironwoods. The area is called "Keaniani Kilo" in the park's descriptive literature; here you have superb views of Kahana Bay and the surrounding mountains. A *kilo* is a lookout point, and *keaniani* is said to refer to sparkling—the sparkling of the bay's waters caused by schools of fish swimming just beneath the surface. A watchman posted here would alert the village when he spotted a school. All the villagers would join in the fishing: men in canoes would stretch nets around the school and pull the nets shoreward, where the rest of the people would take the ends of the nets and pull them to shore *(hukilau)*, heavy with the catch which all would share equally.

After returning to the main trail, you continue your loop by turning left. Almost immediately you begin to switchback down, sometimes steeply, into *hala*, octopus trees, and mango trees. The soil is crumbly and may give way underfoot. After the last switchback turn, the trail becomes very faint under mango debris as it bears downslope, and it almost vanishes by a thicket of tropical almond trees that buffer the trail from the highway. Routes that seem promising lead nowhere useful from here. Instead, there's a ditch between you and the highway; carefully scramble across the ditch and bear right to walk along the highway's shoulder to get back to the park's entrance. Follow the road's shoulder back to your car, keeping as far away from the traffic as you can.

Lono....As explained in the "Geology and History" chapter, the god Lono had sailed away from Hawaii, promising to return on a floating *heiau* (or, in some versions, on a floating island). But why did Lono leave Hawaii?

One version says that from the Hawaiians' ancestral home, Lono sent his brothers to find for him an earthly wife. After searching for a long time, they found the beautiful Kaikilani in Waipio Valley on the Big Island of Hawaii, dwelling beside the twin waterfalls, Hiilawe.

Lono descended to Hawaii on a rainbow to wed Kaikilani. They lived at Kealakekua on the Big Island, deeply in love and filled with happiness, until one day Lono overheard a chief trying to steal Kaikilani's heart with a love song. Maddened by rage and jealousy, Lono slew Kaikilani, though she protested her innocence and assured him of her love as she died. Upon recovering from his madness, Lono was overwhelmed by horror and grief at his crime. He wandered about the island wrestling with every man he met (hence the origin of the *Makahiki* games).

His wanderings were in vain: he could not escape his sorrow. At last, perhaps to escape the place of his sorrow, he built a great canoe, provisioned it, and sailed away alone. Before he vanished into myth, he promised the people of Hawaii he would someday return—on a floating *heiau*, some myths say, or on a floating island, an island of plenty.

Instead, Captain Cook arrived in 1778, and the rest is history.

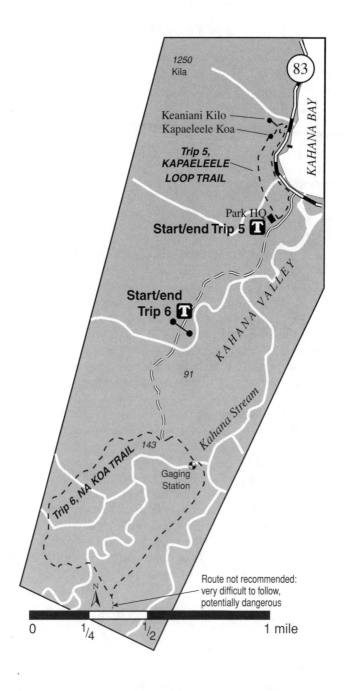

Trip 6. Kahana Valley State Park—Na Koa Trail

Distance: 4¹/₂ miles

Elevation gain: 320'

Hiking time: 2¹/₄ hours

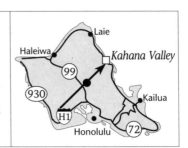

Topos: *Kahana*

Trail map: At the end of Trip 5.

Highlights: An out-and-back segment with fine views of Kahana Valley leads to a lush, wet, adventurous rainforest loop where the trail is occasionally hard to follow. At least one member of your party needs to be an experienced hiker with good navigation skills. A couple of fords late in the hike can be real foot-soakers; you may want to carry wading shoes for these crossings. At the last crossing you'll find swimming holes by a gauging station and low dam. Check at headquarters to learn if the water is high; take this hike another day if it is. The loop is in a part of the valley that is open to hunting at times, so be prepared to be seen.

Driving instructions: Follow the driving instructions of Trip 5, but continue 0.7 mile more down into the valley, to signs instructing you to park here and walk another 15 minutes (about ¹/₂ mile) to get to the trail. Park off the road as indicated.

TheBus routes: Take TheBus routes of Trip 5.

Permit/permission required: None.

Description. On foot now, continue south-southwest down the road past homes and gardens. You reach a gate that bars the public's vehicles, ¹/₂ mile from where you parked. Circumvent the gate and continue on the road, ascending gradually, and shortly reach a hikers' and hunters' check-in station. Sign in here. Your route curves left, signed SWIMMING HOLE, and in another 50 feet reaches a junction. If all you want to do is go to the swimming hole, go left here, reversing the last paragraph of this description. To continue on this hike, take the right fork south-southwest on a narrow trail under swamp mahogany trees and past banks of ferns.

The trail begins traversing above a beautiful gully filled with big hala trees, *hau thickets,* guava trees, and—alas—Koster's curse. The gully is hidden at times by the dense growth of *hapuu, palapalai,* and sword ferns, as well as *ti, koa,* and ginger.

Nearing 1¼ miles, the trail makes an abrupt, steep, slippery descent to continue as a faint track under hala. If the mosquitoes haven't found you earlier, they surely will here! On you go as the trail wanders the steep slopes above Kahana Stream, now through *hala* forests, now through tunnels hacked through *hau* thickets. Views are very rare because of the dense rainforest vegetation.

You descend moderately at 2 miles and shortly cross a tiny stream above a pretty little pool. Circumventing the pool, you slop up the streambank to regain the trail. After a sometimes-steep descent, at 2¼ miles you ford a small stream and descend to a trail junction in a *hala* thicket. Turn left (north-northeast) and descend gradually past a steep, fern-draped bank on your right. The trail grows faint as you traverse a ridgetop in dense *hala*, hearing the noisy stream below.

At 2¾ miles you reach a major stream crossing with steep, slippery banks on both sides. Once across and up the other side, you thrash through more hau thickets. Soon you're out of them and climbing gradually to a signed junction at 3 miles, where the Na Koa Trail goes left (northeast) under schefflera trees. After the trail curves northwest and makes a gradual descent, you reach a low cement dam by an old gauging station on Kahana Stream at 3¾ miles. Scramble down to cross the top of the dam. Often this dam-top is just under the swift-moving water, and, if it is, it will be slick with algae. There's a rope strung across the stream here to help with the crossing, and there are swimming holes on either side of the dam.

On the other side, you climb steeply away from the stream on a ruined, slippery old roadbed. You close the loop at 4 miles, regaining the road you walked up here on. Turn right and retrace your steps to your car, 4½ miles.

The Marchers of the Night.... In a place like Kahana Valley where Hawaiian families live in a more traditional way than you'll find elsewhere on Oahu, it seems appropriate to relate the Hawaiian legend of the Marchers of the Night.

"If a man is found stricken by the roadside a white doctor will pronounce the cause as heart failure, but a Hawaiian will think at once of the fatal night marchers," said scholars Mary Pukui and Martha Beckwith in "The Marchers of the Night" (in *A Hawaiian Reader;* see Bibliography).

The old Hawaiians believed that death did not sever family ties and that the dead returned as spirits in their earthly forms to the places familiar to them during life. In particular, the spirits would return in processions on certain sacred nights or to welcome the spirit of a dying relative and conduct it to the afterworld. The gods might also appear in procession on sacred nights; the processions of the gods were far more brilliant than those of mere spirits. Sometimes the procession was silent; more often, it seems, the procession was accompanied by music: a procession of gods with chanting; a procession of spirits with drumming, the playing of the nose flute, and chanting. The marchers' goal was the area in the district that had been set aside for sports, and there they would enjoy the dancing and the games they had enjoyed in life.

To meet the Marchers of the Night is almost certain death to the living. A living person must escape the marchers as quickly as possible without being noticed. If that is not possible, the person might strip, lie face up, and breathe as little as possible in order to seem dead. If there is no time to strip, the person can only sit still with eyes closed, hoping for mercy. For one of the marchers, seeing the living person, will call out, "Strike that one!" and the person will be slain. But if the person has a relative or an *aumakua* (a family god) among the marchers, the relative or the *aumakua* will shout, "No, that one is mine!" and the person will be spared.

Formerly, many Hawaiians and even some non-Hawaiians heard and saw the marchers of the night and lived to tell about it. Pukui and Beckwith tell of a young man who twice watched such marches; each time, one marcher said of him, "There is the grandson of Kekuanoi!" and another marcher, evidently a relative, responded, "Never mind! we

Kahana Bay

do not mind him!" Upon his returning home, his grandfather Kekuanoi reported having seen it all—the marchers and his grandson—from afar. A woman told Pukui and Beckwith that she was terrified of the marchers when told about them as a child. But now that she is older and can hear them, she has lost her fear in the sound of the beautiful chanting, the music of the flute, and the "drumming so loud that it seems beaten upon the side of the house beside her bed. The voices are so distinct that if she could write music she would be able to set down the notes they sang."

Today, the marchers are rarely seen or heard. Perhaps the familiar places to which they might have returned have been destroyed. Or is it because Hawaiians no longer believe in them? I think not. Several Hawaiian friends have warned me to be sure to be done with my hike and safely indoors before the hours of the marchers—typically, from about half-past seven to about two in the morning. I take that seriously when I'm in Hawaii, even if "indoors" is just my tent.

Consider yourself warned, too.

Trip 7. Hoomaluhia Botanical Garden

Distance: Just under 2 miles

Elevation gain: 140'

Hiking time: Just under 1 hour

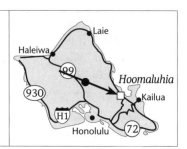

Topos: Optional: *Kaneohe*

Trail map (route approximated based on park literature): At the end of this trip.

Highlights: Hoomaluhia Botanical Garden invites you to stroll numerous trails through its lush landscape. The garden—or park, as some maps call it—is currently open from 9:00 AM to 4:00 PM daily except Christmas Day and New Year's Day. Note that in addition to the trip described here, the park offers guided nature hikes on Saturdays at 10:00 AM and Sundays at 1:00 PM. Call in advance to register for these hikes (1-808-235-6636).

Hoomaluhia is one of four botanical gardens maintained by the City and County of Honolulu. Others are Koko Crater (Trip 11), Foster (Trip 33), and Wahiawa (Trip 42). Each is different; I hope you'll have time to visit all of them.

Driving instructions: From the intersection of McCully Street and Kapiolani Boulevard just outside Waikiki, continue northeast on McCully, crossing over the Lunalilo Freeway (H1) on a narrow bridge. Just across the bridge, follow the signs to get on H1 westbound (a quick left turn onto Metcalfe Street that leads to a westbound freeway on-ramp). Take H1 westbound to the intersection with the Pali Highway. Take the Pali Highway northeast across the Pali toward Kailua but, before reaching Kailua, turn left onto the Kamehameha Highway (Highway 83). Take the Kamehameha Highway northwest toward its intersection with the Likelike Highway. Just before you reach the Likelike Highway, you'll see a left-turn lane for Luluku Street. Turn left onto Luluku Street and follow it through a residential area to Hoomaluhia Botanical Garden's gate. Follow the main access road from the gate through the park to the Visitor Center, on your left almost a mile from the gate. Park here in front of the Visitor Center, 11²/3 miles.

TheBus routes: Not served by TheBus.

Permit/permission required: None.

Description. Much of the trail system at Hoomaluhia has vanished from lack of maintenance, but you can still enjoy a pleasant and varied walk here. After stopping at the visitor center, retrace your steps toward the parking lot but, where the steps lead up to the lot, turn left on a paved path. The path zigzags down past marked plants. Palms with fronds that have lipstick-red stems and ixoras with clusters of colorful blooms are especially striking here.

The pavement ends, but the path continues winding downhill on grass, passing hau, heliconia, and arums, as it heads toward a huge old mango tree and some buildings—first a restroom, then a picnic pavilion. You can't see the lake until you're at the interpretive displays overlooking it, but you'll have no trouble picking out the cropped green slope of the earthfill dam on the lake's far side.

After taking in the view, bear right (southeast) toward the distant spires of lovely Mt. Olomana. Using a broad, grassy strip as your trail, you pass benches overlooking the lake. Stay high above the lake until your route dips to cross a culvert and then a footbridge.

The loop part of this trip begins at 1/3 mile, on the far side of the footbridge, where the path forks. Arbitrarily, go left (lake-ward) here, tracing the shoreline past a bank bright with the pink-powderpuff flowers of bashful plant, the yellow corollas of a daisy-like ground cover, and several kinds of ferns. Ducking under greenery, you cross another footbridge where numerous ducks and geese are apt to waddle up to you, looking for a handout. Expect a noisy reception here!

The path makes a **T**-junction with another grassy lane. Left takes you to a dead end with a nice view across the lake to the pali west of Hoomaluhia. But, to continue with this hike, you go right, a little uphill, and then almost immediately left past octopus trees and into a thicket of rose apple trees. In a few more steps you reach a **Y**-junction at the base of a small peninsula. The right fork is a shortcut across the peninsula; you go left, in the dense shade of rose apple trees, to trace the peninsula. Views may be poor here, but this is an excellent opportunity to hear birdsong.

Near the tip of the peninsula at 1/2 mile, you go right at a junction where the left fork is blocked off. At the next junction, you meet the other end of the shortcut across the peninsula. Turn left (south) as the trees begin to thin. The damp path curves along the mostly unseen and noisy stream, emerging at a little over 3/4 mile at a broad lawn with a fine view of the pali southwest of Hoomaluhia. A grassy road cuts along the edge of the lawn opposite where you've just emerged, so cross the lawn to pick it up. The road's left fork blends into the lawn's edge and hooks right to a dead end at impenetrable shrubbery.

Take the road's right fork past hedges of ginger. The fork shortly makes a **T**-junction with a gravel lane, where you go left to Kahua Lehua camping area. You stroll out onto Kahua Lehua's lawn a little shy of 1 mile, by a double powerline tower. Proceed across the lawn, past hibiscus plantings and toward the pali. There are a restroom, water taps, picnic tables, and marked plants to enjoy—surely, no one will object if you linger to have your lunch here, as long as there are no campers. A little knoll behind the restroom offers benches with fine views to the pali and over the adjacent countryside.

You reach Kahua Lehua's parking lot at a little over 1 mile and proceed up its access road to Hoomaluhia's main access road, at a point opposite a small knoll signed KILONANI MAUKA. Views of the pali are excellent along this stretch.

Now you turn right on the garden's main road, keeping to the shoulder, and head carefully downhill past abundant and beautiful plantings—exotic palm trees are especially intriguing. Beyond a small culvert and then an automobile bridge over a little stream, you reach the parking lot for Kahua Kuou. You could close the loop on the main road, but it's more fun to turn right here at a little over 1 1/4 miles, toward Kahua Kuou's restroom. Behind the restroom you'll find a pair of dirt roads diverging to camping areas.

Take the left road ahead (north) toward the as-yet-unseen lake, past another restroom and another double powerline tower, as the road soon fades into a beaten track. At the edge of a bluff affording a delightful view over the lake at 1 1/2 miles, there are benches for a welcome rest. From here, a grassy ramp angles hard left and downward, switchbacking right to close the loop by the first footbridge you crossed.

Turn left over the footbridge to return to your car from here, just under 2 miles total.

Hoomaluhia: nature undisturbed?.... Hardly. It's more a symptom of the endless human war on nature than of any farsighted effort to live with nature. Hoomaluhia Botanical Garden is the result of a U.S. Army Corps of Engineers project to provide flood control for greater Kaneohe, a town apparently built—*whoops!*—on a floodplain. After a particularly disastrous flood, the Corps of Engineers scooped out a flood-control basin and built the dam, thus creating the lake. The current garden is the culmination of years of citizens groups' planning, landscaping, and planting in the flood-control basin. They've done a wonderful job.

Still, Hoomaluhia, delightful as it is, does not exist primarily to preserve ecosystems. Rather, Hoomaluhia probably will be destroyed by the next flood, in order to protect suburbs and shopping centers.

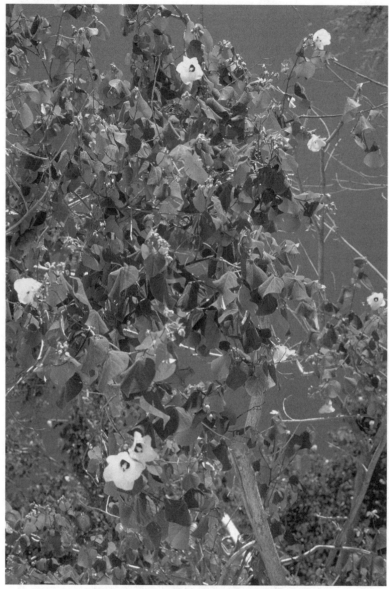

Hau (Hibiscus tiliaceus), introduced by the Polynesians

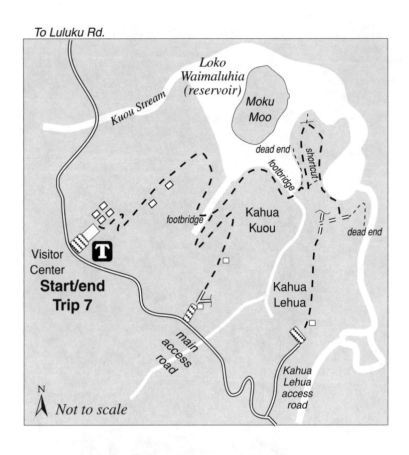

To Luluku Rd.

Loko Waimaluhia (reservoir)

Kuou Stream

Moku Moo

dead end

shortcut

footbridge

footbridge

Kahua Kuou

dead end

Visitor Center

Start/end Trip 7

Kahua Lehua

main access road

N

Not to scale

Kahua Lehua access road

Banana

Trip 8. Kailua Beach Stroll

Distance: Up to 5 miles	
M **Elevation gain:** Negligible	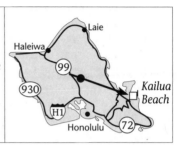
Hiking time: Up to 2¹/₂ hours	

Topos: *Kailua*

Trail map (route approximated): At the end of this trip. There's no trail; you just walk along the beach. Note that there are many more streets in the Kailua area than the map shows. The map shows only those streets that are important in getting to the trailhead or that are used as part of Trip 9. The starting point is arbitrary. You can use any of the many signed public rights-of-way branching off Kalaheo Avenue, the street that roughly parallels the beach, but please don't park on narrow Kalaheo Avenue itself. Either park in the lots mentioned under the Driving instructions or where legal on a side street.

Highlights: Many people consider Kailua Beach to be the finest on Oahu. How can you beat a tranquil walk along one of Oahu's loveliest beaches? You can't, so you will just have to take this stroll! (Of course, you won't take this walk during storms or at any other time when the surf is high and dangerous.)

Driving instructions: From the intersection of McCully Street and Kapiolani Boulevard just outside Waikiki, continue northeast on McCully, crossing over the Lunalilo Freeway (H1) on a narrow bridge. Just across the bridge, follow the signs to get on H1 westbound (a quick left turn onto Metcalfe Street that leads to a westbound freeway on-ramp). Take H1 westbound to the intersection with the Pali Highway. Take the Pali Highway northeast across the Pali toward Kailua.

The Pali Highway turns into a suburban road after it passes the junction with the Kalanianaole Highway (Highway 72) and then rolls into Kailua. Continue on this road to its end at a **T**-junction with Kalaheo Avenue; turn right here to a junction with Kailua Road; turn left onto a spur road into the beach parking lot. Or, to lengthen the hike, continue on Kalaheo Avenue, cross over a bridge, jog left toward Lanikai, and then turn left into the boat-ramp parking lot (the beach's easternmost parking lot). Park here to start your hike at the east end of Kailua Beach County Park ('Kailua Beach Pk.' on the map), almost 15 miles.

TheBus routes: Take Route 19 or 20 into downtown Honolulu and transfer to Route 57 to Kailua. Get off at the stop nearest Kailua Beach County Park—ask your driver. (Even on the same route, some buses go farther than others.) If your bus doesn't go all the way to the beach, you can get off on Kailua Road and walk from there.

Permit/permission required: None.

Description. Hikers who start at the extreme east end of Kailua Beach will find that black lava rocks jut into the sea here, cupping a few tidepools and inviting fishermen to try their luck. Low bluffs that sport wind-battered beach *naupaka, koa haole,* Chinese violet, and *ilima* shield the beach from the road. Walk over the boat ramp and pass a ruined restroom. Walk across the boat ramp and past some buildings. Be sure to linger to enjoy Kailua Beach's exquisite turquoise water and fine white sand! The beach is known not only for its beautiful sand and its length but also for the distance its sand extends out into the sea—perhaps as far as a football field is long.

Looking across the fringe of ironwoods and coconut palms, you have dramatic views of the fluted, sheer windward side of Oahu's famous *pali* (cliffs) and of the jagged peaks of the Koolau Mountains. Windsurfing is very popular here, and the bay is often dotted with brilliantly colored sails. Out in the bay you'll also see a tiny island that truly deserves the description "flat as a pancake." It's known locally as Flat Island; its official name is Popoia Island, and it's a state seabird sanctuary.

Approaching the outlet of Kaelepulu Pond, you may find that you can cross its mouth on a sandbar. Otherwise, you can turn inland and cross on the bridge. While the outlet's water is too polluted for swimming, it's great for canoeing. After work is done, semiprofessional canoe teams like to practice here.

Continue northwest along this lovely strand, passing grass-topped dunes. Restrooms and picnic benches are just over these dunes. Kailua Beach County Park ends soon; this is where hikers who park in the westernmost lot will start their hikes. Continuing northwest from here, private property prevents your cutting inland. The beach, however, remains public to the high-water line (true of all Hawaiian beaches except for a very few that have never had public access). You'll probably have a number of fellow strollers and joggers here as you pass one attractive beach home after another. Views up the bay toward massive Mokapu Point are impressive.

The beach ends at a low shelf of rock topped by *akulikuli kai* and a chain-link fence. Turn around and retrace your steps. Good news: the views are even more dramatic when you are walking in this direction!

The inconstant beach.... The movement of sand due to natural processes has been studied for many years along Kailua Beach. According to *Volcanoes in the Sea*, the beach has three sections: the south end, where you started, a middle section you're probably walking on now, and the north end near Kaneohe. Currents sweep the sand from one end and apparently deposit it at the other end, while the middle section remains relatively undisturbed. Which end loses sand and which end gains it? It depends on the long-term weather patterns. Over the time that the beach has been watched, each end has lost at some times, gained at others. *Volcanoes in the Sea* reports that one researcher has observed total changes in shoreline of as much as 79 feet (24 meters) at places along the north end and of 174 feet (53 meters) along the south end.

Perhaps more constant is the tendency of people to build their homes too close to the beach and then to cry "Foul!" when Nature moves the sand out and the sea in. Another constant tendency is to try to control the movement of sand. Waikiki Beach has fallen victim to that. Waikiki was once as famous as a fishing area as it is as a surfing area now. Natural processes sweep the sand from Waikiki toward Diamond Head; over the long term, the natural supply of sand was being swept away faster than it was being replenished. Enter the promoters: Waikiki must be preserved as a beach! Now, sand is brought to Waikiki from elsewhere (Molokai, for example). And, of course, the imported sand continually moves out to sea in its turn. Some people, like Rabbit Kekai (see Trip 32), judge that the excessive, unnatural supply of sand is killing Waikiki's once-flourishing reef and is destroying its fishery.

Native ilima (Sida spp.) grows in dry, sandy areas. Its yellow flowers were favored for royal leis

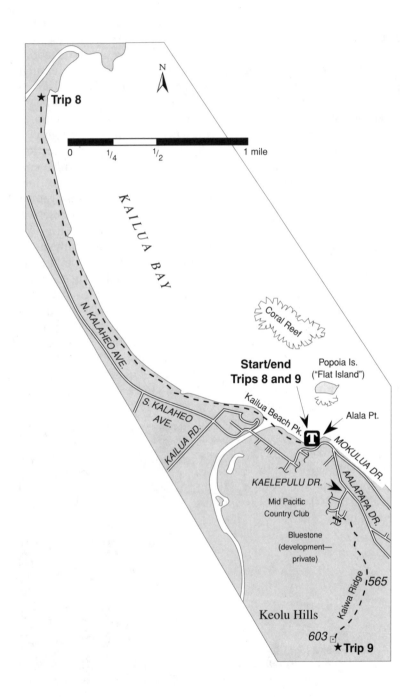

N

★ Trip 8

0   1/4   1/2   1 mile

KAILUA BAY

N. KALAHEO AVE.

S. KALAHEO AVE.

KAILUA RD.

Coral Reef

Popoia Is.
("Flat Island")

**Start/end
Trips 8 and 9**

Kailua Beach Pk.

Alala Pt.

T

MOKULUA DR.

KAELEPULU DR.

AALAPAPA DR.

Mid Pacific
Country Club

Bluestone
(development—
private)

Kaiwa Ridge

1565

Keolu Hills

603

★Trip 9

Trip 9. Keolu Hills

Distance: 2³/4 miles

Elevation gain: 580'

Hiking time: A little over 1¹/4 hours

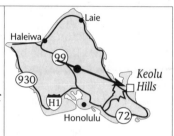

Topos: *Mokapu*

Trail map (route approximated): At the end of Trip 8.

Highlights: Walking along Kaiwa Ridge on the Keolu Hills above Kailua, you enjoy magnificent panoramas of the windward side from an unofficially maintained, but well used, trail. It's quite popular with local people—you're sure to meet a few—but it's no place for acrophobics and it requires a little boulder-scrambling.

Driving instructions: Follow the driving instructions of Trip 8. There is no parking to speak of where the trail starts, so you may as well park at Kailua County Beach Park and enjoy a stroll through the community of Lanikai, too.

TheBus routes: Take TheBus route of Trip 8.

Permit/permission required: None as of this writing. (However, this looks like a classic case of a route at least partly on private land and subject to being shut off at a moment's notice.)

Description. From the easternmost parking lot at Kailua Beach County Park, walk back to the shoulder of the road you drove in on and turn east-northeast along it toward Alala Point and the old stone monument labeled LANIKAI. Bicycling/jogging lanes help you stay out of the way of the cars as you walk past the monument, where Mokulua Drive goes left and you turn right, up Aalapapa Drive to its intersection with Kaelepulu Drive.

Turn right (uphill) onto Kaelepulu Drive and walk past the entrance to the country club, almost to the gate that keeps the public out of Bluestone. About 50 yards before the gate, look to your left for a private driveway. Walk up the driveway. Where the driveway turns left, look for a beaten path going steeply uphill along a chain-link fence. Take this path, which curves right when the chain-link fence does and then, some 15 yards later, takes off very steeply up a deeply eroded slot, going east and south-southeast through scrubby *koa haole*. As you can see from the remains of *koa haole* that other hikers have clung to or stamped on or both, you're not the only one who's had trouble with the footing on this segment! But soon the grade eases and, on this narrow ridge, you make your way through tall grasses and stunted shrubs. The views in almost all directions are well worth the climb!

At a **Y** junction (not shown on the map), you go right. On the eroded stretches, look for boulders that show an "onion" pattern of erosion (more below). After walking along the narrow edge of a cliff overlooking the ocean, you veer right to pass behind a lichen-spattered outcrop of dark rock. Trails-of-use lead to viewpoints with dizzying drops. You pass behind a ruined pillbox overlooking the ocean. The local kids party here now, but you can imagine how, during World War II, the guards here—just kids themselves back then—stared seaward for long hours, wondering when the enemy invasion would come.

You bob over knolls and cross saddles, eventually scrambling up to another ruined pillbox. There's a true 360° view here: Kailua Bay to the west, Mt. Olomana and the Koolaus to the south over Kaelepulu Pond, Mokapuu Point and Manana Island to the east, and the little Mokulua Islands offshore. Fabulous!

But the high point on the ridge lies farther on, so you continue generally south along it. There's a knob where you may think you must continue by scrambling very steeply down its south face, but in fact the beaten track descends on the seaward side of the knob. You dip in and out of head-high *koa haole* scrub and finally reach a semi-open spot where you can see what looks like another concrete structure slightly to your left. Head for it. I think it's the remnant of the marker for point 603, but there's nothing left to say for sure. The views you get when you climb up onto it are splendid (test it to be sure it's still safe to climb on). In addition to the views you've been enjoying so far, you see the crossed runways of inactive Bellows Air Force Base at the foot of the hills to the south-southeast and beyond Bellows, Waimanalo Bay. One small drawback: there are biting ants here.

Retrace your steps after enjoying the view.

"Onion" boulders....are formed by a process called spheroidal weathering. Water seeps into invisible fissures on the surface of a boulder and interacts with the minerals under the surface to form a sort of clay. The clay expands as it absorbs more water, and that expansion separates the outer surface from the remaining core of the boulder. The outer surface breaks away, exposing the core so that water can seep into invisible fissures and interact with the minerals under the surface to form a sort of clay. . . .Layer by layer, the boulder peels away. Boulders that are partly exposed often show multiple layers of weathering around the core. They look a little like an onion sliced across its middle—hence the term "onion" boulders.

Bellows site: the oldest?...As related in Patrick V. Kirch's *Feathered Gods and Fishhooks*, evidence of human grave sites was spotted in 1967 from the eroding face of a sand dune on Bellows Air Force Base, which is almost at your feet at the end of this trip. Investigation revealed that the dunes contained not only human remains but habitation deposits, too. Archaeologists excavated the dunes later in 1967 and again in 1976 and found several habitation layers; the site was apparently occupied on and off over many centuries. Two different techniques for dating the recovered artifacts yielded an approximate age for the lowest (and thus oldest) habitation layer of 323–447 A.D. If those dates are correct, then this is one of the oldest habitation sites known in Hawaii. Certain artifacts in the earliest layer were manufactured in styles reminiscent of other early Polynesian societies, styles abandoned (as seen in the later layers) as the settlers adapted to the materials and conditions of Hawaii.

And yet, Kirch observes, it's apparent that as old as this site is, it is not an original colonization site. It was an established village, off and on, for almost a millenium. If development has spared them, then somewhere in this area there may be other sites as early or even earlier. Finding and studying them would push the limits of our knowledge of early Hawaii closer to that distant day when voyagers from the South Pacific looked on Hawaii for the first time and decided to call it home.

Mt. Olomana from Maunawili Trail

Trip 10. Makapuu State Wayside

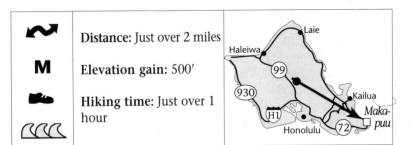

Distance: Just over 2 miles

Elevation gain: 500'

Hiking time: Just over 1 hour

Topos: *Koko Head*

Trail map: At the end of this trip.

Highlights: The incomparable views along this hike, especially those from its destination, are more than enough reward for the steep climb it demands.

Driving instructions: From the intersection of McCully Street and Kapiolani Boulevard, continue northeast on McCully to South King Street. Turn right on South King Street, which soon becomes the *east-bound* Lunalilo Freeway (H1) and then shortly becomes the *eastbound* Kalanianaole Highway (Highway 72). You drive east through Hawaii Kai, pass the turnoff to Hanauma Bay, and curve northeast up the east end of Oahu past striking Koko Crater, hugging the coast. Ahead, on your right (seaward), Makapuu Head looms. The highway curves in-land toward the saddle that separates Makapuu Head from the rest of the island. As you begin the gradual ascent toward the saddle, keep a sharp lookout for an old road that takes off going right (northeast). This is the road you will be walking on, so park near here, a little over 13³/4 miles. As of this writing, there is no developed parking for Makapuu State Wayside, and you may not park where your car will block the gate that bars the public's vehicles from this road. A better bet for parking is along the highway's shoulders.

TheBus routes: Not directly served by TheBus. Take Route 22, get off at the stop nearest Makapuu State Wayside (ask your driver), and walk from there to the trailhead.

Permit/permission required: None.

Description. The sign by the gate advises you that you must keep to the road, so you circumvent the gate and go northward into the draw below the saddle. A dry scrub of grasses, *koa haole*, and *kiawe* rustles on either side of the road as you curve around the draw and head south. Seaward, a number of dirt roads crisscross the draw; the slopes are dotted with clumps of cactus and *ilima*. The road's ascent is gentle at first. This has become a very popular weekend trip, and there is a lot of unsightly litter along the first half-mile or so. But the views are still worth your trouble.

As the road begins to climb more steeply, you must circumvent another gate. Lichen-stained boulders line the road here. Seaward, a large stone monument rises. To the west, you have fine views that get better as you rise: Koko Crater and Koko Head westward and an interesting web of coves and little waterways seaward.

Now the road rounds Puu o Kipahulu and swings north again, and you climb toward views of the wave-cut cliffs that, along with Makapuu Head itself, are the last remnants of the old caldera rim that forms the Koolau Mountains. Waimanalo Bay comes into view, too, as does Makapuu Head's summit. At a saddle, the road swings across the narrow ridge from the Koko Crater side to the ocean side. Constant, brisk sea breezes here may prompt you to put on a jacket even on a sunny day. In season, the roadside is bright with the sweet-scented yellow puffs of algarroba flowers, the white puffs of *koa haole* flowers, and the long, drooping, cream-colored spikes of *kiawe* flowers. The old road is lined with low pylons of rock and cement on the seaward side where the cliffs are very sheer. You can't miss a strange low succulent here with folded, brown-edged leaves; it somehow gives the impres-

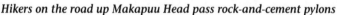

Hikers on the road up Makapuu Head pass rock-and-cement pylons

sion of a cluster of snakes at first glance. Tall, thorny century plants are scattered across the slopes around you.

A spur road (not shown on the map) veers off to your right (seaward) toward a little whitewashed building with a red roof. Together with the arid landscape and the non-native plants, the red-roofed building makes the scene seem more Mediterranean than tropical. You bear left, continuing on the main road past a hedge of that odd and showy cactus, the night-blooming cereus. Cereus and prickly-pear cactus now crowd in around the road, while inland ironwood and shrub-sized jointed firs grow in clumps.

Where the road curves left (inland) below some abandoned bunkers, you bear right on a paved path to a couple of railing-edged platforms poised on the edge of dizzyingly high, sheer sea cliffs. There are breathtaking views over the windward coast here. The old lighthouse is plainly visible a hundred or so feet below your airy perch. Manana (Rabbit) Island and smaller Kaohikaipu Island, both seabird sanctuaries, swim in the dark blue ocean below. This is the perfect complement to the sight you will see at Kaena Point (Trips 38–40): here at Makapuu, the west-trending ocean current crashes against Oahu for the first time, and its waters are forced to divide and flow around the island. Just off Kaena Point, the divided waters rejoin, churning into white foam. How immense is the sea, and how lost in its vastness is this one little island! Reflecting on this, you realize that on a world seventy percent covered by oceans, even the greatest of the continents is just one more lonely island in the sea.

There is a plaque near the lower point, explaining that the pillbox on the ridge to the west-southwest was built by author James Jones (*From Here to Eternity*, 1951) and his Army company in November of 1941. He and they subsequently manned the pillbox on December 7, 1941—Pearl Harbor Day—waiting for the Japanese invasion that never came but which must have seemed inevitable at the time.

You must at last turn away from this grand spectacle and reluctantly retrace your steps.

Trip 11. Koko Crater Botanical Garden

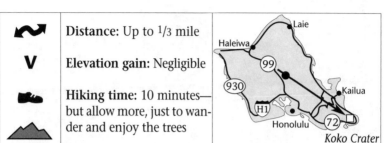

Distance: Up to 1/3 mile

Elevation gain: Negligible

Hiking time: 10 minutes—but allow more, just to wander and enjoy the trees

Koko Crater

Topos: *Koko Head*   *There's also a 2 mile hike*
Trail map: At the end of this trip. *inside the Gardens*

Highlights: Koko Crater is largely undeveloped as a botanical garden, but it has a unique treat for you nevertheless: it lets you plunge into a fragrant, larger-than-life "bouquet"! Koko Crater Botanical Garden is open from 9:00 AM to 4:00 PM daily except for Christmas Day and New Year's Day. It's one of the four botanical gardens maintained by the City and County of Honolulu (see also Trips 7, 33, and 42).

Driving instructions: From the intersection of McCully Street and Kapiolani Boulevard, continue northeast on McCully to South King Street. Turn right on South King Street, which soon becomes the *eastbound* Lunalilo Freeway (H1) and then shortly becomes the *eastbound* Kalanianaole Highway (Highway 72). You drive east through Hawaii Kai, pass the turnoff to Hanauma Bay, and curve north up the east end of Oahu past striking Koko Crater, hugging the coast. Just past Koko Crater, look for Kealahou Street on the inland side. It may also be marked by a sign pointing to Koko Crater Stables. Turn left onto Kealahou Street and follow the signs to Koko Crater Stables (1/2 mile to a narrow, unmarked road onto which you turn left, then 1/3 mile down that road, at first paved and then dirt, to the parking lot at the stable), a little over 13 1/2 miles. Watch out for large vehicles on that one-lane road (pickups pulling horse trailers, for example).

TheBus routes: Not served by TheBus.
Permit/permission required: None.
Description. The entrance to Koko Crater Botanical Garden is currently unmarked, but it's just to the right of the entrance into the stables (just before the parking lot).

And if your eyes can't spot it, let your nose lead you away from the smell of horses toward the heavenly scent of plumeria—non-native but nowadays almost synonymous with Hawaii. For here at the very beginning of Koko Crater Botanical Garden is a grove of plumeria

Plumeria trees bursting with blossoms in Koko Crater Botanical Garden

trees whose flowers are of all the colors and shapes you can imagine plumeria taking. The grove is dedicated to producing plumerias, including new hybrids. Little paths (not shown on the map) wander in and out among the trees; they, like the ground beneath the trees themselves, are covered with shredded bark and may be hard to spot, so wander as you will. Plumerias bloom almost all year around, so you're likely to find a good display whenever you visit.

Look around you at the varied shapes and colors. There are stiff, narrow-petaled, starlike blossoms of a pink so deep and rich that it's almost red. Another has orangey-pink flowers. There are oval-petaled blossoms brushed with tints of gold, pink, and cream, each petal twisted slightly to clear its neighbor. There are the charming, white-blossomed, yellow-throated plumerias that you commonly see elsewhere. And then there are the full-bodied, Rubensian blossoms: sweet, almost palm-sized wheels of round, soft, creamy petals overlapping one another, each luxuriantly curved away from the center, irresistibly inviting you to feast your senses on their unabashed sensual beauty. You can easily spend half an hour or more just sampling the blossoms of each tree. The ground is covered with fallen blossoms, so it's easy to find a perfect one to tuck into your hair or your buttonhole.

And from this bursting, ripe, seductive loveliness comes some of the weirdest, ugliest fruit imaginable. Yes, those huge, awkward, boomerang-shaped double pods in tacky black or sickly green are the fruit of the plumeria—probably lethal if thrown at your head.

Dirt roads leading farther into the crater will bring you to other parts of the garden, where unmarked plantings are scattered in unmarked plots here and there among the scrub and the dust. It's not particularly interesting as of this writing. Climbing on the crater walls is reportedly very dangerous because the soil is extremely loose. So I suggest that you confine your visit to the plumeria grove.

Retrace your steps when you're ready to leave.

The cleverest thief of old Hawaii....was Iwa of Oahu, some fourteen generations before Kamehameha I. Thievery was an honorable profession in those days; there were even some chiefs who supported themselves by theft. The only shame was in being caught.

The boy Iwa grew up on Mokapu, the curiously shaped peninsula that juts north from Kaneohe. Mokapu is the site of some of the oldest vents of the episode of volcanism that also created Koko Crater—which lets me tack a good story about Iwa onto the end of a trip into Koko Crater.

This particular story begins on the Big Island of Hawaii when Umi was king of the island. A fisherman on the Big Island had a wonderful cowrie-shell lure with which he caught many fine squid and octopus. Umi heard about Keaau's wonderful cowrie and sent messengers to fetch it for him. Now, Keaau was only a commoner, and, according to *kapu*, everything—even a poor man's squid lure—belonged solely to the chief. Keaau had no choice but to give up the cowrie, but in his heart he swore to get it back.

Keaau filled his canoe with the finest of his remaining treaures and went in search of a thief to steal the cowrie back. He found no thief skillful enough until he paddled to Oahu, and there he heard about the amazing skills of the young thief Iwa. Iwa agreed to help him, so Keaau gave Iwa the canoe full of fine things.

They paddled back to the Big Island, where Umi was fishing with Keaau's lure. Iwa dove into the water, sank to the sea floor, and walked along the ocean bottom till he was under

A spray of fragrant plumeria blossoms

Umi's canoe. There, he took hold of Umi's fishing line, took off the cowrie, and tied the line to rocks. Feeling the line pay out, Umi assumed he had hooked an enormous squid. But when he tried to pull the "squid" in, the line refused to budge. Meanwhile, Keaau and Iwa escaped to Keaau's house.

Umi sent messengers all over the island to find a diver who could go down and free his line with the wonderful cowrie shell, but none were able to. Finally, Umi's messengers came to Keaau's house and asked Iwa's help. Iwa told them the cowrie was gone and the line was tied to a rock.

Umi then sent for Iwa, who told him the whole story. Umi engaged Iwa to steal the shell back and, that night, Iwa did so. Umi set many arduous tasks to test Iwa's skills, and Iwa succeeded at even the most difficult. As a final test, Umi built two houses of equal size and declared a contest. In a single night, Umi's six best thieves must fill one house with stolen goods, while Iwa must fill the other. Who ever had stolen more would live; the loser(s) would die. Six against one! Iwa agreed.

At nightfall Iwa lay down to sleep. Umi's six thieves, passing by with their arms full of stolen goods, felt sorry for Iwa. Toward morning, their house filled, the six thieves feasted and drank themselves into a stupor. Iwa got up, took the loot from their house to fill his own, slid Umi's *kapa* bedclothes off the sleeping king and put them on top of the other stolen things in his house, and lay down again as if asleep.

At daybreak Umi summoned the people to see the results of the contest. The six thieves were astonished to find their house empty and Iwa's house filled not only with the things they themselves had stolen first but also with the king's own sheets. Umi put the six thieves to death and invited Iwa to stay with him as a dear friend and the best thief in his kingdom.

And Iwa stayed for some time. But finally his longing for Oahu and for his parents overcame him. With Umi's blessings and with many gifts, the greatest thief of old Hawaii returned to the lovely green *pali* of Oahu.

Map shows general location of garden but does not detail the non-existent trails. Wander as you wish!

Trip 12. Waahila Ridge

Distance: 3¹/₂ miles

M

Elevation gain: 1000'

Hiking time: 1³/₄ hours

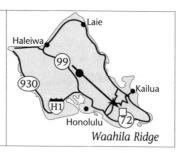

Waahila Ridge

Topos: *Honolulu*
Trail map: At the end of this trip.
Highlights: Views, interesting plants, and a little boulder-scrambling make for a lively and interesting trip. Steep dropoffs along some sections demand cautious hiking. Waahila Ridge State Recreation Area, from which this trip starts, has an enchanting forest of Cook Island pines. Mainlanders homesick for the "piney woods" will especially enjoy a visit here. Waahila Ridge State Recreation Area is open from 7:00 AM to 6:45 PM (winter) or 7:45 PM (summer). However, you should not take this trip on a rainy day, because the trail can be very slippery and exposed, especially where you walk on protruding tree roots. Bouldering skills are desirable.
Driving instructions: Getting to Waahila Ridge State Recreation area involves corkscrewing up through a hillside suburb of Honolulu called St. Louis Heights. From the intersection of McCully Street and Kapiolani Boulevard just outside Waikiki, continue northeast on McCully, crossing over the Lunalilo Freeway (H1) on a narrow bridge. Almost immediately turn right onto Dole Street. Follow Dole east past a miserable intersection with an offramp from H1, through the University of Hawaii Manoa Campus, and then southeast to its intersection with St. Louis Drive near Chaminade University. Turn left onto St. Louis Drive and begin working your way uphill on a web of steep, narrow little streets. There is no single "correct" route, so keep your street map handy! Your goal is to get almost to the top of St. Louis Heights—specifically, to the intersection of Peter Street and Ruth Place. Turn left (west) onto Ruth Place and follow it through the gates of Waahila Ridge State Recreation Area, where the now-one-lane road curves northeast and uphill. (What—not on your street map? Several otherwise adequate street maps I have, and the topo, fail to show the road continuing into Waahila Ridge State Recreation Area—but it does.) Follow it to the park-

ing lot for the picnic area and park here, about 5 miles depending on your exact route. The trail is 1/4 mile farther ahead.

TheBus routes: Not directly served by TheBus. Take Route 14 to the end of the line, which is near the intersection of Peter Street and Ruth Place. Walk west on Ruth Place and then northeast through Waahila Ridge State Recreation Area.

Permit/permission required: None.

Description. Be sure to admire the view over Manoa Valley from the picnic area before you head off. Now head northeast away from the parking lot and into the Cook Island pines. A number of trails of use soon converge on the official trail, which is more like an old dirt service road for now. There are good views if you peer out from underneath the canopy of pine branches. You soon pass a water tank, and the old road becomes very eroded as ironwoods intrude among the Cook Island pines.

Beyond the water tank, the trail quickly shrinks to footpath size

and is shut in by strawberry guava. A power line runs along this ridge, and you approach a supporting tower, then veer off to pass below it on its left side. Descend steeply on a natural staircase formed by the half-exposed roots of the ironwoods that densely clothe this side of the knob. The next saddle and knob are undistinguished, but the saddle after that is

From a trail high above Honolulu, the view sweeps over a steep, lonely valley and down to the city's highrises

very narrow—barely a foot and a half wide in places, with steep dropoffs to either side! Nevertheless, the views over the adjacent ridges and valleys are more than enough compensation for the trail's little hazards.

The ascent of the next knob is very steep, but you can rest in the shade of a *koa* tree on top. The succeeding knob demands some boulder-scrambling on either side. Look for *koa*, silk oak, strawberry guava, and Christmas berry trees growing here. You pass below another power line tower and enter a dense thicket of strawberry guava that obscures the fine views. It's a relief when, near the end of the ridge, you emerge at a relatively large, level spot that makes a fine picnicking place— maybe on your way back, as you're almost at the end of the trail now.

Descending and then ascending a little, you now enjoy good views from this *ohia*- and *koa*-clad ridge. You top out under a big *koa* that's festooned with the fascinating *ieie* vine, which looks like a miniature, climbing *hala*. In a few more steps you reach the junction of the Waahila Ridge and Kolowalu trails on a saddle at the head of a tributary of Manoa Valley. The views over Honolulu are wonderful; take a break here to savor them. Trails-of-use lead farther inland, into the Koolaus, but it is illegal to take them (you would be trespassing into a protected watershed). I don't recommend the Kolowalu Trail; see Appendix B.

Retrace your steps to the picnic area at the trailhead. Waahila Ridge State Recreation Area is a place you'll want to linger in!

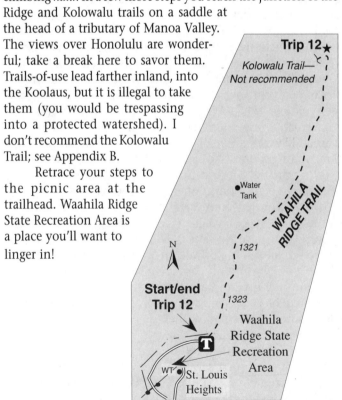

Trip 12★

Kolowalu Trail— Not recommended

●Water Tank

WAAHILA RIDGE TRAIL

N

1321

Start/end Trip 12

1323

Waahila Ridge State Recreation Area

WT● St. Louis Heights

0   ¼   ½   1 mile

Trip 13. Puu Pia

Distance: Just over 1 mile

Elevation gain: 480'

Hiking time: 1/2 hour

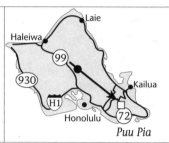

Puu Pia

Topos: *Honolulu*

Trail map: At the end of this trip.

Highlights: A pleasant rainforest walk leads to the summit of Puu Pia, a lovely peaklet deep in misty Manoa Valley, and to great views. Rain gear is a must for this hike!

Driving instructions: The trailhead is hard to find; it's not marked on the street where you have to park. From the intersection of McCully Street and Kapiolani Boulevard just outside Waikiki, continue northeast on McCully, crossing over the Lunalilo Freeway (H1) on a narrow bridge. Keep going to Wilder Avenue. Turn left onto Wilder, and drive northwest to Punahou Street; turn right onto Punahou. Punahou curves northeast around Punahou School and soon becomes Manoa Road. At a **Y** junction, bear right on East Manoa Road. Follow East Manoa Road up-valley, taking the right fork at two more **Y** junctions and passing near a Chinese cemetery. Shortly thereafter, you reach a **T** junction with Alani Drive. Turn left onto Alani Drive and follow this narrow residential street up to a point where it makes a 90° right turn and runs into Woodlawn Drive, near the latter's 3700–3600 block. You'll notice a one-lane drive, almost like a private driveway, that veers northward away from the 90° right turn of Alani-Woodlawn; it's an extension of Alani Drive and you'll need to walk it. Park as best you can on Alani-Woodlawn without blocking the street or anyone's driveway, 4.2 miles.

TheBus routes: Not served by TheBus.

Permit/permission required: None.

Description. Walk to the driveway that's an extension of Alani Drive and follow it north past several homes, downhill past the last house on the right, and northwest into a forest of rose apple trees. Step over a cable gate and follow the road—now gravel—along a streambed (not on map), uphill to the junction of the Kolowalu and Puu Pia trails, near a picnic shelter. Avoid the Kolowalu Trail; see Appendix B.

Go left on the Puu Pia Trail, under the damp shade of the rose apple trees, climbing gradually. The road presently becomes steeper and deeply eroded. You curve west-northwest around a gully, cross a tiny saddle, and climb steeply on a footpath that curves out onto a ridge—Puu Pia—from

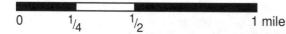

which there are breathtaking views in all directions: south and southwest to city and sea, southeast to Waahila Ridge (Trip 12), east to north along the steep green face of the Koolau Mountains, and northwest to the Manoa Cliffs. If Manoa Valley's rain obscures the view, wait for the clouds to part here and there. The views are worth your time.

Return the way you came.

Adapted from DNLR handout

0   ¼   ½   1 mile

Along a shady trail in the hills above Manoa Valley

Trip 14. Lyon Arboretum—Inspiration Point

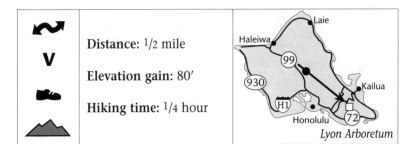

Distance: 1/2 mile

Elevation gain: 80'

Hiking time: 1/4 hour

Lyon Arboretum

Topos: *Honolulu*

Trail map (route approximated): Near the end of this trip.

Highlights: Charming Harold L. Lyon Arboretum, part of the University of Hawaii at Manoa, offers you an opportunity to stroll through beautiful grounds planted with a wide variety of interesting plants. It's more a botanical garden than an arboretum: the latter would be dedicated exclusively to trees, and Lyon Arboretum offers far more than trees. Inspiration Point, the goal of this hike, has a unique view over upper Manoa Valley. Bring plenty of jungle juice!

The arboretum is open Monday through Saturday from 9:00 AM to 3:00 PM except on state holidays; call (808) 988-0456.

Driving instructions: From the intersection of McCully Street and Kapiolani Boulevard just outside Waikiki, continue northeast on McCully, crossing over the Lunalilo Freeway (H1) on a narrow bridge. Keep going to Wilder Avenue. Turn left onto Wilder, and drive northwest to Punahou Street and turn right. Punahou curves northeast around Punahou School and soon becomes Manoa Road. At a **Y** junction, bear left on Manoa Road (the right fork is East Manoa Road). You reach an **X** junction with Oahu Avenue; bear right on Manoa Road here. (Going left would put you on Oahu Avenue, but it curves back to meet Manoa Road in a few blocks.) You pass under the footbridge that leads from the Paradise Park parking lot (you may not park here for hiking). The signed spur road to Lyon Arboretum soon comes in from the left, shortly before Manoa Road ends. Turn left onto the spur road and drive up into the arboretum parking lot, a little over 4 1/2 miles. You may not park here for hiking the Manoa Falls Trail, either. Stop in at the visitor center at the lower end of the parking lot to sign in, make your donation, and pick up maps of the arboretum.

TheBus routes: Take any route that goes to the Ala Moana Shopping Center and transfer to Route 5. Take Route 5 as far as it goes into

Manoa Valley (ask your driver) and walk to Lyon Arboretum from there (see the driving directions above).

Permit/permission required: None.

Description. From the west (upper) end of the parking lot, head uphill on cinderblock paving stones and into a rain shelter. Bear left out of the shelter, toward a sign that says FERN VALLEY. Go uphill, past benches signed JESSICA RAE WOULD HAVE LIKED TO REST HERE. Reaching the signed bromeliad plantings, on a slope to your right, you climb up past them on one of the faint paths on either side of them. Above the bromeliads, you bear left to an open, grassy hillside known as Inspiration Point (sometimes there's a sign here, too). From Inspiration Point, over bright-flowered impatiens and under the lacy foliage of huge old trees in the foreground. there are beautiful—yes, inspiring!—views east over upper Manoa Valley. As seen from Waahila Ridge (Trip 12) and Manoa Cliffs (Trips 21 and 22), Manoa Valley looks like a typical over-built suburb. From Inspiration Point, however, you see only the ex-

quisite pali and the leafy green canopy in the valley's upper end, making the valley seem lush, idyllic, and remote.

After enjoying this view, retrace your steps to your car or to the next trip..

Jessica Rae....was a volunteer at the Lyon Arboretum some years ago and dearly loved the arboretum. Her son lived in South Africa, and she went there to visit him. While in South Africa, she fell ill and died. Her son gave the arboretum the funds for the plaques to honor her memory.

Yes, Jessica Rae would have liked to rest on any of these pleasant benches.

*Intensely fragrant, non-native spider lilies
(Hymenocallis littoralis) grace a garden path*

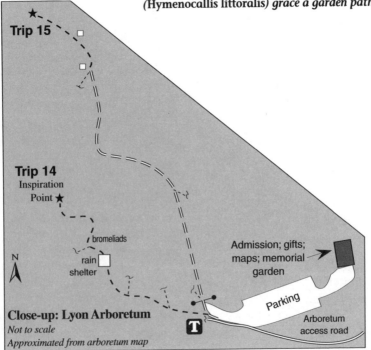

Trip 15

Trip 14
Inspiration
Point ★

bromeliads

rain
shelter

N

Close-up: Lyon Arboretum
*Not to scale
Approximated from arboretum map*

Admission; gifts;
maps; memorial
garden

Parking

Arboretum
access road

T

Trip 15. Lyon Arboretum—Cascade

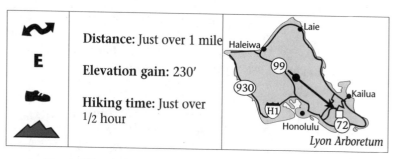

Distance: Just over 1 mile

Elevation gain: 230'

Hiking time: Just over 1/2 hour

Lyon Arboretum

Topos: *Honolulu*

Trail map (route approximated): At the end of Trip 14.

Highlights: An easy walk through Lyon Arboretum brings you to a little cascade in a pretty setting. I like this walk because it winds through a part of the arboretum that seems less artificially tidy and a little more wild.

Driving instructions: Follow the driving instructions of Trip 14.

TheBus routes: Take TheBus routes of Trip 14.

Permit/permission required: None.

Description. From the upper end of the parking lot, curve right past a gate and onto a service road, away from the Inspiration Point trail (Trip 14). You'll stay on this old road for most of this hike, avoiding the occasional trails that come in on either side. The stroll is a pleasant one, curving along banks of attractive plants and passing under shady trees.

The road shortly forks by clumps of palm trees; take the right fork here. You walk between jungle-like plantings of ti, ferns, tree ferns, heliconia, ginger, arums, birds-of-paradise, peperomia, palms, and other exotic plants. At a signed turnoff right to the Economic Section (for plants with economic uses), you stay on the road (left) to reach another fork, this time by a cinderblock building. Go right at this fork. The road dwindles to a weedy little track that bears right, and you climb this wet, slippery, increasingly rocky path past a ruined stone building, through a grove of palm trees and then a grove of heliconias, to a nest of boulders in a niche bright with impatiens and green with mosses and ferns. The boulders are at the foot of a black basalt ledge over which a tiny stream slips noiselessly into a tiny pool—you couldn't get your ankles wet in it if you tried—from which the water flows away into the boulders and disappears.

Stroll leisurely back to your car from here.

The War of the Owls.... There are many myths about Manoa Valley; here is one I especially like.

Long ago there was a treeless plain dotted with small farms where Honolulu now rises, and there was a great marsh inland of Waikiki. Many birds nested among the marsh reeds, and tough *pili* grasses used for thatching grew there. A poor farmer named Kapoi came to the marsh in search of *pili* grass to repair his house. As he cut bundles of the grass, he happened upon an owl's nest full of eggs. Glad for the unexpected food, Kapoi took the nest of eggs home.

That night, as he prepared to cook the eggs, an owl flew down and landed on the wall. "Kapoi," said the owl, "give me my eggs." Kapoi said, "How many of these eggs are yours?" "Seven," said the owl, and indeed there were seven eggs in the nest Kapoi had taken. Kapoi's heart sank, for he had nothing to eat. He said to the owl, "But I have already gotten them ready to be cooked." Said the owl, "Have you no heart, Kapoi? Do you feel no sorrow for me? Give me my eggs."

Kapoi was moved by the owl's plea and returned the eggs to their mother. The owl, acknowledging Kapoi's kindness, became Kapoi's personal god *(aumakua)*. There is a long tradition of family and personal gods in Hawaii, and the owl, revered as a powerful protector in battle and danger, is one of the most ancient. The owl commanded Kapoi to build a *heiau* (a temple) where he could make offerings to his owl *aumakua* in Manoa Valley, where the king of the owls lived. Kapoi set about building the *heiau*, observing all the proper rituals and *kapu*, dedicating it, and making offerings to the owl as he had been commanded.

Kakuhihewa, the high chief of Oahu at that time, was living at Waikiki, where he was building a great *heiau* to his own god. Kakuhihewa had laid a *kapu* on all the people of Oahu: while his *heiau* was being built, no one else might build and dedicate a *heiau*. To have done so would have been an act punishable by death. When he heard of Kapoi's *heiau*, Kakuhihewa imprisoned Kapoi and planned to sacrifice him.

Kapoi's *aumakua* went to the king of the owls for help, who beat his drums to summon all owls from the islands to make war on the high chief of Oahu. Within a day, all the owls of Hawaii island, Lanai, Maui, and Molokai had gathered near Diamond Head. All the owls from Kauai and Niihau gathered near Moanalua. All the owls of Oahu gathered in Nuuanu Valley.

On the day Kakuhihewa had set for Kapoi to die, the owls rallied around Kakuhihewa's temple. So great were their numbers that they obscured the sun as it rose. As Kapoi was about to be slain, the owls attacked. The chief, his warriors, and his priests battled in vain to drive the owls away, but the owls flew at them again and again, scratching their eyes and faces and covering them with dirt and droppings. Kakuhihewa and his forces fled, and Kapoi was set free. The owls had defeated the high chief and had saved the poor man's life!

Trip 16. Manoa Falls

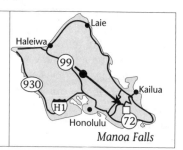 **E**	Distance: 2 miles Elevation gain: 390' Hiking time: 1 hour

Manoa Falls

Topos: *Honolulu*
Trail map: At the end of Trip 14.
Highlights: Those anxious to see a genuine tropical waterfall but lacking the time to go to Sacred Falls, for example, will enjoy this short trip to lovely Manoa Falls. Jungle juice is a must!
Driving instructions: Follow the driving instructions of Trip 14 and continue past the turnoff to Lyon Arboretum and beyond Paradise Park, to a small parking lot at the trailhead, about 4 1/2 miles from your start in Waikiki. If the lot is full, park in the residential area back up Manoa Road, where the road is wide enough, and walk up the road to the trailhead; don't block anyone's driveway, please.
TheBus routes: Take TheBus routes of Trip 14.
Permit/permission required: None.
Description. After carefully winding your way up the rest of Manoa Road, trying not to get run over, walk down that stub of dirt road that extends from the end of Manoa Road. Posts soon bar further vehicle progress, but you easily slip through them, curving along under *hau*, pothos, and bamboo. You cross a bridge over Aihualama Stream; the trail may become very muddy and slippery beyond here. If you've spent all your time in Waikiki till now, you may have wondered when you'd get to see anything like a tropical rainforest. Well, this is it!

At a fork, you bear right (left is just a trail-of-use). Crossing a streamlet on stones, you continue gradually uphill under vine-draped giant trees: *kukui*, African tulip tree, guava, and mountain apple. The understory is largely palm grass and ferns. You pick your way carefully over tangles of muddy roots and boulders, ducking under *hau* thickets. In season, the trail is littered with the tiny white blossoms of *kukui* or lavishly strewn with the shocking-pink stamens of mountain apple flowers. Waihi Stream, the stream that forms Manoa Falls, flows merrily on the right, providing a fine bass tune that complements the lively bird songs.

Nearing 2/3 mile, what looks at first to be a dreadful scramble hand-over-hand up muddy tree roots turns out to be a little switchback turn around an immense banyan—the owner of those impressive roots. Metal ramps have been laid in the trail to help you across the next segment, through a bamboo thicket. You slip and slop up another switchback turn, ignore a trail-of-use that goes steeply up through the bamboo on the left, and continue generally north to the falls.

Metal-clad "stairs" help you over a short but very steep and muddy section that hauls you well above the stream to your first view of the falls—a pair of long, delicate, upper and lower cascades. Nearing the one-mile point, you pass the junction with the Aihualama Trail (left) and continue ahead (right) toward the falls—less than 50 yards away.

The falls lie nestled in a deep green amphitheater. At the base of the falls, a pool—shallow but big enough to splash in—lies in a nest of broken rock. You may want to splash around yourself or find one of the drier rocks to perch on while you have a snack and enjoy watching the falls and the people frolicking in the pool. As at all such waterfalls, watch out for falling rock (see the end of Trip 4).

When you're ready, retrace your steps.

A break in the dense rainforest frames delicate Manoa Falls

Trip 17. Aihualama Trail

Distance: 6 miles

Elevation gain: 1100'

Hiking time: 3 hours

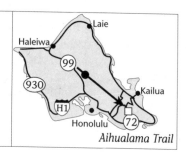

Aihualama Trail

Topos: *Honolulu*

Trail map: At the end of Trip 14.

Highlights: This is a trip of delightful contrasts: the intimate, damp rainforest around Manoa Falls; the far-ranging views over Manoa Valley and Nuuanu Valley from the middle trail; and the almost-claustrophobic forest of giant bamboo, especially as you approach Pauoa Flats.

Driving instructions: Follow the driving instructions of Trip 14 except that, as explained in Trip 16, park in the residential area, not at the trailhead proper, Lyon Arboretum, or Paradise Park.

TheBus routes: Take TheBus routes of Trip 14.

Permit/permission required: None.

Description. Follow Trip 16 to Manoa Falls. It's only about 50 yards to visit the falls and then return to the junction with the Aihualama Trail, so be sure to see the falls.

Returning from the falls, the Aihualama Trail is now on your right (west), and you turn onto it. Its first few feet are very rough, resembling a rockslide more than a trail and requiring a little boulder-scrambling. You contour into a bamboo forest and zigzag across a gully, through *ti*, ginger, fern, and palm grass. (Palm grass is the tall grass with long leaves that look as if they've been fan-folded, like palm fronds.) Because of the general dampness here, the trail can be muddy and slippery.

You presently cross another gully, this one with *uluhe* and taro. Near the 2/3-mile point, you have a fine view over Manoa Valley and beyond, all the way to the tip of Diamond Head, over a slope clothed in *uluhe* and juniper berry. Gray patches in the *uluhe* reflect a die-off, possibly due to a recently-arrived plant parasite. The die-off is cause for concern, because the *uluhe* helps stabilize these fragile slopes. Along the trail you'll see thimbleberry, Koster's curse, redwood sorrel (sometimes called "shamrock"), *kukui*, *koa*, *ieie*, tree ferns, and eucalyptuses—a varied display, but only the *uluhe*, *ieie*, and *koa* are native to Hawaii.

Listen for the magnificent song of the white-rumped shama. Look for its white "flashes," too: as it sits caroling on the branch, it flicks its tail, displaying the white-feathered fanny that gives it its common name.

You and the trail wind gradually up, up, up. Small landslides may have erased the maintained tread on some switchbacks. If so, use your own best judgment to decide whether it's safe for you to proceed. The Aihualama Trail tops out in a dense forest of giant bamboo that presses in close and dark around you. It descends slightly as it reaches a junction with the Puu Ohia Trail on Pauoa Flats.

Turn right (northeast) onto the Puu Ohia Trail through bamboo, eucalyptus, and mountain *naupaka*, and follow the trail to its end at Nuuanu Overlook. Far below, the Pali Highway roars through Nuuanu Valley past a large reservoir and toward Kailua through a deep notch in the green cliffs of the Koolaus. Around you, steep green cliffs and sharp green peaks—so near and yet so far because the terrain is loose and dangerous—speak more eloquently than the noisy highway of this island's volcanic origin and its tropical nature.

When you can tear yourself away from this Nuuanu Valley panorama, retrace your steps.

The water of life of Kane....Hawaiian legends of "little people," mysterious and magical beings like the Menehune and the Mu, have been especially popular with mainland visitors because of the little people's resemblance to Ireland's leprechauns. Sometimes they helped human beings; the Menehune are famous in legend for having built great *heiau* (temples) in a single night, for example. Often they were troublesome, making mischief among the humans. There were more kinds of them than just the Menehune and the Mu, and in a tributary valley of Nuuanu Valley—seen at the end of this trip—lived a race of little people called the Eepa.

I can't say whether the little man who figures in the following myth was an Eepa—but he may have been. This is the story: A king of Oahu fell ill and was near death. A wise man passing by said, "He must drink of the water of life of Kane." Kane was one of the principal gods, and the water of life of Kane, which could restore life, was to be found only on a mysterious land over the horizon, or perhaps in the realm of the clouds, where it formed a lake.

The king had three sons. When the eldest of the brothers heard this, he longed to fetch the precious water, but not because he loved his father. No, he wished only to ensure that his father would leave the kingdom of Oahu to him alone. Putting on his most loving face, he begged his father to let him try to find the water. At first the king refused, preferring death to risking his son's life. At last he gave in, and the eldest brother set out through the forest. Suddenly a little man appeared on the path and asked him where he was going. The eldest brother rudely pushed the little man aside and ran on. The dwarf was angry and made the path grow ever more narrow, twisting, and overgrown. The eldest brother fell to his knees to try to crawl under the dense vegetation that closed in on him. At last he lay helpless, trapped by it.

When the eldest brother failed to return, the second brother appealed to his father. He, too, wished only to win the kingdom. Reluctantly, the king gave in again. As it happened to the eldest brother, exactly so did it happen to the second brother, until he, too, lay imprisoned by the forest.

Now the youngest brother, who cared only that his father might live, entreated the king to let him fetch the life-giving water. The king gave his permission with the greatest reluctance. The boy sped off, soon meeting the little man on the path. When the dwarf asked where he was going, the boy explained courteously and requested the dwarf's help. The little man not only told him how to get to the magic land and its lake—a long and perilous way—but gave him magic weapons.

With the dwarf's advice and weapons, the boy at last reached the lake and filled his bowl with the water of life of Kane. Then he began the long journey back to his beloved father. Upon meeting the little man again, the boy related his adventures and thanked the dwarf for his help. Then the boy asked if he might have one more favor: his lost brothers to be restored to their family. The dwarf warned the boy that his brothers were evil, but the boy pleaded, and the dwarf finally yielded.

Reunited with his brothers, the boy excitedly told them he now had the true water of life of Kane. Little did he realize that in their wicked hearts, they were not glad but angry and jealous! As they traveled homeward together, they met in succession three chiefs each of whom faced a dangerous and difficult situation. Each time the youngest brother was able, with the help of the dwarf's magic weapons, to rescue the chief and his people.

And as they traveled, the older brothers sought opportunities to kill the boy, but the magic weapons defended him. So the older brothers stole the bowl with the water of life of Kane, poured the water into their own bowls, and filled the youngest brother's bowl with seawater. Upon reaching their home, the boy rushed to his dying father's side and bade him drink from his bowl, which he believed still contained the true water of life of Kane. The king drank deeply and became sicker than ever. He cursed his youngest son and ordered one of his officers to take the boy into the forest and kill him. Then the older brothers, all loving smiles, approached the king and offered him the true water of life of Kane. The king again drank deeply and this time was restored to health at once.

The officer ordered to kill the youngest son instead took the boy far away and hid him safely. The boy remained in hiding for a long time. The three chiefs he had saved came to his home to offer him their thanks along with many splendid gifts. They were sorry not to find the boy at home, and they told the king what a wonderful son he had. The king, realizing that he had been mistaken about the boy, summoned the officer to ask if the boy were dead. Upon learning that his youngest son still lived, the king rejoiced and sent messengers to bring him home.

It became clear to all how treacherously the older brothers had acted, and they fled when the boy returned. They were never heard of again. In time, the youngest brother became the king of Oahu and ruled long and wisely.

Stalks of giant bamboo tower over a trail, nearly cutting off the sunlight

Trip 18. Kanealole Trail

Distance: A little under 1¹/₂ miles

Elevation gain: 530'

Hiking time: ³/₄ hour

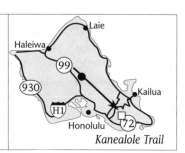

Kanealole Trail

Topos: *Honolulu*

Trail map: At the end of this trip.

Highlights: This pleasant walk along Kanealole Stream in charming Makiki Valley offers an easy visit to what I think is Honolulu's best hiking area.

Driving instructions: From the intersection of McCully Street and Kapiolani Boulevard just outside Waikiki, continue northeast on McCully, crossing over the Lunalilo Freeway (H1) on a narrow bridge. Keep going to Wilder Avenue. Turn left onto Wilder and go west to Makiki Street, where you turn right. (It's a little hard to spot: look for a church on the *left* side of Wilder.) Go north on Makiki Street to a **Y** junction at the narrow end of a wedge-shaped park. Take the left fork here; it's Makiki Heights Drive. Follow Makiki Heights Drive uphill to a hairpin turn from which a narrow spur road leads north. It's a right turn to get onto this spur road, which leads you into Makiki Valley past the green trailers that house the offices and classrooms of the Hawaii Nature Center (see below). *Don't* park in the lot that's the Hawaii Nature Center's "front yard." Instead, just beyond the Hawaii Nature Center, there's a parking lot on the right side of the road just before the PRIVATE ROAD and NO PRIVATE CARS BEYOND THIS POINT signs. Park here, less than 2¹/₂ miles. Or, if it's full, park along the road.

TheBus routes: Not directly served by TheBus. Take Route 8, 19, 20, or 58 to the Ala Moana Shopping Center and transfer to Route 17. Get off at the stop nearest the start of the spur road that leads to the Hawaii Nature Center (ask your driver).

Permit/permission required: None.

Description. Continue on foot up the spur road, past some buildings and vehicles belonging to the Department of Land and Natural Resources and past a chlorinator station. The road presently dwindles to a footpath. Look around you for the odd plant called Job's Tears. It's a grass, and it's perfectly capable of growing head-high. The seed capsules begin as hard, green ovoids and mature to bluish-black, then white. It's considered a weed—it's not native to Hawaii—and people are reported to collect the seed capsules and to string them like beads.

The lower half of the trail is pleasant though not particularly distinguished. The upper half is steep and may be deeply eroded in places. Following an archaeologist up this trail one day, I wondered how anyone would have the slightest clue that there might be something of historical interest here. So I asked her. She said she looked for *ti* plants. The *ti* is not native to Hawaii; the Polynesians brought *ti* with them when they colonized Hawaii. It stands to reason that, not knowing what plants might be growing on the strange, lonely islands they might find, they felt compelled to carry with them the plants they knew would supply them with food, medicine, and materials for clothing and shelter. *Ti* was essential for lining the pit oven *(imu)*, for wrapping food for cooking and serving, and for thatching. Dried *ti* leaves fastened to a fiber network made an efficient rain cape. And much later on, after Europeans had introduced distilled liquors, the juice of the huge, sugary *ti* root became the source of a fine native brandy, *okolehao*—the local moonshine. Finally, *ti* is believed to protect a house and those who dwell in it; even today, Hawaiian homes have their protective hedge of *ti*.

So when an archaeologist searches through a now-abandoned valley looking for old Hawaiian home sites, she naturally looks for *ti* plants. They're the tipoff that a particular area might have once been a home or even a *heiau*. Following her through the dense tangles of *kukui* and coffee plants (Makiki Valley was home to a coffee plantation in the 19th Century; see the end of Trip 19), we indeed came upon the ruins of stone walls, finely laid with no help from mortar, as is typical of Hawaiian stonework. Some day, when more work can be done, we may know for sure whether these were old Hawaiian home sites. (In the meantime, I recommend that you not go rummaging off-trail without such a guide, in order to preserve potential study sites and to keep from getting lost— it's easier to get lost in the dense growth than you think!)

Almost 3/4 mile from your start, you meet the Makiki Valley Trail. From here, retrace your steps to the trailhead.

The Hawaii Nature Center....makes an excellent place to start your Makiki Valley hikes for a number of reasons. It's at both the Kanealole and Maunalaha trailheads and couldn't be more convenient. It invites you to learn about the environmental and conservation needs of Hawaii through displays about the plants and animals of Hawaii as well as hands-on exhibits that let you touch and feel plant and animal materials. You may be able to buy maps and pamphlets about the area you'll hike through, and these can greatly add to your hiking pleasure.

You can ask questions of knowledgeable people. And then there are their hikes. . . .

The Hawaii Nature Center sponsors organized hikes on weekends and holidays. Some hikes are specifically for children; others are suitable for fit adults only. None is ordinary: your trip leader will probably be an expert in some aspect of Hawaiian ecology or history. Normally, I avoid organized hikes. But when the Hawaii Nature Center offered a hike in the Waianaes with a botanist and another hike in Makiki Valley with the archaeologist who had surveyed the valley, even I couldn't resist. More recently, I joined a Nature Center hike led by Dr. Mark David Merlin, whose works include two guides to Hawaiian plants that every hiker will want to have (see Bibliography).

There is a modest fee for the trip, payable just before the hike starts. The fee, which helps support the Center, is money well-spent.

The Hawaii Nature Center is particularly dedicated to ensuring the future health of Hawaii's environment by educating her children. They also work with the community and its businesses to raise everyone's awareness of Hawaii's unique environment and the need to preserve it.

Write to the Center for its calendar of upcoming hikes (include a stamped, self-addressed envelope so they can send you the calendar). Then call to reserve a place on the hike you're interested in—space is limited. All hikes require that you bring good hiking shoes (closed toes; no sandals), water, a snack, sunscreen, insect repellent, and other items as noted for that particular hike. *Be sure to call and cancel if you cannot go on a hike for which you have made a reservation, so that someone else can have a chance to go!*

The Hawaii Nature Center on Oahu is at 2131 Makiki Heights Drive, Honolulu, HI 96822; telephone 808-955-0100. The Hawaii Nature Center opened a new facility on Maui in April of 1992 at 875 Iao Valley Road, Wailuku, Maui, HI 96793; telephone 808-244-6500.

I'm indebted to Dave Hill, Community Program Coordinator of the Hawaii Nature Center. He wrote to Wilderness Press about the Center, and that's how I found out about it. Thanks, Dave!

The **place for hiking!**...As this book organizes its hikes, this is the first of the hikes in the wonderful Makiki Valley-Tantalus-Round Top-Nuuanu Valley area. The hikes I've described here (Trips 18 through 27) are just the beginning. A look at the map at the end of this trip and at the end of Trip 14 shows a wealth of possible trips. How about making a loop out of the Manoa Cliffs, Nahuina, Makiki Valley, and Moleka trails? Or how about starting at the Manoa Falls trailhead (Trip 16) in Manoa Valley, working your way over the Aihualama Trail, picking up the Nuuanu and Judd-Nuuanu trails, and finishing in Nuuanu Valley on the Judd Memorial Trail? Now, *that* should keep you busy for a while!

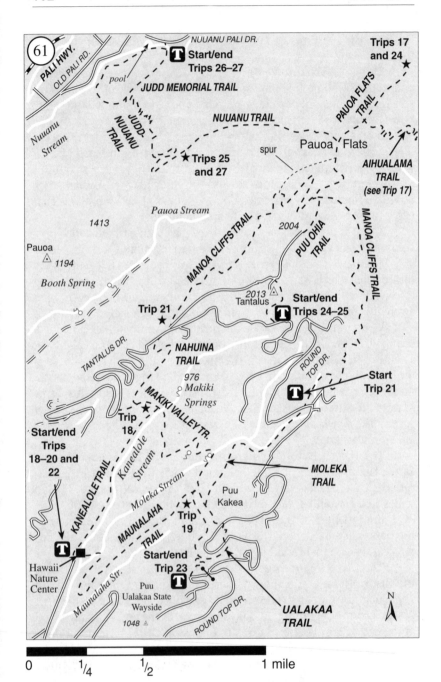

Trip 19. Maunalaha Trail

Distance: Almost 2 miles

Elevation gain: 740'

Hiking time: 1 hour

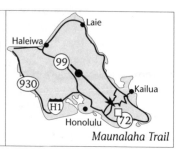

Maunalaha Trail

Topos: *Honolulu*
Trail map: At the end of Trip 18.
Highlights: Unlike the Kanealole Trail, which is safely tucked into Makiki Valley, the Maunalaha Trail winds out of the valley proper and then marches steeply up a ridge that offers superb views over the adjacent valleys of Moleka and Maunalaha streams, over to Round Top ridge, and over Honolulu.

Driving instructions: Follow the driving instructions of Trip 18.
TheBus routes: Take TheBus routes of Trip 18.
Permit/permission required: None.
Description. Walk back to the Hawaii Nature Center's restrooms (between the Center and the parking lot) and pick up the trail that starts as a paved path and crosses Kanealole Stream on a footbridge just east of the Center. This is the Maunalaha Trail. At a junction not shown on the map, a trail of use veers off to the right down Kanealole Stream's east bank for a short way. You, however, go left and stay on the Maunalaha Trail here, following it uphill into the forest past *ti*, banana, Norfolk and Cook pines, and past other vine-draped trees. You pass a taro patch opposite which there is a big tree that in season bears large, globular fruits covered by enlarged green sepals—the elephant apple, not a true apple and not particularly edible but certainly an eye-catching oddity.

You soon hop over Moleka Stream and reach another trail-of-use junction not shown on the map. The Maunalaha Trail (right) makes a hairpin turn here and climbs away from the stream, while the trail-of-use (left) goes a short way upstream to the remains of the Herring coffee plantation (see below). A sign saying MAKIKI LOOP TRAIL points downhill here, the way you came, directing downhill travelers away from the trail-of-use. You take the righthand fork, and the trail climbs under the shade of rows of Norfolk pines, broad as an old road—which it is, part of the carriage road built to the coffee plantation.

You make another hairpin turn, pass a volcanic outcrop, and walk by some bamboo and ironwood. Almost imperceptibly, you gain the ridgeline and find yourself climbing steeply, perhaps puffing a little. The wonderful views here make perfect excuses to stop and catch your breath often. In season, the adjacent stream valley slopes are brilliant with the golden flowers of the silk oak. The ridge itself sports a few silk oaks as well as guava and plenty of eucalyptuses. You find yourself switching to one side of the ridge and then the other to circumvent outcrops of rock.

The trail presently abandons the ridgetop and continues to ascend steeply just below it. A look over your shoulder reveals the towers of downtown Honolulu through the shady branches of the forest. You reach a four-way trail junction under kukui trees. The left (north, down) and straight-ahead (northeast, up) branches are part of the Makiki Valley Trail, while the right (east-southeast, level) branch is the Ualakaa Trail.

You, however, turn around and reluctantly retrace your steps from here. The views are even more enjoyable on the way down!

The Herring coffee plantation.... According to a brochure available at the Hawaii Nature Center, a Mr. J.M. Herring tried to establish a coffee plantation in Makiki Valley between 1864 and 1876. The trail-of-use that leads away from the first hairpin turn in the Maunalaha Trail is part of the carriage road that Herring built to his plantation, as is the segment of the Maunalaha Trail it branches away from.

The plantation failed: Makiki Valley, like adjacent Manoa Valley, is too wet for coffee. The coffee plants have gone wild and infest the valley in places. You'll find this evidence of failed coffee plantations in many valleys throughout the islands. Only in Kona on the Big Island of Hawaii has coffee-growing been commercially successful.

But Mr. Herring didn't know that. Now, all that remains of his efforts besides the plants are the spring that bears his name (the one on Moleka Stream just below the Makiki Valley Trail), a few ruined foundations, and the fragments of "pipes" for a water system he laid. They aren't true pipes. Instead, they are old-fashioned ceramic ginger-beer bottles. (Ginger beer is a carbonated, nonalcoholic drink similar to ginger ale.) Breaking off the narrowest part of the bottle's neck as well as the bottle's bottom, he fashioned pipes by joining the broken ginger-beer bottles. Please leave the ginger-beer bottle fragments where they are, so that they will be available for historians to study when funding is available.

You'll notice that Herring built his plantation on the old Hawaiian agricultural terraces that already existed here. They seem to be withstanding the years far better than the house Herring also built here, traces of which are hard to spot except for the pipes.

I recommend you not explore any farther up Moleka Stream than the plantation because it has been thoroughly invaded by a noxious weed called "cats claw," a shrub with large, strong, vinelike branches studded with vicious, curved thorns. If you are caught in them, you'll probably get cut trying to free yourself. It's not the same as the catclaw of the Mojave desert—though both are legumes—but *this* cats claw's thorns are even nastier. I have the scars to prove it.

A trailside display of ti (Cordyline terminalis) *(lower left—stalks with rosettes of long, oval leaves),* uluhe (Dicranopteris spp.) *(lower right— the fern), and* koa (acacia koa) *(background—tree overarching from right to left). The Polynesians introduced* ti; koa *and* uluhe *are native to Hawaii*

Trip 20. Makiki Valley Loop

Distance: 3 miles

Elevation gain: 760'

Hiking time: 1¹/2 hours

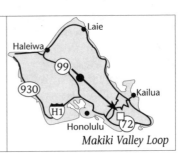

Makiki Valley Loop

Topos: *Honolulu*
Trail map: At the end of Trip 18.
Highlights: Add a scenic and interesting segment of the Makiki Valley Trail to the pleasant ramble up the Kanealole Trail and the view-filled delights of the Maunalaha Trail, and what have you got? The Makiki Valley Loop!

There's an inexpensive guide to the Makiki Valley Loop available at the Hawaii Nature Center; having it will add considerably to your enjoyment. It describes the loop in the counterclockwise direction; this trip describes it in the clockwise direction because the elevation gain is more gradual when hiked that way and because the views from the Maunalaha Trail are better as you're going downhill.

Driving instructions: Follow the driving instructions of Trip 18.
TheBus routes: Take TheBus routes of Trip 18.
Permit/permission required: None.
Description. Follow the description of Trip 18 up the Kanealole Trail to its junction with the Makiki Valley Trail. Turn right onto the Makiki Valley Trail here and almost immediately make a muddy little crossing of a branch of Kanealole Stream. You're above much of Makiki Valley now, and you'll be climbing gradually as you contour in and out of the gullies and around the ridges that water and shape the valley. Listen for songbirds, particularly the irresistible white-rumped shama, and pause to enjoy the view over Honolulu from the noses of the ridges. You shortly cross another branch of Kanealole Stream.

Ironwoods predominate along the next segment, and their soft, droopy needles lie fallen in brown mats on the trail, while their knobby, twisted roots protrude from the trail. Looking around you, it's difficult to believe that by the early years of the twentieth century, Makiki Valley and the slopes around it had been almost completely deforested as a result of the sandalwood trade and, later, of efforts to supply firewood for homes in Honolulu. The native forest was destroyed. Reforestation began in 1910, and it has been successful, as you see, though unfortunately it used non-native trees almost exclusively.

You cross another stream as you dip into the next gully. Native *koa* trees put in an appearance on this trail segment. You can identify them by their long, narrow, curving "leaves," which in fact are not true leaves at all but flattened and enlarged leaf stems. Their true leaves are fern-like compound leaves and are found on very young *koa* but only occasionally on full-grown trees. Or, if you can't identify them by leaf, sniff the air for traces of the oniony-garlicky scent of damp *koa* roots—the most uniquely Hawaiian of all island scents, I think.

Out you go around the ridge nose, then back into another gully and another little stream crossing. As you approach the crossing of Moleka Stream, look for the thin, narrow, shiny leaves of the mountain apple. In season, it sports shocking-pink flowers—actually clusters of long stamens—that sprout from both branch and trunk and, later, a red-skinned fruit that was prized by the old Hawaiians, whose Polynesian ancestors introduced it. You may also spot a close relative of the mountain apple tree, the rose apple, with flowers that look similar but are white and with a yellow fruit.

You climb to the four-way junction of the Makiki Valley, Ualakaa, and Maunalaha trails. The rightmost trail is the Maunalaha Trail. Turn right onto it and close the loop by reversing the steps of Trip 19.

Native ohia lehua (Metrosideros collina, *subsp.* polymorpha), *with striking red "powderpuff" blossoms*

Trip 21. Manoa Cliffs

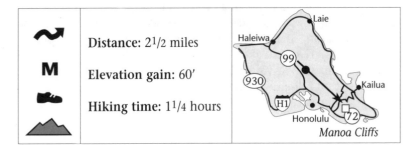

Distance: 2¹/₂ miles

Elevation gain: 60'

Hiking time: 1¹/₄ hours

Manoa Cliffs

Topos: *Honolulu*
Trail map: At the end of Trip 18.
Highlights: No other trail in the Makiki Valley-Tantalus-Round Top-Nuuanu Valley area offers views as sweeping and as breathtaking as the Manoa Cliffs Trail does. There's a fine display of interesting plants along the trail, too. If you have time for only one hike in this area, this one or Trip 22, the next, should be it, unless you're seriously acrophobic.
Driving instructions:
To take this as a shuttle trip or to pick up friends who have taken this hike as a shuttle trip, you need to shuttle the first car or drive the pick-up car to the end of the trip. Start by following the driving instructions of Trip 18: From the intersection of McCully Street and Kapiolani Boulevard just outside Waikiki, continue northeast on McCully, crossing over the Lunalilo Freeway (H1) on a narrow bridge. Keep going to Wilder Avenue. Turn left onto Wilder and go west to Makiki Street, where you turn right. (It's a little hard to spot: look for a church on the *left* side of Wilder.) Go north on Makiki Street to a **Y** junction at the narrow end of a wedge-shaped park. Take the left fork here; it's Makiki Heights Drive. Follow Makiki Heights Drive uphill past the hairpin turn from which the spur road to the Hawaii Nature Center takes off. You, however, continue corkscrewing steeply uphill to a junction with Tantalus Drive, where the hood of your car seems pointed almost skyward. Turn right onto Tantalus Drive and continue uphill past the west end of the Makiki Valley Trail and past the Nahuina Trail to the west end of the Manoa Cliffs Trail. Park off the road here, a little over 6¹/₄ miles.
To get to the east end of the Manoa Cliffs Trail from the west end, where this hike starts, drive the second car almost 1¹/₂ miles farther on Tantalus Drive and then Round Top Drive, passing the start of the Puu Ohia Trail, to a small parking area that serves the upper end of the Moleka Trail and the east end of the Manoa Cliffs Trail. Park here.

If you're plannning to retrace your steps rather than set up a shuttle, start by following the driving instructions of Trip 18: From the intersection of McCully Street and Kapiolani Boulevard, continue north-northeast over the freeway and turn left at Wilder Avenue. Go west on Wilder to Makiki Street, where you turn right. Go north on Makiki Street to a Y junction at the narrow end of a wedge-shaped park. Starting here, you depart from the driving instructions of Trip 18. Take the right fork here; it's Round Top Drive. Follow it as it twists uphill past the turnoff to Puu Ualakaa State Wayside and past an unmarked trailhead (it's part of the Ualakaa Trail) to a small parking area at the upper end of the Moleka Trail and the east end of the Manoa Cliffs Trail. Park here, 6 miles.

TheBus routes: Not served by TheBus. Or see the Manoa Cliffs Trail as part of Trip 22, which starts in Makiki Valley.

Permit/permission required: None.

Description. The beginning of the Manoa Cliffs Trail (labeled CONNECTOR on some maps) is directly across the street from the parking lot. The trail heads off through dense forest to a Y junction; turn right here and ascend well-engineered, gravel-filled "steps." You climb steeply as you negotiate a switchback turn along a strawberry-guava-filled gully. Then the trail twines downhill through strawberry guavas, thickets of *ieie, koa,* a few *ohia,* presently leveling out—more or less—along the cliff face. Where the vegetation permits, there are marvelous views east over Manoa Valley and beyond, and north to the Koolaus.

A wooden walkway helps you cross a tiny but steep gully past which there's a bench by a signpost that says 101 MANOA CLIFFS BAMBOO REST. Rest and enjoy the surroundings. Around you, the breeze rattles the stems of giant bamboos so that they make an eerie clatter. Across Manoa Valley and Waahila Ridge, the city glitters in the sunlight and the ocean stretches out to meet the sky.

Another bench and another superb view soon greet you at a hairpin turn overlooking the valley, and more wooden walkways carry you over damp sections. Up and down you go, now in sun, now in shade, now wrinkling your nose at the *koa's* oniony-garlicky scent, now inhaling with delight the perfume of the world's only fragrant hibiscus (native to the Waimea Canyon region of Kauai). There are brief but amazing glimpses right through the Koolaus to the windward side of Oahu along this stretch, too.

At the east junction with the Puu Ohia Trail, continue ahead (right). The Manoa Cliffs and Puu Ohia trails meet here, and the Puu Ohia Trail briefly merges with the Manoa Cliffs Trail. At their west junction, the Puu Ohia trail diverges, going right. A sign says TO TANTALUS

DRIVE, pointing west—the direction you're going in—and TO ROUNDTOP DRIVE, pointing east—you just came from there. Continue ahead (left) on the Manoa Cliffs Trail. This area is almost a rainforest, and the *koa* trees are especially beautiful here.

Now you switchback gently down, enjoying great views west to Honolulu Airport and Honolulu Harbor. Take the left fork to stay on the main trail at an unmarked junction (not on the map) at a hairpin on the Manoa Cliffs Trail; the right fork is a signed spur trail to Pauoa Flats and may be labeled "shortcut" on the DLNR literature about the area. (This area is honeycombed with trails-of-use that offer added zest for island residents but are the bane of visitors.) You stroll through ginger, guava, *ieie*, bracken ferns, maidenhair ferns where it's very shady, *ti, koa,* and the red-flowered *ohia.* Take a view-filled break at a bench under a big ferny-leafed tree. Another bench soon offers similar splendid views over the west side of the island to the Waianaes.

You shortly pass a taro patch sustained by a tiny seep and then

some handsome, white-flowered rose apple trees. It's not long now before you meet Tantalus Drive by a big old banyan tree, just below a turnout. Your shuttle car or pick-up ride should be waiting for you here (or, retrace your steps from here).

High banks and overarching trees create an appealing little tunnel of greenery along a Honolulu trail

Trip 22. Makiki-Manoa Cliffs Adventure

Distance: Just over 6 miles

Elevation gain: 1260'

Hiking time: Just over 3 hours

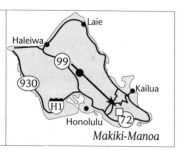

Makiki-Manoa

Topos: *Honolulu*

Trail map (route partly approximated): At the end of Trip 18.

Highlights: This long but wonderfully scenic and varied trip has it all: rainforest vegetation, sweeping views, and that "edge of the world" feeling that comes from walking on ridgetops and cliffs. So it lacks a waterfall or a swimming hole? Plenty of other places to find *them*. This is one of my favorite three hikes on Oahu and a must-see for sturdier hikers! (My other two favorites are Trips 36 and 45.)

Driving instructions: Follow the driving instructions of Trip 18.

TheBus routes: Take TheBus routes of Trip 18.

Permit/permission required: None.

Description. Begin your loop on the Maunalaha Trail as described in Trip 19 (not the Kanealole Trail of Trip 18). At the four-way junction with the Makiki Valley and Ualakaa trails, turn right onto the Makiki Valley Trail (the rightmost trail here is the Ualakaa Trail). You curve southeast in dense forest on an easy grade, passing a huge banyan tree, and soon reach the junction with the south end of the Moleka Trail (not on the topo).

Turn left (almost due north) onto the Moleka Trail, still deep in the forest. Old guava trees overhang the trail, and maidenhair ferns sprout from the rock face below. It certainly feels like a rainforest here! Where openings in the forest permit, you have views across the adjacent gully to luxury homes on the surrounding slopes. Look for a tiny white-flowered begonia along the trail, too—when the terrain permits. The trail is very narrow and the slope below it very steep in places.

You descend slightly and then curve southeast through the forest under *kukui* and *koa*. There's a small, bamboo-filled gully on the downhill (left) side of the trail. Blue ageratum and bracken ferns fill in the understory. Giant bamboo presently crowds in on both sides of the trail, so high and so dense that light filtering through it seems tinted green. Then, as the bamboo gives way to a more open forest, you curve around the head of the gully and emerge at the small parking lot on Round Top Drive at the north end of the Moleka Trail.

Cross Round Top Drive and pick up the east end of the Manoa Cliffs Trail just across the street. (This first part of the east side of the Manoa Cliffs Trail is marked as the CONNECTOR trail on some maps.) Follow the description of Trip 21 to take in the many pleasures of the Manoa Cliffs Trail.

At the west end of the Manoa Cliffs Trail, you emerge on Tantalus Drive. Turn right and cautiously walk about 100 yards down Tantalus Drive, which briefly becomes one lane, then widens to two again. Pick up the north end of the Nahuina Trail (not on the topo) on the left (southeast) side of Tantalus Drive and twine southeast and downhill on the shady trail, through *hau* thickets and under *koa*, guava, and mango trees. It's pretty if unexciting, and it's a short way to the south end of the Nahuina Trail at a junction with the Makiki Valley Trail.

Turn *left* onto the Makiki Valley Trail—the right branch goes to Tantalus Drive—and begin descending under large mango trees while enjoying some outstanding views of the towers of downtown Honolulu. The going gets a bit steep, but you're soon at the junction with the Kanealole Trail.

Turn right (southwest) onto the Kanealole Trail and reverse the steps of Trip 18 to close the loop and end this long and satisfying trip.

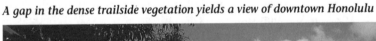

A gap in the dense trailside vegetation yields a view of downtown Honolulu

Trip 23. Ualakaa Loop

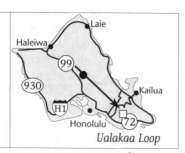

Distance: 1 mile

Elevation gain: 180'

Hiking time: 1/2 hour

Ualakaa Loop

Topos: *Honolulu*

Trail map (route approximated): At the end of Trip 18.

Highlights: The Ualakaa Loop rewards you with a most pleasant mile of woodsy hiking—except for having to cross Round Top Drive a couple of times. I think you'll enjoy it.

Driving instructions: From the intersection of McCully Street and Kapiolani Boulevard just outside Waikiki, continue northeast on McCully, crossing over the Lunalilo Freeway (H1) on a narrow bridge. Keep going to Wilder Avenue. Turn left onto Wilder and go west to Makiki Street, where you turn right. (It's a little hard to spot: look for a church on the *left* side of Wilder.) Go north on Makiki Street to a **Y** junction at the narrow end of a wedge-shaped park. Take the right fork here; it's Round Top Drive. Sometimes there are no signs on Round Top Drive for the turnoff to Puu Ualakaa State Wayside (which I'll refer to as "the park"). I hope there will be a sign when *you* go there. If not, note that as you twine up Round Top from the **Y** junction, the turnoff is at the apex of the fourth *major* hairpin turn, almost 4 1/4 miles. It comes after a relatively long, straight stretch of Round Top Drive that offers excellent views southeast over the city to Diamond Head. Another clue: look for the gate on the park's access road. Turn left through the gate into the park.

Inside the park, you shortly reach another hairpin turn by a good-sized stand of Norfolk pines. Park off the road here, 4 1/4 miles. The trailhead is on the right side of the hairpin as you face west (toward the Norfolk pines). Or, if there's not room to park here, drive to the picnic area at the high point of the park, where the road ends, and walk back down the road to start your hike. This high point, "1048" on the map, is the summit of the crater-less cinder cone now called Round Top (to the Hawaiians, it was Puu Ualakaa—hence the park's and trail's names). The park is open from 7:00 AM to 7:45 PM from April 1 to Labor Day and to 6:45 PM from the day after Labor Day to March 31.

TheBus routes: Not served by TheBus. You can get to the loop from the Maunalaha Trail (Trip 18), which would add 2 miles and 740 feet to your hike and make this trip a strenuous semiloop.

Permit/permission required: None.

Description. The trail begins with a very short segment that leads north away from the hairpin but soon curves northeast. Ascend through Norfolk pines, palm grass, impatiens, the blue flowers and reclining green stems of wandering Jew (dayflower), and a large shrub called Christmas daisy. Christmas daisy has wide, almost maple-like leaves and—surprise!—produces clusters of white, daisy-like flowers around Christmas time. Lazy switchbacks soon take you up into ironwoods and Christmas berry trees to the junction with the loop part of this trip. You could go left or right here; arbitrarily, go left (west). (This puts off the street crossings till near the end of the hike.)

At a cliff edge under Norfolk pines, the trail hooks sharply right (northeast) and descends slightly, then levels out as it curves northwest. Duck under a huge ficus, perhaps a strangler fig, that's engulfing a *koa* tree. The dense forest is almost wholly non-native: *ti, kukui,* banana, octopus tree, banyan, guava, mountain apple, and the native *koa.*

In a little less than 1/2 mile, you reach the four-way junction with the Maunalaha and Makiki Valley trails. You'll now find a bench and a trail map here. The leftmost trail is the Maunalaha Trail; the trail ahead and the trail that goes sharply right are both parts of the Makiki Valley Trail. Turn sharply right (east-northeast) on the Makiki Valley Trail and ascend moderately as the trail curves southeast, almost paralleling the previous leg of your hike but above it. You shortly reach a junction with the Moleka Trail (left); you continue ahead (right) on the Makiki Valley Trail.

You presently teeter over the roots of big banyans, walk under a banyan-root arch, and descend a little to emerge at Round Top Drive under *koa* and through Christmas daisy. Bear right, carefully cross the road, and walk about 100 feet down the road to an unmarked trail signified by a low tunnel hacked into a dense *hau* thicket. Duck into the tunnel and shortly find yourself at a junction where the right fork goes uphill about 120 feet to a nice viewpoint overlooking Diamond Head. You go left (east) to continue your trip, The trail zigzags down-hill, making a shortcut across a hairpin turn on Round Top Drive. You meet Round Top Drive again, this time at a turnout, where the trail is marked but unnamed. Pick up the trail again immediately across the road. Back on the trail, you stroll gradually downhill and southwest to close the loop.

From here, it's a short walk down the out-and-back segment to your car.

Round Top cinder cone and the Tantalus-Round Top loop.....Round Top cinder cone is one of a series of three cinder cones on this particular ridge: Round Top (Puu Ualakaa), Sugarloaf (Puu Kakea), and Tantalus (Puu Ohia). (Puu means "hill.") They lead almost north into the Koolaus and are remnants of the same series of eruptions that produced Diamond Head, Koko Crater, and other cones of the Honolulu Volcanic Series, which occurred well after the final building of the Koolau volcano. The term "series" suggests that these events occurred close together, but the evidence is that they were spread out over hundreds of thousands of years and ended as recently as 32,000 years ago. Of course, in geological terms, that *is* very close together. *Volcanoes in the Sea* quotes an age of about 67,000 years for Sugarloaf and offers the opinion that Tantalus is about the same age, Round Top a little older.

Round Top's coarse cinder is exposed along the park's access road, and formations that may have been the conduits that fed lava to Round Top are exposed in Makiki Valley. However, no lava is reported to have flowed from Round Top itself; it just belched cinders. Sugarloaf and Tantalus spewed both lava and cinders. Lava from Sugarloaf flowed eastward into Manoa Valley, pushed the course of Manoa Stream from the valley's midline over to its east side, and raised the floor of the valley. Lava from Tantalus, on the other hand, flowed westward into upper Pauoa Valley. The upper part of this flow is little eroded and today forms Pauoa Flats, through which Trips 17, 24, and 25 pass. Trips 24 and 25 also pass just below the summit of Tantalus.

If you haven't figured it out by now, the Tantalus Drive-Round Top Drive loop offers wonderful views over Honolulu. The city has thoughtfully put many turnouts along the road so that we visitors can pull over, enjoy the view, and take photos. Don't miss it!

Trip 24. Puu Ohia Trail to Nuuanu Valley View

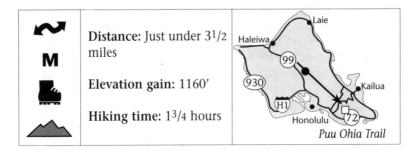

Distance: Just under 3¹/2 miles

Elevation gain: 1160'

Hiking time: 1³/4 hours

Puu Ohia Trail

Topos: *Honolulu*

Trail map (route partly approximated): At the end of Trip 18.

Highlights: This rainforest adventure takes you practically over the top of Tantalus (Puu Ohia) cinder cone and down through Pauoa Flats to that wonderful view over Nuuanu Valley that you enjoyed in Trip 17.

Driving instructions: From the intersection of McCully Street and Kapiolani Boulevard just outside Waikiki, continue northeast on McCully, crossing over the Lunalilo Freeway (H1) on a narrow bridge. Keep going to Wilder Avenue. Turn left onto Wilder and go west to Makiki Street, where you turn right. (It's a little hard to spot: look for a church on the *left* side of Wilder.) Go north on Makiki Street to a **Y** junction at the narrow end of a wedge-shaped park. You can go right (on Round Top) or left (on Makiki Heights Drive and then right on Tantalus Drive). It's just under 7 miles via Makiki Heights and Tantalus drives, and the same via Round Top Drive. You may as well drive the loop by going up one and down the other. In any case, at the top of the road loop, you'll find a wide turnout on the seaward side of the road. Park here.

TheBus routes: Not served by TheBus. You need to drive to this trailhead.

Permit/permission required: None.

Description. The Puu Ohia trailhead is directly across the street from the turnout where you parked. On the trail, head northwest and uphill past night-blooming jasmine, ginger, avocado, and Christmas berry. After a switchback turn, you climb steeply on rude "stairs" cut into the coarse, gray-brown soil. The grade eases as you step over tree roots and contours around a hillside where at times you must duck under guava branches. *Ti* and bamboo join the vegetation, while breaks in the forest offer magnificent views over Honolulu to Diamond Head.

Soon you're in a dense forest of giant bamboo. Be alert here: this area is full of trails-of-use that the locals probably think are great fun but which can ruin a visitor's hike; they are not shown on the map. A little past the 1/3-mile point, there's a junction where an unmarked trail-of-use goes off through the bamboo to the right (east-northeast). Don't take it. Stay on the main trail by going left here. Contour through ginger, *koa*, and bamboo and presently meet another trail-of-use veering off to the right. Stay on the main trail by taking the left fork and shortly make a steep climb on high steps around the trunk of a big old *koa* tree.

At the top of this climb, you find yourself on a paved road. Note this junction; it can be hard to spot on the way back. The Puu Ohia route turns right, down the paved road. However, you may wish to divert from the main route briefly to climb Tantalus: turn left and go uphill on the road a little to a pair of telephone relay stations. Look for a use trail that may be marked by a "railing" improvised from lengths of bamboo held together by duct tape—how long can *that* last?—and that leads southward between the relay stations. On it, climb a short distance through ginger and ageratum to the top of Tantalus, where there's a ruined concrete monument—the remains of the benchmark, perhaps. (See the end of Trip 23 for more on Tantalus and its fellow cinder cones.) Retrace your steps after taking in the view.

Back at the junction of the foot trail and the paved road at the big old *koa* tree, walk north-northeast and downhill on the paved road, which almost immediately meets another paved road. Stay on the same road (right), continuing north-northeast and dipping down to a saddle. Climb northeast to another telephone relay station. Behind the station, the route becomes a footpath again and leads downhill very steeply over slippery clay and through bamboo to a junction with a trail-of-use that goes left. Go right, contouring through bamboo, *koa, ti,* and strawberry guava to an unmarked junction with the Manoa Cliffs Trail (Trip 21). Note this junction for your return. Turn left onto the Manoa Cliffs Trail.

At the next trail junction, turn right (north-northeast) onto the Pauoa Flats Trail and make a gradual descent on long switchback legs, through dense ginger, guava, *ieie*, and thimbleberry. The path traverses a complicated, living lacework of exposed tree roots as it passes a junction with the Nuuanu Trail (coming in from the left, west) and then a junction with the Aihualama Trail (coming in from the right, east). Continue ahead (northeast), emerging at Nuuanu Overlook as described in Trip 17. What a view you have over Nuuanu Valley here!

Retrace your steps when you're ready, being careful to avoid the trails-of-use.

Tangle of tree roots at Pauoa Flats

Trip 25. Puu Ohia-Nuuanu Trails

Distance: 4 miles

Elevation gain: 1110'

Hiking time: 2 hours

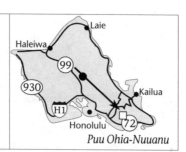

Puu Ohia-Nuuanu

Topos: *Honolulu*

Trail map (route approximated): At the end of Trip 18.

Highlights: Give your Puu Ohia Trail trip a different twist by taking in the Nuuanu Trail instead of continuing out to the Nuuanu Overlook. Or see both of them! The lovely but remote Nuuanu Trail, inaccessible except from the far ends of other trails, offers pleasant views and native plants.

Driving instructions: Follow the driving instructions of Trip 24.

TheBus routes: Not served by TheBus.

Permit/permission required: None.

Description. Follow the description of Trip 24 to the junction of the Puu Ohia and Nuuanu trails. Turn left (west) onto the Nuuanu Trail. Stroll along under banyans, then curve west-southwest through some paperbarks with their attractive layers of white, peeling, papery bark. The paperbarks give way to Norfolk pines, then the native *ohia*, and there's a patch of the native sedge *uki* (on the uphill side).

Views open up over Pauoa Valley to the city below as you curve around the valley's head. Southeastward, high on the ridge from which you recently came, are the telephone relay stations you passed on the Puu Ohia Trail. After rounding the nose of a ridge, you have some wonderful views to the east. Curve around the head of a tributary valley and arrive at an open area surrounded by *ohia* and a small *koa* tree, all on the nose of another small ridge. There's an obscure junction here, too: the Judd-Nuuanu Trail (Trip 27) leads downhill from here (left fork, through the *ohia*), while a trail-of-use leads a short way around this ridgelet (right fork).

After enjoying a rest at this remote, peaceful spot, retrace your steps to the Puu Ohia trailhead.

Silk oaks (Grevillea robusta) *are native to Australia and were brought to Hawaii for use in reforestation. They have naturalized widely in Hawaiian forests. With their deeply cut leaves and seasonal displays of bright golden flowers, they are striking sights on many Hawaiian hillsides*

Trip 26. Judd Memorial Trail ("Jackass Ginger Pool")

Distance: A little over 1 mile

Elevation gain: 250′

Hiking time: A little over 1/2 hour

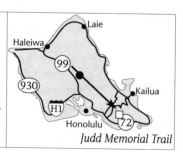

Judd Memorial Trail

Topos: *Honolulu*

Trail map (route approximated): At the end of Trip 18.

Highlights: A delightful forest walk is capped by a visit to one of Honolulu's most popular swimming holes, Jackass Ginger Pool. Bring some jungle juice as well as a swimsuit!

Driving instructions: From the intersection of McCully Street and Kapiolani Boulevard, go northeast on McCully, cross over the H1 freeway, and almost immediately turn left on Metcalfe in order to get onto the H1 freeway westbound. Take H1 to the Pali Highway (Highway 61) and get onto the Pali Highway going north-northeast toward Kailua. Keep your eyes peeled for the turnoff (on the right—east) to Nuuanu Pali Drive; if you get to the turnoff to the Pali Lookout, you have gone too far. Turn right onto Nuuanu Pali Drive, which promptly angles northeast. At a **Y** junction, take the right fork, which continues to be Nuuanu Pali Drive (the left fork is Old Pali Road). The drive presently makes a hairpin turn. Beyond this turn, keep a sharp lookout for a small trail sign on the right (east) side of the narrow, forested drive. It marks the start of the Judd Memorial Trail. Turn into the damp little parking lot at the trailhead and park here, 6 1/4 miles, just past Poli Hiwa Place.

TheBus routes: Not directly served by TheBus. Take Route 8, 19, 20, or 58 to the Ala Moana Shopping Center and transfer to Route 4 (be sure to get a Route-4 bus that is going all the way to Dowsett, not to Pauoa Road). Get off at the stop nearest Nuuanu Pali Drive (ask your driver) and walk up Nuuanu Pali Drive a little less than a mile to the trailhead.

Permit/permission required: None.

Description. Bear southeast on a beaten path past banyans and mango trees under a cool green forest canopy. Descend over roots and rocks toward the sound of rushing Nuuanu Stream, which you soon cross. The crossing is wide and the rocks slippery, so pick your way across carefully to the dense forest of giant bamboo on the far side. Clamber up the bank and regain the trail.

The loop begins here, just across the stream. You could go left or right; arbitrarily, go left for now. Head up through the bamboo, avoiding any side trails-of-use. Curve around the bamboo grove and into a grove of spicy-smelling swamp mahogany trees. The trail becomes faint as you reach an area where the ground slopes gently downward. Bear left (west-southwest) across the slope, then curve around a small, dry gully. Wander southwest under the friendly shade of Norfolk pines, so reminiscent of a mainland evergreen forest—except for the occasional octopus tree or strawberry guava. Beyond another gully, there are pillows of pale green moss here and there on the moist ground, while bracken and sword ferns join the understory. You soon dip across another gully, this one damp and ferny.

At the Judd-Nuuanu Trail, which goes left (south-southwest), you go right (southwest) to stay on the Judd Memorial Trail. Soon, a glimpse of a house up ahead suggests that the trail is practically in someone's back yard. Fortunately, the trail curves right, taking you away from the house and the possibility of a homeowner's wrath. The trail now descends a little, then curves left along a gully to your right (it's mostly hidden in vegetation). You presently curve west-southwest down a little ridge and swing across another gully. The presence of silk oaks, largely hidden by the *hau*, is betrayed by their distinctive large, deeply divided leaves lying on the trail.

Soon you find yourself looking down to your left to a big swimming hole. It's a short but very steep scramble of about 70' down to this overused, well-loved pool, Jackass Ginger Pool. Rose apple and banyan trees overhang Jackass Ginger Pool, which is bordered on the far side by someone's backyard fence (see photo on page 124). Watch out for broken glass and hungry mosquitoes!

Back on the main trail, well above the stream, it's apparent that there are a number of good-sized, quieter pools upstream from Jackass Ginger Pool. Steep trails-of-use lead down to some of them. Then the main trail descends to meet the streambank, parallels it into the bamboo forest, and emerges at the beginning of the loop. Cross the stream and retrace your steps to the parking lot to conclude this enjoyable hike.

The Judd Memorial Trail....is named for Charles S. Judd, Hawaii Territory's chief forester from 1915 to 1939. Judd planted the grove through which you've been hiking. The grove and the trail were named in his honor in 1953. For another Judd of Hawaii, see the note at the end of Trip 27.

Jackass Ginger.... According to *Place Names of Hawaii*, the Jackass Ginger Pool got its name in the early 1900s for a donkey that was tethered by it and for the yellow ginger that grew around it.

Trip 27. Judd-Nuuanu Semiloop

Distance: Just under 3³/4 miles

Elevation gain: 1070'

Hiking time: A little over 1³/4 hours

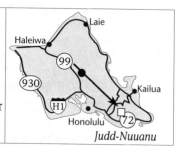

Judd-Nuuanu

Topos: *Honolulu*

Trail map: At the end of Trip 18.

Highlights: Interrupt your swimming-hole loop on the Judd Memorial Trail (Trip 26) to hike steeply up into the forest on the Judd-Nuuanu Trail. It's a real treat because of the opportunity it offers to see native plants and birds.

Driving instructions: Follow the driving instructions of Trip 26.

TheBus routes: Take TheBus routes of Trip 26.

Permit/permission required: None.

Description. Follow the description of Trip 26 to the junction with the Judd-Nuuanu Trail (it may say only NUUANU TRAIL on the marker). Turn left on the Judd-Nuuanu Trail and twist uphill through Norfolk pines. The trail ascends in tight, moderate to steep switchbacks. Views open up and then disappear as the dense vegetation permits. Near the halfway point, there's a *very* steep pitch up to some ironwoods. Catch your breath at the ironwoods, for there are now about three very steep, loose switchback turns to negotiate. They carry you around the ridge and into palms and eucalyptus. The grade eases as you contour around a gully, cross a tiny stream, and continue climbing.

Native trees appear as you gain altitude. Look for the *kopiko* with its blackish bark and narrow, dark green leaves and for the *mamaki* with its large, heart-shaped leaves with their prominent palmate veins. You pass above a huge banyan and walk—very steeply at times—northeast up a narrow ridge on which grow the native *koa, kopiko,* and *ohia* trees and the native *uluhe* fern. Listen and look for native birds along this ridge, too: the red *apapane* and the greenish *amakihi*.

The grade levels out at an open spot under *ohia* and *koa* where the Judd-Nuuanu Trail meets the Nuuanu Trail (Trip 25), which goes right (east) from here to meet the Puu Ohia Trail. You, however, take a rest, enjoy the view, and then return to the Judd Memorial Trail, where you turn left to resume the loop as in Trip 26 and to enjoy a well-deserved swim in Jackass Ginger Pool.

"Who is the despotic Dr. Judd?"....asked the British during the reign of Kamehameha III. "Dr. Judd" was Gerrit Parmele Judd (1803–1873), a New England physician who became a missionary to Hawaii. Judd and his wife, Laura, arrived in Hawaii in 1828. They arrived at a time of great political and cultural upheaval in Hawaii. Hawaii was finding it increasingly difficult to resist foreign intrusion and to maintain her sovereignty. The major powers competing for dominance in Hawaii—America, Britain, and France—couldn't make up their minds about Hawaii. Was Hawaii a sovereign nation worthy of their respect? Or did she need the protection of one of the major powers? Or was she fit only to be seized and exploited?

Eager to exploit Hawaii, many foreigners violated Hawaiian law and mistreated the Hawaiian people—and then screamed to their own governments for help when the Hawaiian government tried to protect

its land and people by enforcing Hawaiian law. Time and again, the other nations responded to Hawaii's efforts to defend herself by sending a warship into Honolulu harbor to point its guns at the town and to wring concessions for its citizens—American, British, or French—from the Hawaiian government.

King Kamehameha III, raised when Hawaii's king had been an absolute monarch under

Pretty cascades tumble into Jackass Ginger Pool

the *kapu* system, found the nation's problems so bewildering and un-manageable that he preferred to withdraw into the bottle. He needed competent help, and Judd was at hand. Judd and his wife had taught themselves Hawaiian on the voyage over, and they quickly became flu-ent in it. Judd was strong-willed, incorruptible, hard-working, and de-termined to see that Hawaii and her people were treated fairly. Kamehameha III came to know and respect the Judds; so did the *kuhina nui* (queen regent), the chiefess Kinau.

In 1842 Judd resigned from the mission and accepted a govern-ment post, the presidency of the Treasury Board. He brought fiscal re-sponsibility to the kingdom, and he strove to keep the king sober and out of trouble. Says Edward Joesting in *Hawaii: An Uncommon History,* "[Judd's] admirers thought he held the kingdom together. . . .His very presence probably scared some persons about him into remaining hon-est." His detractors accused him of usurping the king's powers and called him King Judd. In his single-minded pursuit of the good of the king-dom as he saw it, Judd eventually alienated almost every other leading citizen in Honolulu. After eleven years of remarkable service in those trying times, he resigned in 1853, driven out by a host of enemies.

Judd died in 1873. On his tombstone is inscribed "Hawaii's Friend." Indeed he was. Consider a specific incident in his service to the nation: In February of 1843 the British frigate *Carysfort* sailed into Honolulu harbor to investigate complaints by British subjects. Her commander, Captain Lord George Paulet, exceeded his brief: he pointed the *Carysfort's* guns at the town, annexed Hawaii to Great Britain, and set up himself as ruler. While Hawaii grieved and Paulet rewrote her laws, Judd smuggled the Hawaiian government's papers into the royal mausoleum to safe-guard them. There he worked in secret at night, using Queen Kaahumanu's coffin as a desk while preparing petitions to the British, French, and American governments and arranging for a secret mission to those nations to plead for their help in restoring Hawaii's indepen-dence. (See "Geology and History" for more on Kaahumanu.)

Judd's envoy reached Britain safely, where news of the unautho-rized annexation was ill-received. In July of 1843 the British frigate *Dublin* sailed into Honolulu harbor. Her commander, Rear Admiral Ri-chard Thomas, had been charged to restore Hawaii to the Hawaiians. During the restoration ceremonies, Judd read in Hawaiian the declara-tion restoring Hawaiian sovereignty, and Kamehameha III uttered the words that have since become Hawaii's motto: "*Ua mau ke ea o ka aina i ka pono* (The life of the land is preserved in righteousness)."

While he may have been "the despotic Dr. Judd" to others, Gerrit Parmele Judd was truly Hawaii's friend.

Trip 28. Old Pali Highway

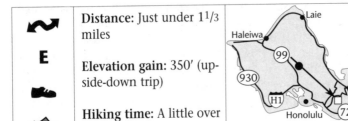

Distance: Just under 1¹/₃ miles

E

Elevation gain: 350′ (up-side-down trip)

Hiking time: A little over ²/₃ hour

Old Pali Highway

Topos: *Honolulu*

Trail map: At the end of this trip.

Highlights: Who will have the finest views of windward Oahu and of the famed Nuuanu *Pali?* Not drivers on the Pali Highway—though the views they get are hard to beat. No, the winner is you on this short, though sometimes steep, trip on an abandoned segment of the old Pali Highway.

Driving instructions: From McCully Street and Kapiolani Boulevard, drive northeast over the H1 freeway and almost immediately turn left onto Metcalfe in order to get on H1 westbound. Take H1 west to the Pali Highway (Highway 61). Turn north-northeast on the Pali Highway toward Kailua. As the suburbs of Honolulu give way to forest, look for the turnoff to Nuuanu Pali State Wayside (which I'll refer to as "the park") on the right (east) side of the road. Get off here, drive up the access road to the parking lot, and park here to start your hike, just under 8¹/₂ miles.

TheBus routes: Not served by TheBus.

Permit/permission required: None.

Description. Walk away from the parking lot and out to the windy viewing platforms a few steps away. The views from this spot are justly famous. The south end of windward Oahu stretches out before you, the land dominated by the steep green *pali* on which you're standing and by the sprawling town of Kailua. Beyond Kailua lie the long white beach and clear turquoise waters of Kailua Bay. Northward, the suburbs of Kaneohe spread over the plain, and huge Kaneohe Bay sparkles in the distance.

From the viewing platform, either descend a few steps on the right side or zigzag down a gentle ramp on the left to the lower platform. The routes converge almost immediately, and you stroll downhill out of the worst of the wind and toward a locked gate. Climb up and step through a frame on the outer edge of the gate—careful of that drop!

Beyond the gate, you amble down, seemingly on the very edge of the *pali*. The old road is slowly being commandeered by plants, some of which were probably planted long ago as roadside adornments. Now, ficuses, morning glory, vervain, *kukui*, sweet fern, and juniper bush vie for space on and along the old roadbed. A heavily overgrown section precedes a turn into a recess where a tiny stream slips northward down a high, sheer cliff face to an unromantic end in a roadside culvert. Air plants, *koa haole*, Indian pluchea, *ti*, palm grass, bashful plant (stroke a leaf and you'll see where it gets its name), ficus, an occasional palm, and cup-of-gold jostle for room.

This world of growth and greenery seems hidden from the noisy highway below like a flowerbox in a second-story window, unnoticed by the passerby on the busy street. Too soon, however, the old highway reaches the ruins of a hairpin turn—your turnaround point for this trip, though you may continue (see below).

Retrace your steps from the ruined hairpin turn. If anything, the views are even better going uphill than going downhill. No other vantage point offers such a continuous, and yet changing, view of the *pali* and such a chance to appreciate how sheer and delicately fluted these stream-cut cliffs are. And if the day is overcast or it's late in the day, there's an extra treat: from some vantage points, the lighted mouths of the Pali Highway tunnels seem to glow like immense orange eyes in the cliffs. Stop to admire the view from the lookout at the top again!

If you continue beyond the ruined hairpin turn. . . .You can now continue around the turn to meet the Maunawili Demonstration Trail (Trip 29). This option adds just over 2/3 mile, 1/3 hour, and 140 feet of elevation loss/gain to this trip. Uninteresting in its own right, the continuation trail's main attraction is that it lets you start Trip 29 at Nuuanu Pali State Wayside. The continuation trail dips in and out of damp recesses, then descends steeply to meet the Maunawili Demonstration Trail coming up from the Pali Highway switchback above St. Stephen's Seminary.

The Nuuanu *Pali*....is famous as the site of Kamehameha's final battle for Oahu. In 1795, after having consolidated his grip on the Big Island and having conquered Maui and Molokai, Kamehameha was ready to subdue Oahu. Kaiana, a high chief who had sometimes been his ally and sometimes his rival, now deserted Kamehameha and joined the defenders of Oahu.

Kaiana was not just a political rival. Kaahumanu, Kamehameha's favorite wife, had taken the handsome Kaiana as a lover. In a society where both men and women, particularly *alii*, were permitted more than one spouse, this liaison ought to have caused no stir. Kamehameha, however, was terribly jealous. Although Kamehameha and Kaahumanu eventually reconciled (with the help of British Captain George Vancouver, a friend to both), the hostility between Kaiana and Kamehameha was never laid to rest till Kaiana's death.

Undeterred by Kaiana's desertion, Kamehameha and his armies crossed the channel between Maui and Oahu in a great fleet of canoes, landing on either side of Diamond Head ("Leahi" to the Hawaiians). Kamehameha and his men were superior in numbers and were armed with Western as well as traditional Hawaiian weapons. They pushed the defenders back across the plains where modern Honolulu now sprawls, back past a stone fort at the mouth of Nuuanu Valley, and up the valley toward the *pali*. As Oahu's warriors were driven up into the head of the valley and defeat became inevitable, some fled into the wild peaks surrounding the valley or found their way down steep paths to the windward side. Some held their ground and fought to the death, including Kaiana. And still others, in the tragedy that is inextricably associated with the Nuuanu *Pali* now, leaped to their deaths a thousand feet below rather accept defeat.

Kamehameha was victorious. Now only Kauai (and thus also Niihau) remained for him to conquer. It must have seemed inevitable that Kauai would shortly fall. Little did he know that this victory on Oahu marked the height of his military career. Twice he tried to invade Kauai; twice he failed. Rough seas in the channel between Oahu and Kauai defeated him

View over Nuuanu Valley, reservoir, and, barely visible crossing left-right at center, the Pali Highway

in 1796, disease in 1804. In the end, Kamehameha added Kauai and Niihau to his crown peacefully in 1810 when the king of Kauai agreed to recognize his sovereignty. By then, Kamehameha was an older and wiser ruler; he may well have understood that peace is more profitable than war. The warrior-king of Nuuanu *Pali* had become the greatest statesman of the new nation.

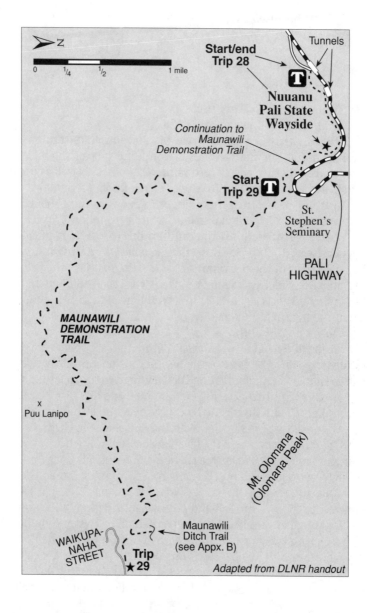

Adapted from DLNR handout

Trip 29. Maunawili Demonstration Trail

Distance: A little over 9 miles

Elevation gain: 300′ net on rolling trail

Hiking time: 4 1/2 hours

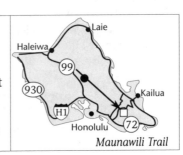

Maunawili Trail

Topos: *Honolulu, Koko Head*
Trail map: At the end of Trip 28.
Highlights: The relatively new Maunawili Demonstration Trail—Maunawili Trail for short—offers a wonderful mix of splendid views over windward Oahu and of lush rainforest gullies, as well as the thrill of trekking along the beautiful slopes of the Koolau Mountains all the way to Waimanalo. Strictly speaking, this is a windward-side trip, but its connection to Trip 28 makes it a "natural" to follow Trip 28.
Driving instructions: You can start this trip at Nuuanu Pali State Wayside (see Trip 28). However, the *recommended* start is just beyond the "turn" part of the big windward-side switchback on the Pali Highway, above St. Stephen's Seminary. There's a sizeable pullout and parking lot there. This is a shuttle trip, so you'll need to shuttle a car to the end of the trip, in Waimanalo.
To set up the shuttle—
To get to the end in Waimanalo. With both cars, follow the driving instructions of Trip 28 as far as the turnoff for Nuuanu Pali Wayside and then continue over Nuuanu Pali and down toward windward Oahu, swooping around a big switchback as you descend. Note this switchback: your starting point for this shuttle trip is near the switchback's turning point. For now, continue past the junction with the Kamehameha Highway (Highway 83) to the junction with the Kalanianaole Highway (Highway 72) and turn right onto the Kalanianaole Highway; note the mileage here. Follow the highway southeast, past Olomana on your right and then Olomana Golf Course on your left, to the outskirts of Waimanalo. Nearing 2.9 miles from the junction of the Pali and Kalanianaole highways, look on your right for Kumuhau Street; turn right onto Kumuhau. Follow Kumuhau to a T junction with Waikupanaha Street; turn right onto Waikupanaha. A little past a junction with Mahiku Place, on your right, you'll see a metal fence with a big gate that's signed GOVERNMENT PROPERTY/NO DUMPING, CAMPING OR MOTORIZED VEHICLES IN AREA. . . .This is the ending, Waimanalo trailhead;

park near here, about 15 miles from your start.

Now hop into the second car and head for the starting trailhead— *To get from the Waimanalo trailhead to the start.* Backtrack from the ending trailhead—but note that you can't turn left into the parking lot at the switchback on the Pali Highway. Instead, continue up the Pali Highway and take the turnoff for Nuuanu Pali State Wayside and head up to the wayside's parking area, where either you can leave your car if you prefer to start here or you can turn around and get back on the Pali Highway headed for Kailua and Kaneohe in order to start at the recommended point. Just past the switchback turn, pull into the lookout/trailhead parking, about 9 1/3 miles from the Waimanalo trailhead. Park and start from here, the Pali Highway trailhead.

TheBus routes: Not served by TheBus.

Permit/permission required: None.

Description: From the Pali Highway trailhead above St. Stephen's Seminary, look south-southwest toward the uphill entrance into the parking lot, for an opening in the lot's cliffside guard rail. Pass through this opening, cross a cement-lined ditch, and head south on a muddy trail lined with ferns, grasses, mangoes, and guavas, soon crossing a stream. You'll cross so many streams on this trail that I'm not going to map or mention them all.

Curving west and climbing moderately, you pass a viewpoint under a mango tree and shortly reach a junction: right (west) to Nuuanu Pali State Wayside, left (south) to Waimanalo. Go left, crossing a large gully, then strolling through swampy nooks on wooden walkways, and passing a water tank (not on map). There's a wonderful view seaward over Kailua town. Now you've had a taste of the two principal treats of this trail: lush rainforest nooks, often tucked into steep gullies, and sweeping views over windward Oahu. It just gets better!

You wander along the trail, which follows the contours of the steep north wall of Maunawili Valley—a wall that's also the north face of the Koolau Mountains. Around 1 mile, you swing into a grove of rose apple trees, then into a grove of *ieie*-festooned *koa* and *kukui* trees. Beyond 1 1/2 miles, the trail switchbacks down a little, taking you into and out of some very wet gullies where you'll need to watch your footing. The gullies get bigger and their vegetation lusher; mongooses rustle through the undergrowth; shama thrushes carol from the branches. The views from the intervening ridges are often breathtaking, especially of Mt. Olomana, which you are "circling" on its south.

This gully-and-ridge pattern persists mile after mile, yet each gully is different from any other, and each ridge offers a different view. Nearing 3 miles, the trail begins a moderate climb under *koa* trees, and around 4 miles you approach a ridge on which there are a number of powerline

A view from the Maunawili Trail sweeps over the forest to the impossibly steep cliffs of the windward, east end of the Koolau Mountains, above Waimanalo

towers. Between 4 and 5 miles, you pass under sets of power lines. It becomes obvious that you're headed for Anianinui Ridge, which connects Olomana to the back of Maunawili Valley.

Around 7$\frac{1}{2}$ miles, you pass under more power lines and reach a potentially confusing area where there's a trailhead marker and a sign that says NO HORSES. Forty yards ahead there's a junction with a very rough road that goes northeast, while, to the right (east) there's another NO HORSES sign and more trailhead signs pointing to the next trail segment. Bear right on this next trail segment and swing across Anianinui Ridge to a spectacular overlook of Waimanalo.

At 8 miles you finally begin a steep descent that will take you to the western outskirts of Waimanalo. At a **Y** junction (not on map) where another trail comes in sharply from the left and is gated, you go ahead (right) on the **Y**'s tail. The descent moderates and the trail becomes increasingly like an old jeep road—which it is. Around 8$\frac{3}{4}$ miles you pass a junction: hard left (north) on the Maunawili Ditch Trail—see Appendix B—or ahead (right, southeast) on the Maunawili Demonstration Trail. You shortly come to an umarked **Y** junction; go right (east) behind some houses.

A little beyond 9 miles you meet a road, Waikupanaha Street, at a metal fence with a big gate. You'll take a hiker's pass-through to get through the fence. This is the Waimanalo trailhead described in the driving directions, and your shuttle car should be waiting for you here.

Trip 30. Diamond Head

Distance: Just under 1³/4 miles

Elevation gain: 520'

Hiking time: 1–1¹/2 hours (some parts very steep)

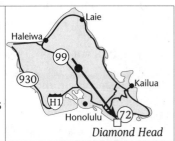

Diamond Head

Topos: *Honolulu*

Trail map (route approximated): At the end of this trip.

Highlights: A steep hike through hot, dusty brush and dark, musty rooms culminates in glorious views over east Oahu. Military history buffs will appreciate this hike for its glimpses of long-abandoned World War II defenses. *Bring a flashlight, as it can get very dark inside the command posts and pillboxes.* Diamond Head State Monument is open from 6 AM to 6 PM. A morning or late afternoon start is best in order to avoid the heat of midday.

Driving instructions: Your starting point for this drive is different from the McCully Street-Kapiolani Boulevard starting point for most of the other hikes. Assuming you're staying in Waikiki, this drive starts at the intersection of Kaiulani Avenue and Kalakaua Avenue, which is approximately where Kalakaua emerges from the dark hotel canyons at Kuhio Beach Park. You want to be on Kalakaua Avenue driving south-southeast. As you pass the intersection with Kapahulu Avenue and come abreast of the Honolulu Zoo, you reach a **Y** junction with Monsarrat Avenue. Bear left (east) on Monsarrat, which is one-way eastward at this point. You drive through a residential area as Monsarrat turns into Diamond Head Road, curving around the north side of the cone. You reach the marked entrance to Diamond Head State Monument just *before* Diamond Head Road intersects 18th Street.Turn right into Diamond Head State Monument. Follow signs that lead you through a tunnel in the northeast rim of the cone and bring you to a parking lot. Park here to begin your hike, just over 2³/4 miles.

TheBus routes: Take Route 58 toward Kahala. Get off as close to the entrance to Diamond Head State Monument as you can (ask your driver). Walk carefully up the road into the monument to the parking lot described above.

Permit/permission required: None.

Description. The trail begins at the far end of the parking lot as a paved path past the restrooms, seeming at first to be very easy as you stroll through dusty stands of *koa haole* on the floor of the cone. Soon it reaches the cliffs that form the rim of the cone, and here the trail quickly degenerates into a rough, unpaved track with a guardrail on the downhill side.

The trail contours along the cliffs and then climbs moderately and then steeply up the cliffs. Switch on a flashlight to light the way as you climb steeply up through a tunnel. Beyond the tunnel there's an extremely steep haul up a staircase to a concrete-lined room chopped out of the cliffs.

Switch on your flashlight again, for this room is dark! Within it, ropes and railings guide you to a steep, dark climb up a spiral staircase to a pillbox. The narrow slot in the pillbox through which spotters once watched and gun barrels extended is wide enough to let you crawl out—which you do. Outside the pillbox, you find that the slot is at ground level. Turn left on a beaten path and ascend a gradually climbing stairway that leads to a set of viewing platforms.

The view from these platforms is a knockout, which explains why there are lots of other people here. You may even have to wait for some space to open up on the very highest perch, though plenty of views almost as good are available below it. Luxury homes line the coast below, if you can bear to look down. Waikiki and downtown Honolulu stretch away to the west. To the northeast, across the floor of the cone and its far rim, are the deeply fluted cliffs of the Koolaus. Koko Head rises majestically on the east. And on three sides—west, south, and east—the blue Pacific lies shimmering in the tropical sun, its restless surface striped here and there by the white streaks of breaking waves.

Diamond Head got its present name from British sailors who, exploring the tuff cone, mistook calcite crystals they found for diamonds. The Hawaiian name for the cone is Leahi. It was formed by steam explosions about 100,000 years ago.

Trails-of-use that once led to other sites around the cone's rim are now blocked off, so, after taking in the view, retrace your steps to the parking lot.

The Battle of Niihau.... Today, Diamond Head is an icon that symbolizes Hawaii. You can't see images of Diamond Head without thinking both of Hawaii's image as a tropical paradise and of Sunday, December 7, 1941, "a date which will live in infamy," as President Franklin D. Roosevelt put it. Imperial Japan had carried off a surprise air attack on the American military forces on Oahu, destroying much of the Pacific Fleet and devastating the Army Air Force on Oahu. American radar had detected the incoming Japanese planes nearly an hour before they struck Oahu. But the U.S. and Japan were not at war, and the officer in charge dismissed the blips as something else—probably a flight of B-17 bombers due in from the mainland that day. No one took any further action. Three hours later, the same radar set saw the victorious Japanese planes as they flew back to their carriers. Again, no one took any action: nothing was left to take any action with. Oahu's defenders were stunned, disorganized, and frantically trying to deal with the flaming ships, burning planes, and thousands of wounded and dying men. It was a brilliant tactical success—it nearly knocked the United States out of the North Pacific—and a fatal strategic blunder. The U.S. got angry. And then it got even.

Sunday, December 7, 1941, was like any other Sunday on Niihau (Nee-ee-hau), the oldest and farthest northwest of the major Hawaiian islands. Niihau had no radios then. Even if it had had them, the English-language broadcasts from Oahu would have been meaningless to most Niihauans, who spoke Hawaiian, not English. Niihau's owners, the Robinsons, made weekly visits by sampan from Kauai. It was Niihau's only connection with the outside world. And after the Japanese attack, the Army forbade the weekly sampan visit—all of which was unknown to the isolated Niihauans.

One Japanese plane, damaged and unable to return to its carrier, landed in a plowed field on Niihau. The pilot gave his papers to a Niihauan, Hawila Kaleohano—in effect surrendering. And then, it seemed, there was nothing else to do except to wait for the sampan to come. A week passed. No sampan. No news.

The pilot went on the offensive. There were only two other Japanese people on Niihau. The pilot appealed to their patriotism, sure that they would help him. One refused; the other, Yoshio Harada, agreed and helped the pilot take the machine guns from the crippled plane so the guns could be used to control the island. But he never got to use the guns because Benehakaka ("Benny") Kanahele stole the guns' ammunition, rendering them useless.

Now the pilot wanted his papers back, but Hawila Kaleohano had disappeared with them. So the pilot burned down his house, took Benny Kanahele and his wife hostage, and sent Benny to look for Hawila. When Benny returned without Hawila, the pilot tried to shoot Benny and his wife. Benny, then fifty-one, jumped the pilot, taking three bullets in the stomach as he seized the pilot and dashed his brains out against a stone wall. Yoshio Harada shot himself. The Battle of Niihau was over.

The indestructible Benny Kanahele became one of Hawaii's heroes. Many years later, our friend Dan Masaki, then a kid, worked in a grocery store with Benny. He remembers Benny as a cheerful,

hardworking, massive man with a huge bald head and huge hands. Benny would say of the Battle of Niihau, "When he shot me the second time, I got *really* angry!" And then he got even.

Looking down the steep staircase inside Diamond Head

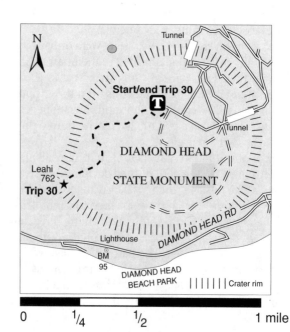

Trip 31. Ala Wai Canal Stroll

Distance: Up to 3³/4 miles

Elevation gain: Negligible

Hiking time: Just over 1³/4 hours for the full stroll

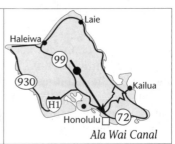

Ala Wai Canal

Topos: *Honolulu*

Trail map: At the end of this trip. (Note that I've left out most of the little streets that crisscross Waikiki in order to emphasize the more important streets.)

Highlights: The level, paved walkway along the south bank of the Ala Wai Canal provides easy walking, while the canal itself mirrors the fields and buildings alongside it, even the steep, green Koolaus far to the northeast. I recommend an early morning or an early evening start, as Waikiki can be fiery hot at midday. You can start almost anywhere along the Ala Wai Canal and shorten this stroll to suit yourself. You'll have plenty of other walkers, as well as joggers, for company.

Driving instructions: I've assumed you're staying in Waikiki, so you don't need to drive at all. Walk from your hotel to the south bank of the Ala Wai Canal and start from wherever you happen to be—just adapt the description below.

TheBus routes: You don't need TheBus: you're already in Waikiki!

Permit/permission required: None.

Description. This description starts at the southeast end of the Ala Wai Canal, near the Waikiki Branch of the Honolulu Public Library, but you can pick it up just about anywhere you wish. Begin walking northwest, toward the city's towers and away from Diamond Head, under *hau* and palm trees. The paved path, somewhat cracked and uneven, is paralleled by a dirt-and-grass curb strip. Occasional benches offer a chance to rest and enjoy the scenery on the other side of the canal. It's especially good at this end of the canal, where there are few buildings on the north bank to impede your view of the Koolaus. (The large open space on the north bank is the Ala Wai Golf Course, and you can't walk through it. That's one of the things that prevent a loop hike completely around the canal.)

Swarms of zebra doves and white pigeons patrol the sidewalk. The canal is a popular site for canoe practice, and it's a treat to watch the sturdy paddlers propelling their craft swiftly through the water.

Clomp, clomp, clomp—that's a jogger passing you, probably with head-phones firmly clamped over ears. Here, a bench holds a pair of elderly ladies chatting quietly. There, on one of the staircases that leads down to the water's edge, a couple smile as they crumble bread for the little gray fish that school so thickly they make the water bubble and froth with their frantic activity. Toss them some stale bread scraps yourself and watch the resulting miniature feeding frenzy. On a perch over-looking the canal, a child sits, holding a fishing pole and intently watch-ing for signs of fishy interest at the far end of the line. You take a closer look at the canal, find it unappetizing, and hope the kid's parents will throw the fish away uneaten.

At the intersection of Ala Wai Boulevard and McCully Street, make a dicey three-stage crossing of the wide intersection, two stages with the help of lights. Drivers turning right onto McCully from Ala Wai are particularly oblivious to pedestrians. It's not long before you reach the intersection of Ala Wai and Kalakaua. Here, you can't cross on the ca-nal side—don't ask me why—so cross the long way: cross Ala Wai away from the canal, then cross Kalakaua, and finally cross back over Ala Wai to the canal bank.

Now you begin the loop part of your walk along a shady stone-work embankment. You presently reach a short staircase, ascend it to Ala Moana Boulevard, turn right to cross the canal on a bridge, and turn right to descend on the other side. This walkway is called the Ala Wai

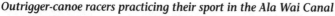

Outrigger-canoe racers practicing their sport in the Ala Wai Canal

Promenade. Stroll toward Diamond Head along the ficus-shaded walk-way—this is surely the nicest section of the walkway, though the shade trees and buildings shut off most of the other scenery. Too soon, you reach Kalakaua again, climb a shallow flight of stairs, turn right, and cross the canal on the Kalakaua-Ala Wai Bridge to close the loop part.

Take the long crossing back to the seaward side of the Ala Wai Canal and then retrace your steps from here.

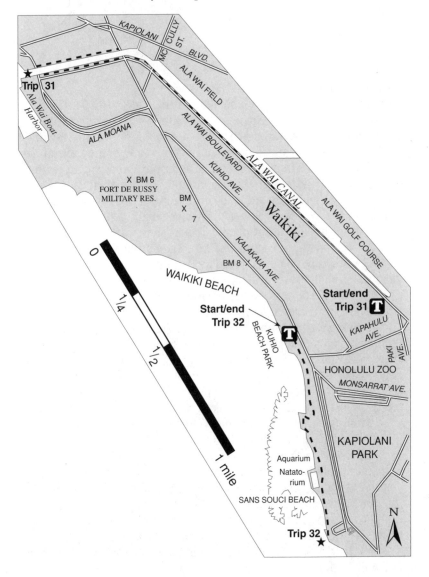

Trip 32. Rabbit Kekai's Waikiki Beach Stroll

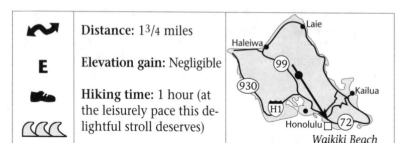

Distance: 1³/4 miles

Elevation gain: Negligible

Hiking time: 1 hour (at the leisurely pace this delightful stroll deserves)

Laie
Haleiwa
99
930
H1
Kailua
Honolulu 72
Waikiki Beach

Topos: *Honolulu*

Trail map (route approximated): At the end of Trip 31. (There is no trail. You follow the beachfront sidewalk or walk on the sand.)

Highlights: Waikiki Beach is the most famous beach in the world. Its warm waters and outstanding surfing and canoeing opportunities have drawn visitors from the mainland and from abroad since the nineteen-teens. Waikiki has changed enormously since then. But one of Waikiki's most enduring and endearing features is its corps of unofficial hosts, the Waikiki beachboys. They've taught generations of visitors to surf, canoe, and just plain *have fun*. Their antics and their feats in the water have amused and amazed visitors from all over the world.

On this trip, you'll see Waikiki's present as you stroll along. And you'll catch a glimpse of Waikiki's past through the stories of legendary surfer Rabbit Kekai. It's best as an early morning or an evening walk, when the air is cooler and the crowds smaller.

Driving instructions: Assuming you're staying in Waikiki, you don't need to drive at all. Walk from your hotel to Kuhio Beach Park to start your stroll. Kuhio Beach Park is located about where Kalakaua Avenue breaks free of the high-rise canyons of Waikiki. A fine statue of one of Hawaii's greatest athletes, Olympic champion Duke Kahanamoku, stands on the seaward side of Kalakaua Avenue at Kuhio Beach Park.

TheBus routes: You don't need TheBus: you're already in Waikiki!

Permit/permission required: None.

Description. Start your walk where my friend, whom I'll call Kate, and I met Rabbit Kekai near sunset: on a bench under the big old banyan tree at Kuhio Beach Park. We had chosen to meet during the quiet interlude between the bustle of the beach crowd and the noise of the nightlife crowd. After enjoying the scenery here, do as we did: stroll along the sidewalk in the general direction of Diamond Head.

We had planned to do some walking and some talking story about old Waikiki. Kate had met Rabbit many years ago at a Waikiki surfing meet. Her boys—both avid surfers—were wild to have the meet's official T-shirt, but she was told they were sold out. Then she noticed that people were walking behind the T-shirt booth and calling to someone in the back, "Hey, Rabbit, save me a shirt!" A gruff voice would answer, "Okay!" So she walked behind the booth and yelled, "Hey, Rabbit, save me a couple of shirts!" "Okay!" After the meet she went to collect the shirts. She introduced herself, and they've been friends ever since.

When Kate introduced me to Rabbit, I was awed. With his silver hair, mustache, and goatee, Rabbit looks like a sage whom you should approach saying, "O Master, how can I find the meaning of life?" His answer might be, "Surf!" Rabbit Kekai is a legend I had known only from books like Grady Timmons's *Waikiki Beachboy* and from magazines like *H3O*—whose cover he happened to be on that month, photographed as he slid skillfully across the face of a huge blue wave. In his seventies now, Rabbit surfs every day as he always has since he took to the water at about age six. Why slow down when you're on a roll?

Awed or not, I had a job to do, so there I stood under the banyan tree, notebook and pencil ready, camera bouncing on chest. Rabbit pointed at me and said firmly but with a smile, "You don't write. You just listen." "Yes, sir!" I said as I put the paper and pencil away and sat down. (Later, I sneaked them back out so I could save a few of his stories to share with you.)

Long before Europeans arrived, Rabbit told us, Waikiki had been prized both for surfing and for fishing. "It was *kapu* for commoners and reserved for the *alii*." The *kapu* had been lifted by the time of Queen Liliuokalani (1838–1917). She had a residence there, "The Queen's Retreat," and enjoyed watching her subjects amuse themselves at the seashore. Today, one of the breaks at Waikiki is called "Queen's" because it occurs near the place where "The Queen's Retreat" stood.

Rabbit took us back in our imaginations to the nineteen-twenties and -thirties, which saw the heyday of the Waikiki beachboys. Hawaii was much harder to reach before World War II. It required a leisurely, expensive ocean voyage on a glamorous steamer like the *Lurline*. A Hawaiian vacation was the privilege of a wealthy few. No highrises pierced the Honolulu skyline then, and it was a more gracious and far less crowded place than it is now. Waikiki was a tranquil community of pretty beach homes, family stores and restaurants, and a few top-notch hotels like the 1927 pink stucco Royal Hawaiian—still there but engulfed by recent "improvements."

Rabbit looked up into the banyan and observed that when he was a youngster, it was much bigger, its branches reaching clear across Kalakaua Avenue. They had cut it back in order to widen Kalakaua when Waikiki development exploded in the Fifties and Sixties. Before that, he and the other beachboys would often stash their boards in the banyan's aerial roots for the night. "Nobody would steal them," Rabbit explained—such was the open, trusting atmosphere of pre-war Waikiki.

The Waikiki beachboys—young Hawaiian men who asked of life only that they be allowed to live it at the beach, surfing all day and partying all night—eked out a living by giving surfing, swimming, and canoeing lessons to visitors for a fee. And more: they freely gave friendship and an entry into the music, laughter, and simple joys of beachboy life. Visitors adored the beachboys, and handsome tips from wealthy patrons might exceed by far the fees the beachboys got for the lessons.

It could be a hand-to-mouth existence for a beachboy, though, and an inexpensive meal meant a lot. It might be his only meal of the day. The Waikiki Tavern had been built nearby in the nineteen-thirties. "It was great," said Rabbit. "$1.25 for all you can eat—pork chops, ribs, you name it. Everything. A restaurant called Dean's used to be where the seawall is now. It was built up off the ground, and we could store our surfboards underneath it. The chef was a big fan of the surfers. He would give us food for free—make a rice dish with some meat in it and slip it out to us. The Biltmore used to be where the Hilton is now. There was a big café there—all you can eat for $1.50, family style." I began to sense just how precarious the beachboy lifestyle could be.

In spite of that, the beachboys had little desire to trade places with the wealthy visitors. Instead, it was the other way around: the visitors longed to join the beachboys. Stories about the Waikiki beachboys as told by those visitors have created some of our most lasting images of Hawaii.

As we strolled toward Diamond Head, Rabbit told us about some of the people besides Queen Liliuokalani who used to have homes at Waikiki. "Judge Steiner had a beach property around here, and the Cleghorns did, too." (Archibald Cleghorn was the father of the lovely Princess Kaiulani, Queen Liliuokalani's heir.) "There were lots of nice cottages. A Mr. Soong had a little snack store over there. The city tore them all down to make Kuhio Beach bigger," Rabbit recalled. "The Fullard-Leos [who own the lonely South Pacific island of Palmyra, scene of the grisly murders described in Vincent Bugliosi's *And the Sea Shall Tell*] used to live on King's Alley in Waikiki. Mrs. Fullard-Leo's parrot was very smart and talked nicely. The beachboys played a joke on Mrs. Fullard-Leo. They would walk by when she wasn't looking and say to the parrot, 'To hell with you!' Soon, when Mrs. Fullard-Leo would come out and talk to it, the parrot would say, 'To hell with you!' to *her*. Actually, what we taught the parrot was worse than that, but you can't print it!" (True.)

Waikiki has lost much of its "Hawaiian-ness" to our modern world. But before tourism exploded, Waikiki was as famous for its fishery as

A forest of masts in Ala Wai Harbor dominates the sweep of the coastline southeastward past Waikiki. Diamond Head in the background

for its surf. Many beachboys helped feed their families by fishing at Waikiki. As the sidewalk curved into Kapiolani Park Beach, Rabbit gestured seaward. "Used to be a great fishing ground," he said. "Waikiki was a lot of sandy areas, not one long beach. Now they truck in all this sand, and the sand gets swept out to sea. Makes the water cloudy, smothers the reef and kills it. No more fishing. I used to come here for my grandfather's favorite fish, *uu*, at a special fishing hole that he showed me. We were the only ones that knew about it. I was careful not to take more than six fish at a time so I wouldn't fish out the hole. I would take the fish home, filet them, wrap the filets in *ti* leaves, and lay them on glowing coals to cook. I did this only for my grandfather. Some other people wanted to know where the fishing hole was, because the *uu* is the best fish to eat. They knew they could make a lot of money by catching and selling a hundred or more fish at a time. That would destroy the fishing hole. I never told them, so they watched me carefully and saw where I went. But when they went out there, they couldn't find the fishing hole. The sea hid it from them."

Rabbit remembers that the waves used to be higher and the breaks used to be one continuous wall instead of sectioned as they are now that Waikiki has been "engineered" for lots of tourists. A skilled surfer back then could catch a wave at the farthest break and by maneuvering his board from one break to the next could ride almost all the way in to shore. "One time, a bunch of us were way out at Bluebirds—so far out

the *Lurline* steamed right between us and the shore. We were getting
15- to 20-foot waves out there! The captain and the passengers thought
we were crazy. Then the wave came—so big it broke right behind the
Lurline. And we rode it all the way in!"

Many beachboys were very musical. On Sunday nights they would
gather at Waikiki to sing and play out on a pier, not for pay but for
pleasure. Visitors were welcome to listen, though, and those who did
soon fell in love with the sweet music drifting across the water, min-
gling with the sound of the waves. It is from the beachboys' music that
the Hawaiian music so beloved today came.

Walking under iron-pipe arches that make a tunnel through *hau*
trees, we passed the old Waikiki Natatorium, where Duke Kahanamoku
had competed in swimming meets. It's a big saltwater swimming pool
right on the waterfront. "There used to be swimming shows here at
night," Rabbit recalled. "It was beautiful—the lights, the music, the
girls, the costumes." Now the ownership of the natatorium is split between a couple of agencies. Neither will take responsibility for it, so it's
closed and going to ruin.

The path along the beach ended, and we walked on the sand in
front of some first-class beachfront hotels and restaurants. "Hello, Rabbit!" called a man dining on the terrace of a fancy restaurant. Rabbit
recognized a friend, went over, and talked surfing. The surfing confer-
ence over, we got a few steps farther before a well-dressed lady hailed
him: "Rabbit, how are you? Good to see you!" And they chatted for a
while. We went a little farther, as you will, only to discover that the
water cut off our route just below the Elks Club. It was time to turn
around. I could see that Rabbit's time for "talking story" was pretty
much over, anyway. The evening crowd had turned out, and people
were coming over to greet Rabbit every few minutes.

Rabbit shared one more story as we retraced our steps. The
beachboys had rolled up their sleeves and gone to work or to war during World War II, but they still surfed when they could get time off.
"The Army put these big rolls of barbed wire all over the beach in case
there was an invasion. And they told us we couldn't surf after six P.M.
Why six P.M. I don't know. It didn't make any sense. But they put these
big machine gun emplacements on the beach, too, and at six P.M. they
would shoot high in the air to make us come in. One time, some smart
guy fired low, *right over our heads!* I got hold of him and told him if he
ever shot over *my* head again, I was going to toss a 'pineapple' [hand
grenade] in there with *him*. He never did it again."

It was dark when we returned to the bench under the banyan
tree. Waikiki is lovely at night, when hundreds of lights make long,
brightly colored streaks on the dark water. People kept coming up to

Rabbit. Now there was a whole family visiting with him. When they moved on, the youngest child, a boy of about ten, went a few yards with them and then stopped in the shadows, turned, and stared back in awe at his hero, Rabbit, until a family member came to collect him.

We went to dinner with Rabbit. A surfer has to keep his strength up, and Rabbit was competing the next day. While Waikiki has changed a lot, it still has some very good restaurants. The host was obviously one of Rabbit's fans and hastened to make him welcome.

Some believe the mystique of the beachboys is gone from Waikiki forever. Watching Rabbit with his friends and admirers made me think it was still here.

Sam Kaninau comes home.... Samson Kealohaaina Kaninau, one of Rabbit's brothers, came home to Waikiki for the last time on a quiet, sunny Monday morning. We had assembled at the Elks Club to hear him praised and to share the laughter and tears of those who knew and loved him. All the brothers had been among the elite of the beachboys in their day, as Rabbit still is. As a kid, Sam had been one of the most fun-loving and mischievous of the beachboys. He was in *so* much trouble that one of his older brothers took him aside and told him to straighten up or else. Sam joined the Marines and became a solid citizen, ending his days in San Diego.

Another surfing legend, Blue Makua, Sr., was there that Monday morning. Entertainer Don Ho sang goodbye to Sam. Sam's cousins sang beautiful old hymns in close harmony. Renowned Hawaiian musician Arthur Lyman played the vibraphone between the songs and the eulogies. "If there's a surf beyond that final horizon," said the minister, "I know what Sam is doing now!"

We gathered again on the beach at Waikiki. Beachboys young and old, joined by strong young women, boarded gaily painted outrigger canoes while the rest of us followed Sam's widow, Shirley, aboard a big catamaran from the Royal Hawaiian. Rabbit captained the first canoe, which carried the brothers, Sam's daughter, Nalani, and Sam's ashes. The flotilla moved out beyond the break called "Popular's," where the boats formed a circle on the turquoise water. A gentle breeze carried the farewell song of the mourners across the swells: *"Aloha oe, aloha oe...."* Nalani scattered Sam's ashes on the waves, and from the boats we tossed armfuls of flowers into the circle: leis of plumeria and poinciana; blossoms of carnation, rose, gardenia, and orchid; and wreaths of evergreen. We bowed our heads in silent prayer. Then, as the boats returned to shore, we looked back to see the flower-strewn circle slowly widening and drifting, riding on the swells, carrying Sam with it. He was home at last.

Trip 33. Foster Botanical Gardens

Distance: Up to you

Elevation gain: Negligible

Hiking time: 2 hours recommended—take your
time here

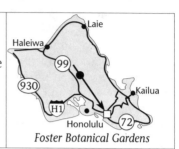

Foster Botanical Gardens

Topos: *Honolulu*
Trail map: At the end of this trip.
Highlights: Talk about a collection of fascinating plants! From
the beautiful to the bizarre—that's Foster Botanical Gardens. The fact
that you can overlook its awful location—next to the noisy, smelly H1
freeway—is further testimony to its great beauty and interest. Open
daily 9 AM–4 PM; there is an admission fee. Free guided tours are given
periodically during the day; check at the entrance for times.

Foster Botanical Gardens is part of the system that includes
Hoomaluhia, Koko Crater, and Wahiawa botanical gardens (Trips 7, 11,
and 42, respectively). I recommend them all!

Driving instructions: From the intersection of McCully Street and
Kapiolani Boulevard just outside Waikiki, continue northeast on McCully,
crossing over the freeway. Just across the bridge, follow the signs to get
on H1 westbound (a quick left turn onto Metcalfe Street that leads to a
westbound freeway on-ramp). Take H1 westbound and get off at Vineyard Boulevard (Highway 98). Follow Vineyard northwest past Nuuanu
Avenue and turn right into the marked parking lot on the inland side of
Vineyard Avenue for Foster Botanical Garden, 3 miles.

TheBus routes: Take Route 19 or 20 and get off at River Street.
Walk inland up River Street to Foster Botanical Gardens.

Permit/permission required: None.

Description. Assuming you're not on a guided tour, there's really
no plan to this hike. You'll realize when you step out of the entrance
building that you can head in just about any direction. A broad, tree-
shaded lawn stretches away in front of and on either side of you. While
there are a few pathways, as you can see on the map, in general you wander across the lawns in search of whatever interests you the most—or
maybe you just stroll along enjoying whatever you pass. Those of you
who have the Hargreaves's *Hawaii Blossoms* will notice that specimens of

the Brownea and the aptly-named Cannonball Tree—two very intriguing non-natives—are planted here, and they're well worth hunting for.

Don't miss the Lyon Orchid Garden in the northwest corner, unfortunately next to the freeway. We mainlanders are accustomed to the standard, unexciting corsage orchids—white cattleyas or sickly green cymbidiums. Here you'll find orchids whose blossoms range from the tiny to the giant. I like the tiny ones best because they bloom in big sprays of dazzling colors. Look for velvety blue-purples, vivid oranges, sprightly pinks, and rich buttery yellows. Alas, none of these are native. Only three species of orchid are native to Hawaii, and all are ground-dwellers with inconspicuous blossoms, not showy ones like those so prominent in this part of the garden. (Even the purple Philippine and white bamboo orchids you often see while hiking are non-native.) Nevertheless, enjoy this orchid display until the noise and exhaust fumes drive you out.

Look for a small and fragrant herb garden in the southeast section. If you like spices and flavorings as much as I do, you'll enjoy searching out the exotic plants from which they come, like the cinnamon, the allspice, the "chocolate trees" (cacao), and the coffee shrubs. The last are fairly common in damp areas in Hawaii where, years ago, people tried to create coffee plantations.

When you're through exploring the garden, retrace your steps to the entrance.

Orchids....didn't disperse to Hawaii as well as might have been expected, considering the infinitesimal size of orchid seeds. How can that be? Sherwin Carlquist offers a reasonable explanation in *Hawaii: A Natural History*: Most orchids have specialized reproductive structures finely adapted to the particular insects that pollinate them. If those insects don't disperse with the seeds and survive in the new location, there may be a single generation of that orchid, but there is virtually no chance of the orchid establishing itself in the new location. Apparently, three inconspicuous orchids have managed to do so.

But the orchids most commonly seen along the trail, the stiffly upright, white-petaled and purple-lipped bamboo orchid

*Non-native bamboo orchid (*Arundina bambusifolia*) is often seen along Hawaiian trails*

with its single flower atop a bamboo-like stalk, and the rose-to-laven-der wind (or Philippine) orchid with its terminal clusters of blossoms, are non-natives. Someone once told me their presence was probably the byproduct of aerial seeding during reforestation efforts in the nine-teen-thirties.

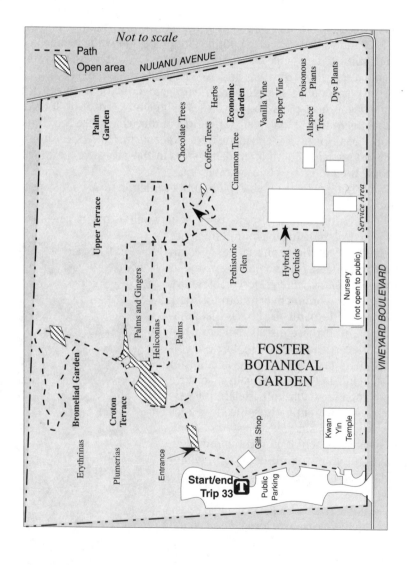

Trip 34. Aiea Loop (Keaiwa *Heiau* State Park)

Distance: 4³/4 miles

Elevation gain: 990', last part steeply uphill

Hiking time: Just under 2¹/2 hours

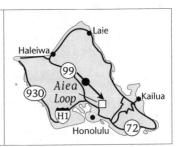

Topos: *Waipahu, Kaneohe*

Trail map (route partly approximated): At the end of this trip.

Highlights: Wonderful views and varied terrain make this hike a winner! Stop and visit Keaiwa *Heiau* (just past the entrance to the park), too. It's believed to have been dedicated to the healing arts, and the plants around it were used in old Hawaiian medicine. The park is open from 7 AM to 7:45 PM from April 1 to Labor Day and from 7 AM to 6:45 PM from the day after Labor Day to March 31.

Driving instructions: From the intersection of McCully Street and Kapiolani Boulevard just outside Waikiki, continue northeast on McCully, crossing over the Lunalilo Freeway (H1) on a narrow bridge. Just across the bridge, follow the signs to get on H1 westbound (a quick left turn onto Metcalfe Street that leads to a westbound freeway on-ramp). Take H1 to the junction with Highway 78 to Aiea (you'll need to be in the left lanes of the freeway to catch Highway 78). Get off Highway 78 at the "Aiea" turnoff, onto Moanalua Road. Turn right at Aiea Heights Drive. Follow Aiea Heights Drive as it twists and turns uphill to the entrance to Keaiwa *Heiau* State Park. After stopping to see the *heiau*, follow the one-way road that initially curves to the right. Follow it uphill to its highest point, where you'll find the trailhead and a parking lot. Start your hike here, just over 13 miles.

TheBus routes: Not directly served by TheBus. Take Route 8, 19, 20, or 58 to the Ala Moana Shopping Center. Transfer to Route 11 and take it to Aiea Heights. Get off as close as you can to Keaiwa *Heiau* State Park (ask your driver) and walk the rest of the way to the park. After stopping to see the *heiau*, walk up the one-way road that initially curves to the right, and follow it uphill to the trailhead. (Near the end of the hike, instead of turning uphill to close the loop at the trailhead, you should turn downhill toward Aiea Heights Drive and your bus.)

Permit/permission required: None.

Description. From the trailhead, walk under swamp mahogany trees toward an old water tank. Shortly after you pass the tank, the trail dips sharply across a saddle and then climbs into a fragrant stand of lemon-scented gums (my favorite tree). Break a fallen leaf and inhale the intense, citronella-like odor! You climb the broad "stairs" formed by eucalyptus roots threading their way through reddish soil and emerge on a ridge overlooking the city. There's a bench here, so you can take in the wonderful view in comfort.

Bear left (northeast) here along the ridge, through strawberry guava, ironwood, Norfolk pine, and *koa*. Ignore side trails-of-use here, even a well-beaten one that may be tagged (it looks as if it might lead to great views, but in fact it leads to a dull walk past some powerline towers, mostly through strawberry guava). The route generally stays on a ridge, passing through *koa*, strawberry guava, paperbark, swamp mahogany, and lemon-scented gum trees. *Uluhe*-clad slopes spill away on either side into gullies splashed with the light green of *kukui* trees and the golden-orange of silk oak blossoms. In the damper nooks, look for tree fern, *ohia, kukui, ti,* sword fern, and even the fascinating *ieie,* looking like a miniature palm tree on a vine. There are outstanding views, some back into the mountains, others out over the city. Noise from H3 is annoying along a couple of segments; one ridge-nose even sports a bench with a fine view of H3!

You pass the high point near Puu Uau. Not long after, you make a hairpin turn and begin a gentle descent into a gulch. The trail leads through eucalyptuses and Norfolk pines; an abundance of young, feathery Norfolk pines here gives the understory the look of ferns. Hello, here's a junction with a trail to a U.S. Marine Corps reservation (to the left and strictly off-limits to *you*; not

*Five white petals surrounding a tuft of yellow stamens distinguish the flowers of guava (*Psidium *spp.), a widespread non-native with tart-sweet, seedy fruit. The yellow and the smaller strawberry guavas are the most common types in Hawaii*

shown on the map). Bear right here and, in about another half mile, cross a ginger-lined streambed at another hairpin turn.

The descent is over, and you now begin an easy to moderate climb out of the Christmas-berry-shaded gulch. You emerge on a ridge overlooking the city and follow a red-dirt path under acacias and swamp mahogany trees to the park's camping area. Here, bear right across the lawn, past the restrooms, and climb a flight of stairs to a spur road. Turn left and follow the spur road to the park's main, one-way road, and then turn right to climb steeply up it to the trailhead to close the loop.

Clusters of rosy-lavender blooms nod atop the non-native Philippine, or wind, orchid (Spathoglottis plicata Blume), a familiar flower along Hawaii's trails

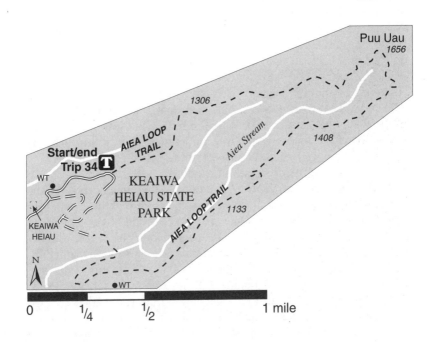

Trip 35. Upper-Lower Waimano Loop

Distance: 2 miles

Elevation gain: 290' (up-side-down trip)

Hiking time: 1 hour

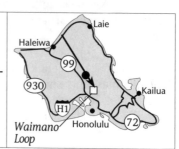

Topos: *Waipahu*

Trail map (route partly approximated): At the end of this trip.

Highlights: This relatively short look at the beautiful and interesting Waimano area gives you a taste of its many pleasures and its boulder-scrambling thrills without your having to walk the entire 14 miles of the Waimano Trail.

Driving instructions: From the intersection of McCully Street and Kapiolani Boulevard, go northeast on McCully, cross over the H1 freeway, and almost immediately turn left on Metcalfe in order to get onto the H1 freeway westbound. Take H1 to the Pearl City exit (Exit 10) and get off on what turns out to be Moanalua Road. Go northwest on Moanalua Road and turn right onto Waimano Home Road. Follow Waimano Home Road up the hill to the fence surrounding Waimano Home, 22 1/4 miles. There's a bare-dirt parking area just outside the fence, on the left side of the road. Park here to begin your hike.

TheBus routes: Take Route 8, 19, 20, or 58 to the Ala Moana Shopping Center and transfer to Route 53. Take Route 53 toward Pacific Palisades and get out as close as you can to the end of Waimano Home Road (ask your driver). Walk the rest of the way up Waimano Home Road to the trailhead (above). Sometimes there's a shuttle to the end of the road; call TheBus and ask (808-848-5555).

Permit/permission required: None.

Description. Starting from the dirt parking area, sign in at the trailhead hunter's/hiker's check station and then pick up the beaten path to the left of the automobile gate and outside of the fence. You walk through swamp mahogany trees and along the fence, roughly paralleling the road on the other side of the fence. At the first junction, go to the right to stay on the upper Waimano Trail (this is the first junction with the lower Waimano Trail, to which the left fork leads, and where you'll close this loop). Veer away from the road at last and stroll along under swamp mahogany, strawberry guava, and Christmas berry, with a fern understory. Step across a runoff channel and head generally northeast, paralleling an old irrigation channel (on your right). Nearing the half-mile point, you curve left, climb briefly to an open spot, and find yourself at another junction.

Go left at this junction—the right fork is a dead-end use trail—and descend a bit. Continue generally east-northeast on the north side of the ridge, still paralleling the old irrigation channel. Where the vegetation permits, views over the adjacent valley of Waimano Stream are excellent.

A little before the 1-mile point, you reach the second junction with the lower Waimano Trail. Take the left fork here to zigzag downhill, sometimes very steeply, until the trail gradually levels out and reaches the streambed. It's likely to be dry, but the forest of tall swamp mahogany trees and the dense understory of ferns give the valley floor a "streamside" feel nevertheless. And at one point, you're almost walking in the streambed because the trail has collapsed into it. The walking here is nearly level, so that it's hard to notice when you begin to ascend very gradually. Eventually, the trail begins angling uphill more steeply. It becomes an open, grassy old road as it curves uphill, offering you views of the next ridge to the north.

You're presently back up on the ridge where you started, closing the loop. From here, turn right; in a few steps, you're back at your car.

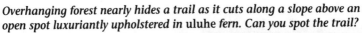

Overhanging forest nearly hides a trail as it cuts along a slope above an open spot luxuriantly upholstered in uluhe *fern. Can you spot the trail?*

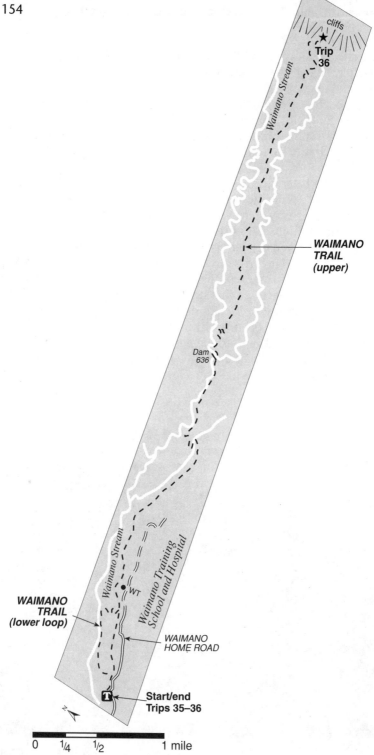

cliffs

Trip 36

Waimano Stream

**WAIMANO
TRAIL
(upper)**

*Dam
636*

Waimano Stream

*Waimano Training
School and Hospital*

WT

**WAIMANO
TRAIL
(lower loop)**

*WAIMANO
HOME ROAD*

T **Start/end
Trips 35–36**

N

0   1/4   1/2   1 mile

Trip 36. Upper Waimano Adventure

Distance: 14 miles

Elevation gain: 1990'

Hiking time: 7–8 hours

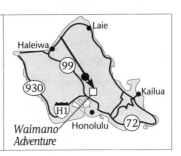

Topos: *Waipahu, Kaneohe*
Trail map: At the end of Trip 35.
Highlights: This is one of my favorite Oahu hikes. You start on leeward Oahu and walk to the crest of the Koolaus for spectacular views of windward Oahu! In the upper reaches, you'll find some of Oahu's increasingly rare native plants. You may find the unmaintained latter part of this trail to be very overgrown and, at times, exposed; because of these conditions, you may want to turn around. Boulder scrambling in the lower reaches adds thrills and chills in both directions.
Driving instructions: Follow the driving instructions of Trip 35.
TheBus routes: Take TheBus routes of Trip 35.
Permit/permission required: None.
Description. Start your trip as described in Trip 35 as far as the second junction with the lower Waimano Trail. Instead of going left to the lower Waimano Trail, go right to continue on the upper Waimano Trail, along the ferny old irrigation channel, sometimes walking on its retaining walls. The Christmas berry thickets become more dense here, and the understory includes clover, vervain, *ti*, and fern. In a couple of places where the ditch ducks through tunnels, you scramble up over slippery, muddy tree roots to meet the trail on the other side. These 'detours' have considerable exposure. Aids have been placed to help you, but I suggest you rely less on them and more on your own boulder-scrambling skills. Wrap an arm securely around a firmly anchored root or trunk before putting your weight on that rope or cable.

As the trail penetrates deeper and deeper into the mountains, you spot new species in the canopy and understory: *koa, kukui, hau,* mango, guava, mountain apple, ginger, Koster's curse. The hiker's curse, mosquitoes, will probably spot *you*. The trail presently angles into a narrow stream canyon, crosses the streambed, and climbs toward a eucalyptus-covered ridge. With the help of some switchbacks, you emerge on a grassy saddle, where there's a welcome picnic shelter.

From here, the trail leads east into a valley on the north side of the ridge, through *ohia, uluhe,* and *koa.* You traverse deeper into the valley, high above Waimano Stream, eventually meeting the old irrigation works again. The trail descends gently as the streambed rises, and they meet near the barely discernable ruins of an old dam. The stream may be dry, which makes it easier for you to boulder-hop upstream a few yards to the confluence of two streambeds, Waimano Stream from the east and a tributary from the south. You're in the tributary's streambed at the moment. Cross the streambed you're in, and pick up a *hau*-shaded trail on the ridge between the streambeds. Now you curve around the ridge into the next valley and begin ascending the south side of the valley, through fern and Koster's curse and under *ieie*-clad *koa.* Look for the light green of *kukui* trees in the forest canopy below.

You round the nose of a small ridge and switchback up through tree ferns, sword ferns, *kukui, ohia,* and palms. Stretches of the trail are, badly overgrown, with poor footing (slippery, full of roots and rocks) that's hidden by the overgrowth. There's also considerable downhill exposure. Proceed with extra care. Soon you're high above the valley, contouring gently up along the ridge, but almost never on the ridgetop. Look for the lacy *palapalai* fern here as well as *uluhe,* mountain *naupaka,* and non-native leptospermum (which nearly dominates the ridgetop in dense, shaggy-barked thickets). In spite of some dicey spots, the going is so pleasant and the scenery so agreeable you may lose all sense of time as you fall into the rhythm of this long, gradual ascent. It comes as a surprise when you make a little switchback turn and cross over to the other side of the ridge. This last segment of the hike boasts some rarely seen native plants like yellow-flowered *ohia lehua, kanawao* (a wild, native relative of the garden hydrangea), *kopiko,* and purple- and white-flowered mountain *naupaka.* Sometimes, mountain *naupaka* flowers are wonderfully fragrant; let your nose search them out here.

The trail ends abruptly at a narrow saddle on the rainy crest of the Koolaus, high above Waihee Valley on the windward side. Hang onto your hat, as the winds are very strong here! Cliffs fall away almost vertically from your windy perch, and the views over the windward side, across Kahaluu to Kaneohe Bay, are magnificent. The leeward side is barely visible behind you.

Any attempt to go farther in any direction except back the way you came would be extremely dangerous, so from here, you reluctantly retrace your steps. On your return, you may wish to visit the lower Waimano Trail (see Trip 35) if you're not too weary. The additional distance and elevation gain aren't included in the icon box for this trip.

Trip 37. Kuaokala Loop

G **S**	Distance: 5 miles Elevation gain: 640' Hiking time: 2¹/₂ hours	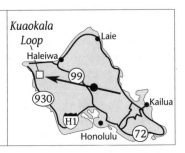

Topos: *Kaena*

Trail map (route partly approximated and not to scale): At the end of this trip.

Highlights: Varied views and colorful volcanic soil highlight this pleasant ramble, most of which is on the back roads of Kaena Point Tracking Station.

Driving instructions: From the intersection of McCully Street and Kapiolani Boulevard, go northeast on McCully, cross over the H1 freeway, and almost immediately turn left on Metcalfe in order to get onto the H1 freeway westbound. Continue westbound on H1, curving around Pearl Harbor, until H1 ends and you find yourself on Farrington Highway. (If you should happen to get off onto Farrington Highway earlier, it's no problem; you'll travel about the same distance and wind up at the same place.) Continue west and then northwest on Farrington Highway through Waianae and Makaha to the turnoff to the Kaena Point Tracking Station, just before the entrance to Kaena Point State Park. Stop at the guard shack and present your Division of Forestry and Wildlife permit to the guard. You'll get another permit and information about visiting Kaena Point Tracking Station. Continuing, you drive steeply uphill to a junction atop a ridge, where you turn right. Follow this road along a ridgetop, first southeast, passing entrances on your right to a huge radome and some satellite-tracking 'dishes,' then around a sharp curve, and finally north toward another large white dome. Before you reach the second dome, you'll pass a signed trailhead and an adjacent side road, both on your right. You'll walk on both of them in the course of this hike. Just beyond the trailhead and road, there's a large, bare parking area on the right. Park here, slightly over 41 miles from your start. There may be a temporary DLNR shack here; it looks like a giant dumpster bearing the DLNR *kukui*-leaf logo on its side.

(*About Farrington Highway:* Your road maps probably show a Farrington Highway along the extreme southwest shore of Oahu as well as another Farrington Highway along the extreme northwest shore. Farrington Highway once went all the way around Kaena Point, but the segment that actually rounded the point is gone, a victim of time and erosion.)

TheBus routes: Not served by TheBus.

Permit/permission required: First, you must get the initial permit in person from the Division of Forestry and Wildlife in downtown Honolulu (see "Getting Permits or Permission" earlier in this book). Second, you must exchange the Division of Forestry and Wildlife permit for an on-site permit and its accompanying helpful maps and instructions at the guard shack at Kaena Point Tracking Station, just after you turn onto the station's access road.

Description. Face the road you drove in on: the 4WD side road that you will return on is sharply to your left and heads downhill past a Smoky the Bear sign. The signed trailhead (1280') is also to your left. Start here by contouring around the head of a gully on a sometimes-narrow trail, through ironwoods and Christmas berry, climbing a little. A little before 1/2 mile, you meet a rough road cut along a ridge. Turn left (generally east) and follow the cut up the ridge, sometimes steeply. Mountain-bike tracks are evident in the soft soil of this road. You soon pass a picnic shelter.

Kaena Point, the extreme west end of Oahu, is generally behind you, but you soon descend to an overlook of Kaena Point State Park. Continue southeast along the ridge, enjoying amazing views, now on your right to the ocean, now on your left across steep, tree-filled gullies. Views vanish as you dip into a gully filled with strawberry guavas. The climb out of the gully ends on a broad saddle overlooking charred trees above another gully, and a path goes right from here, up a steep knob. But you bear left (northeast, away from the ocean), where you may see traces of the former foot trail paralleling the newer road cut. Pursue your way across slopes above gullies aflame in season with the golden-orange of silk oak blossoms. Mongooses rustle in the dry underbrush. From here, the ocean seems (and is) impossibly remote because of the ruggedness of the terrain.

The route veers north up a bare knob dotted with recently-planted pine saplings and with a few surviving *koa* trees. This knob would be dangerously slippery when wet. The area has obviously suffered a recent fire; perhaps fire-fighting was the reason for cutting the road, but no one I spoke to at the Oahu DLNR offices seemed to know much about it. On a footpath now, you soon reach a saddle and a junction near 1 1/2 miles, where the left fork leads to a welcome picnic shelter and the right fork is your continuing route. You traverse a slope behind some odd mud formations, cross a saddle splashed with vivid soil colors—brick reds, dusty gray-greens, oranges—and puff your way very steeply up past bidens, *ieie, ohia, palapalai,* and Christmas berry on a southeast-trending ridge. There are dizzying views at the top into Makua Valley, which is a military reserve and whose rim is lined with boundary markers and signs announcing DANGER DO NOT ENTER HIGH EXPLOSIVES IMPACT AREA SHELLS AND OTHER OBJECTS MAY EXPLODE IF TOUCHED OR MOVED. Traverse the rim of Makua Valley, enjoying views of the valley, the ocean, the tracking station, and flat-topped Mt. Kaala, the highest point on Oahu (4,020 feet, usually hidden in the clouds; see Appendix B). Finally, you wind up to a wattle-crowned knob, which is the high point on this route and which is also the terminus of the Kealia Trail (Trip 41).

Sharing the Kealia Trail, you soon drop steeply down across an eroded saddle and then climb steeply to the top of another knob, where you meet a 4WD spur road. Your route now becomes complicated by the web of 4WD roads, complete with lots of unmarked junctions, in the area you're entering. Few of these roads and junctions appear on the map at the end of this hike—or on any other map. For starters, a couple of other 4WD roads sneak in from either side; ignore them and continue ahead (north).

(Do As I Say, Not As I Do, Dep't. If you read the trail directions from the Division of Forestry and Wildlife, you'll read that you should "Keep taking the left route at any intersections you encounter." I didn't read that, and took a few right turns instead, but still managed to close the loop.)

At a **T**-junction, from where the Kealia Trail continues north (right), go left. Go left again at the next junction and switchback down into a shady valley. You cross a tiny gully, begin climbing again, and,

Precipitous view over Makua Valley

after more several junctions and turns, make a hairpin turn near the top of a ridge and come into view of the white domes of the tracking station. You soon emerge on a ridge where you have splendid views both north and south along the coast. Pass through a fence and go either left or right; they end up at the same place, but the righthand route is easier on the old knees. If you go right, you'll cross a cattle guard, descend, make a hairpin turn, and meet the other route several dozen feet lower down.

At the next junction, go left through the remnants of a fence, noting the richly colored soil layers revealed in the road cut: ochre, reddish purple, gray-black, bluish-gray, rose, and yellow-brown. Following the next left turn, you twine down into Manini Gulch. It's a pleasant doodle along the gulch bottom under *kukui,* Christmas berry, morning glory, Java plum, Indian pluchea, and coffee.

You presently exit the signed game-management area and re-enter Kaena Point Satellite Tracking Station at a little power installation. The road's surface becomes paved as it curves uphill. In another minute, you pass the Smoky the Bear sign, reach the main road, and turn right to the parking area to close the loop.

Trip 38. Kaena Point from the Waianae (South) Side

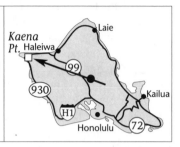

Distance: 4³/4 miles

M

Elevation gain: Negligible

Hiking time: Just under 2¹/2 hours

Topos: *Kaena*

Trail map (route partly approximated): At the end of this trip.

Highlights: A long walk on an old 4WD road through dark lava boulders climaxes with a visit to Kaena Point Natural Area Reserve, where you'll find sand dunes harboring native plants and birds. It's wild, it's scenic, it's different, it's wonderful!

Driving instructions: From the intersection of McCully Street and Kapiolani Boulevard just outside Waikiki, continue northeast on McCully, crossing over the Lunalilo Freeway (H1) on a narrow bridge. Just across the bridge, follow the signs to get on H1 westbound (a quick left turn onto Metcalfe Street that leads to a westbound freeway on-ramp). Continue westbound on H1, curving around Pearl Harbor, until H1 ends and you find yourself on Farrington Highway. (If you should happen to get off onto Farrington Highway earlier, it's no problem; you'll travel about the same distance and wind up at the same place.) Continue west and then northwest on Farrington Highway through Waianae and Makaha to Kaena Point State Park. Just inside the park gates, the road quality deteriorates considerably. Nevertheless, follow it until the pavement ends and the 4WD road begins. There's a sandy area on the inland side of the roadend where you can park, 42¹/3 miles. Start your hike here. (The 4WD road is extraordinarily bad, so don't even *think* about driving any farther on it.)

(*About Farrington Highway:* Your road maps probably show a Farrington Highway along the extreme southwest shore of Oahu as well as another Farrington Highway along the extreme northwest shore. Farrington Highway once went all the way around Kaena Point, but the segment that actually rounded the point is gone, a victim of time and erosion.)

TheBus routes: Not served by TheBus.

Permit/permission required: None.

Description. Head west on the 4WD road through *koa haole* scrub. To the north, the cliffs towering above you have been cut by wave erosion. The dominant flora may seem to be the beer can at first, but as you continue, you find the deep yellow flowers of *ilima papa* and the pale blue flowers of *pau o Hiiaka*, which peep through the dry weeds. The broad sand beach of Kaena Point State Park gives way to steep, rugged shelves of black lava and yellowish coral, battered by fierce seas into arches, bony fingers, and tidepools. An occasional cobblestone "beach" interrupts this shoreline; note that the shoreline itself is very dangerous to walk along when the surf is high.

About halfway to Kaena Point, you pass a pair of Mutt and Jeff blowholes that operate when the tide is just right. The Jeff blowhole shoots up a column of air and fine mist and heaves a dignified, exasperated sigh: "Whuff!" A few seconds later and a few feet away, the less-refined and less-reliable Mutt blowhole may let fly with a low-arcing spitball of water: "Ptui!" Look for a striking arch in the sea rocks, as well as for wooden railroad ties beneath your feet—more on the latter below. As you near the west end of the cliffs and sand dunes come into view, there's a spot where the old road has crumbled away entirely. Call on your boulder-scrambling skills to circumvent this cave-in and continue west to the border of Kaena Point Natural Area Reserve. It's this cave-in that forms a barrier to motorized vehicles and mountain bikes on this side of Kaena Point; while mountain bikes are permitted on the reserve, bikers and hikers must stay on the rock-bordered trails. You can see a sizable cave here, the gaping mouth of an old lava tube, forbidding and dangerous to enter.

From a junction where the old road curves right, the footpath leads west (left) toward the lighthouse visible in the distance. Continue ahead on the footpath, soon passing an old railroad cut (on the left and not shown on the map). *A Nature Walk to Ka'ena Point* explains: From its opening in 1895 to its closure in 1947, when trucking became more economical, a single-track railroad ran from Honolulu on the leeward side of Oahu around Kaena Point all the way to Kahuku on the windward side.

You soon find yourself on a tidy, sandy footpath bordered neatly with stones. Please stay on it as you take it out into the dunes, many of which are graced with crowns of white-flowered beach *naupaka*. Piles of rocks here and there may be shrines, so keep a respectful spirit here. Pause, fall silent, and listen: how wild, how empty is the reserve compared to the crowded, motorized craziness of Honolulu! Along with the beach *naupaka* you'll see the *pohinahina*, its purple flowers cupped in nests of gray-green leaves. Look also for the now-rare *ohai*, which has long, deep orange-red flowers and gray-green leaves. Winter and spring months bring Laysan albatrosses that nest in the sandy areas. It's a thrill to see one of these immense birds cruising overhead or coming in for a landing—though it may be a shock when one of them sweeps right over your head!

If you can do so without trampling plants or disturbing birds, leave the bordered trail briefly to walk up to the lighthouse to see the view. It's the complement of the view at Makapuu Point on the east end of Oahu (Trip 10), where the great ocean currents encounter Oahu and split to flow around the island. Here, they're reunited in a display of dark blue water, white foam, and jagged rocks.

After taking in the view, return the way you came. On the way back, there are great views eastward down the cliff-bound coast.

Kaena Point....took a beating from 4WD and offroad traffic for many years. According to *A Nature Walk to Ka'ena Point*, almost six feet of sand was lost from the dunes around the lighthouse. Yet Kaena Point was one of the last refuges of the beautiful *ohai*, and it was a former nesting site for many seabirds. Many agreed (as you will, too) that the

area was worth preserving for its remote, wild, scenic qualities. Now, it's open only to self-propelled traffic. Those who care about Kaena Point must be very happy that the Laysan albatross has returned to nest here once again.

Tiny "half-flowers" of beach naupaka (Scaevola taccada) nestle deep within rosettes of stiff, shiny, bright green leaves having curled edges. White berries follow the flowers. Beach naupaka not only grows wild but is widely used in coastal landscaping

A member of the morning-glory family, pau o Hiiaka (Jacquemontia sandwicensis) has pale blue flowers strung along its sturdy runners, among its half-folded oval leaves

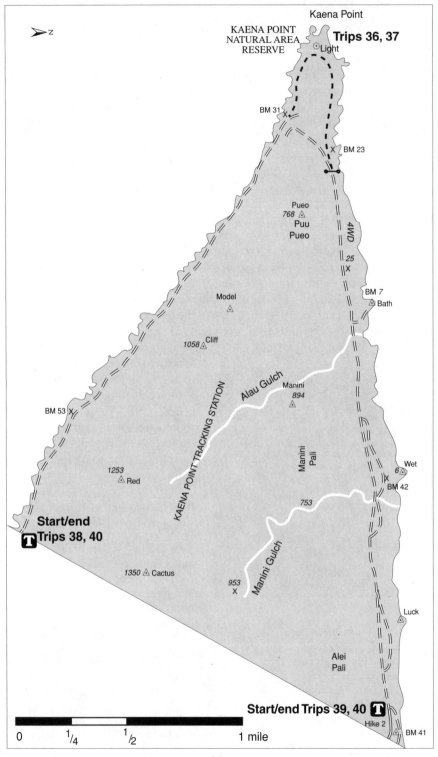

Kaena Point

KAENA POINT
NATURAL AREA
RESERVE

Trips 36, 37

⊙ Light

BM 31 X

X BM 23

Pueo
768 △
Puu
Pueo

4WD

25
X

BM *7*
△ Bath

Model
△

1058 △ Cliff

Alau Gulch

Manini
894
△

BM 53 X

Manini
Pali

Wet
6 △
X
BM 42

1253
△ Red

753

Start/end
🚻 **Trips 38, 40**

1350 △ Cactus

953
X

Manini Gulch

Luck
△

Alei
Pali

Start/end Trips 39, 40 🚻

Hike 2
△ BM 41

N

0   1/4   1/2   1 mile

164

Trip 39. Kaena Point from the Mokuleia (North) Side

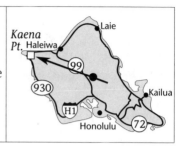

Distance: 5¹/2 miles

Elevation gain: Negligible

Hiking time: 2¹/2 hours

Topos: *Kaena*

Trail map (route approximated): At the end of Trip 38.

Highlights: The intriguing world of Kaena Point can be reached from the north, too. The approach from the north traverses a gentler shore-line than that of the south side featuring sand and dunes instead of black lava rocks, while the tall cliffs on this side are softened by a bit more vegetation—the windward side, after all, is wetter. Personally, I find this side more scenic than the Waianae side (Trip 38). Mountain bikes are permitted on the reserve, but bikers and hikers must stay on the rock-bordered trails.

Driving instructions: From the intersection of McCully Street and Kapiolani Boulevard just outside Waikiki, continue northeast on McCully, crossing over the Lunalilo Freeway (H1) on a narrow bridge. Just across the bridge, follow the signs to get on H1 westbound (a quick left turn onto Metcalfe Street that leads to a westbound freeway on-ramp). Continue westbound on H1 to the junction with H2, which you take toward Wahiawa. Around Wahiawa, the H2 freeway ends and you find yourself confronted with some confusing choices. Your objective is to head for Waialua. The better way is to take Highway 99 out of Wahiawa, and then take Highway 803 just past Schofield Barracks, where Highway 99 veers northeast. You coast northward through cane fields; just outside Waialua, at the junction with Highway 930, you take Highway 930 northwest at a traffic "triangle" toward Waialua. Follow Highway 930 (also called Farrington Highway) past Waialua and Dillingham Airfield to the end of the pavement. The dirt roads beyond are very eroded. Park your car off the pavement in one of the sandy areas here to start your hike, just over 46 miles.

(If you err and take Highway 80 out of Wahiawa, you'll come to a fork near Whitmore Village. Take the left fork, Highway 801, to Waialua. You presently meet Highway 803 to Waialua; turn north toward Waialua here.)

Stop at the beach right before the airfield for bathrooms)

TheBus routes: Not served by TheBus.

Permit/permission required: None.

Description. Here on Oahu's far northwest shore, the shoreline is much less rugged than it is on the southwest shore (Trip 38). It's sandy—dunes topped with typical strand vegetation—rather than rocky. A number of primitive roads thread through the dunes here. Inland there are dirt roads that turn to mud when it rains; along the shoreline, sandier roads. (Many of these roads don't appear on the map at the end of Trip 38 or on any map, as a "road" can be created in a few hours with a bulldozer or by a bunch of 4WD vehicles following one another.) You can pretty much pick whichever one you prefer as long as it takes you westward toward Kaena Point. Just remember that shoreline routes are dangerous when the seas are high.

Circumvent a steel gate and cross a cattle guard to start your hike and take the road that picks up where the paved road ends. You're likely to see plenty of people fishing from the shore if the weather permits. The sea-cut cliffs south of you are the west end of the Waianae Range. Look for huge, spiky, dark-green sisal plants on the talus slopes below the cliffs. Their thorny, succulent leaves, bursting from giant rosettes, are up to six feet long, and their flower spikes can be up to 30 feet tall! They're the remains of efforts to grow sisal commercially in the Islands: the fibers of the sisal were once prized for making rope. The fiber and rope-making industry in Hawaii faltered long ago, but the sisals, native to Latin America, have escaped cultivation and naturalized here.

You presently reach a steel-gate-and-boulder barrier that bars farther travel by motorized vehicles. Hikers and mountain bikers, however, can make their way through the barrier and continue their trip to Kaena Point. Look for grasses, *koa haole,* and *naio* (also called "false sandalwood," with long, droopy, folded leaves) here. Even if the coastline isn't terribly interesting here, it certainly has some intriguing names for its elevation benchmarks, as you'll see on the map and the topo: Bath, Wet, Luck, and—maybe in honor of what you're doing—Hike 2.

Where the road curves left and begins climbing up the talus slopes near the end of the cliffs, continue ahead (right) on a sandy path into Kaena Point Natural Area Reserve. Staying on the path, you stroll through dunes crowned with beach *naupaka* (white "half" flowers), *pohinahina* (purple flowers), and the long, prostrate stems and half-folded leaves of *pau o Hiiaka* (small, pale blue, morning-glory-shaped flowers). As mentioned in Trip 38, winter and spring find Laysan albatrosses nesting in the dunes here, and you may see these immense birds with their very slender wings flying overhead. Or, if the path takes you too close to a nest, an adult bird may take to the air and try to drive you away!

As the path comes near the point itself, it curves left, behind the lighthouse. If walking briefly and directly to the lighthouse will not trample plants or disturb any birds, walk up to the lighthouse to take in the splendid view. It's the counterpart of the view at Makapuu Point (Trip 10): there, the ocean currents divided to flow around Oahu; here, they reunite in a splash of dark water and bright foam on jagged rocks.

After enjoying the view, retrace your steps.

Naio....is often called "false sandalwood," for when the supply of true sandalwood was used up in the early nineteenth century, merchants tried to sell *naio* to the Chinese, who were the principal customers of Hawaiian sandalwood. The Chinese recognized *naio* as an inferior product and refused it; thus, *naio*, unlike true sandalwood, is fairly common today. Contrary to common belief, true sandalwood did survive in Hawaii. If you're lucky, you may spot some true sandalwoods along the Kaunaula Loop (Trip 45).

"When Boki comes back"....The sandalwood may have all but disappeared, but the debts of the chiefs, debts which they had run up acquiring lavish possessions and which they were supposed to repay with sandalwood, did not disappear. As they were unable to repay their debts, the Hawaiian government assumed them, apportioning responsibility for the debts to the governors of the major islands. As related in *Hawaii: An Uncommon History,* Boki, the governor of Oahu, thus became responsible for $48,000 of the debt to the Americans—an immense amount in the late 1820s in Hawaii. To make things worse, Boki was himself an extravagant chief. Though he owned and ran many businesses, he had no resources sufficient to make good on such an enormous sum. So when he received secret word of the discovery of South Pacific islands with abundant sandalwood, he hastened to outfit two ships and to recruit 500 men for a voyage to the islands. It must have seemed his only chance to repay the debt. Boki himself took charge of one of the ships.

Disaster stalked the expedition: poor organization, disease, and hostile natives all took their toll. Five hundred sailed; only twenty ever came back, in just one of the ships. The other, with Boki on it, was never seen again after the two ships parted company north of Fiji. A saying became widespread in Hawaii: "When Boki comes back," meaning "It'll never happen" or "It's impossible."

Trip 40. Kaena Point—Both Sides

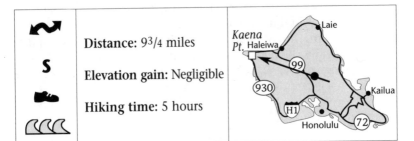

Distance: 9³/4 miles

Elevation gain: Negligible

Hiking time: 5 hours

Topos: *Kaena*

Trail map (route partly approximated): At the end of Trip 38.

Highlights: Having trouble making up your mind whether to see the south side or the north side of Kaena Point? It's easier than you may think, as there's virtually no elevation gain or loss.

Driving instructions: Follow the driving instructions of Trip 38 or Trip 39, depending on where you want to start your trip. (As described, this hike assumes you start from the south side, from Kaena Point State Park.)

TheBus routes: Not served by TheBus.

Permit/permission required: None.

Description. The complete walk all the way around Kaena Point and back again reminds me of a remark attributed to Mae West: "Too much of a good thing can be wonderful!" Assuming you start on the leeward side at Kaena Beach State Park, begin your trip as described in Trip 38 and then continue to the windward terminus by reversing the steps of Trip 39. Retrace your steps to conclude the trip.

Distant mysteries: Nihoa and Necker....As you stand at Kaena Point, look far out to sea, northwest toward Kauai and Niihau. Beyond them lies the rest of the Hawaiian archipelago: a dozen or so islands, islets, rocks, and atolls stretched across more than a thousand miles of ocean, each one increasingly ancient and tiny, all uninhabited except for a few military installations.

The two tiny islands beyond Kauai and Niihau are called Nihoa and Necker. Like the other Hawaiian islands, they are remnants of volcanoes. While Niihau offers an environment of 73 square *miles*, Nihoa offers only 155.5 *acres* and Necker only 39.5 acres. (An acre is ¹/640 of a square mile.) According to Patrick V. Kirch's *Feathered Gods and Fishhooks*, both Nihoa and Necker clearly show signs of having been inhabited in the distant past—the signs on Necker perhaps pointing to a tragic human drama.

Nihoa, about 170 miles from Kauai, was first sighted by Europeans in 1789. It has sea cliffs on three sides; on the fourth, it slopes steeply to the ocean, forming Adam Bay. Fishing is limited to the open ocean. No fringing reef offers a home for shellfish and reef fish or protection from the open sea. No

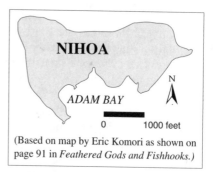

(Based on map by Eric Komori as shown on page 91 in *Feathered Gods and Fishhooks*.)

beach softens a canoe landing, which must be made on a rocky shelf in Adam Bay—possible in fair weather only. Annual rainfall is sufficient for dryland crops like sweet potatoes and gourds but not for taro and other typical Polynesian crops. Other food sources must have included birds and eggs. The island has a native *loulu* palm that can supply wood for canoes. Year-round water supplies are limited to three small guano-contaminated seeps; good fresh water must come from rainfall.

An archaeological expedition in the 1920s found that in spite of these severe limitations, Nihoa had been well populated at one time. Agricultural terraces, house sites, domestic implements, tools, and religious sites dot the island. Archaeologist-author Kirch estimates that Nihoa may have supported 100 to 125 people at most. It is hard to imagine people spending their whole lives on this remote nubbin of rock. Kirch observes that ". . .a protracted drought could have devastated the island's fragile agricultural systems, leading to widespread starvation." Perhaps that is why the island is now uninhabited.

Necker, over 300 miles from Kauai, was first spotted by Europeans in 1786. It is hardly more than a ridge of rock with sea cliffs on one side and a steep slope to the ocean at Shark Bay on the other side. Necker's environment is so limited that it is unlikely it could have supported a permanent population. Year-round water is limited to two guano-tainted seeps. There are no trees large enough to supply wood for canoes; the native vegetation is limited to low shrubs and grasses. Agriculture would be extremely difficult; fish, birds, and eggs are the potential food sources. Landing a canoe on Necker would have been even more difficult than on Nihoa.

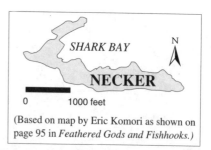

(Based on map by Eric Komori as shown on page 95 in *Feathered Gods and Fishhooks*.)

Yet, to their astonishment, the expedition sent to annex Necker to the rest of Hawaii in the 1880s found over 60 archaeological sites on the island. They were particularly struck by a well-constructed temple with a number of stone images unique in Hawaii but reminiscent of idols from the Marquesas. The same archaeological expedition that investigated Nihoa visited Necker, too, where they found no less than 34 such temple sites. There is no evidence of permanent habitation; however, a cave shows evidence of human occupation. Who, then, was here long enough to build the 34 temples? What brought them here? What became of them? Sherwin Carlquist, author of *Hawaii: A Natural History*, speculates that they were a band of long-distance Polynesian voyagers cast up on Necker's hostile shore:

> I would guess that they were marooned, unable to sail for another island (there are no really woody plants on Necker, so even a raft could not be constructed). They might have survived for a while on birds and eggs and the small seeps of water, but perhaps they eventually died, building their [temples] as a sort of desperate symbol of hope.

No less an authority than Kirch quotes Carlquist's speculation as an explanation for the mysterious temples.

If that is correct, think what it must have been like on Necker in those last days—to have been the last lonely survivor, despair stealing the hope from his heart as hunger and thirst stole the life from his body. It is almost unbearable! Even the heat of Kaena Point cannot rout the chill of horror.

The currents meet at Kaena Point

Trip 41. Kealia Trail

Distance: 6²/3 miles

Elevation gain: 1820'

Hiking time: 3¹/3 hours

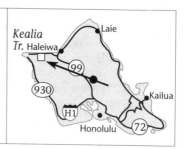

Topos: *Kaena*

Trail map (route partly approximated): At the end of this trip.

Highlights: A dry-forest hike that starts on the north side of the Waianaes climaxes at a dramatic overlook of Makua Valley on the south side of the range. The last segment of this trip overlaps part of Trip 37.

Note: You must drive onto Dillingham Airfield to get to the trailhead, and Dillingham's gates are closed overnight. Schedule your hike exclusively for daylight hours.

Driving instructions: From the intersection of McCully Street and Kapiolani Boulevard just outside Waikiki, continue northeast on McCully, crossing over the Lunalilo Freeway (H1) on a narrow bridge. Just across the bridge, follow the signs to get on H1 westbound (a quick left turn onto Metcalfe Street that leads to a westbound freeway on-ramp). Continue westbound on H1 to the junction with H2, which you take toward Wahiawa. Around Wahiawa, the H2 freeway ends and you find yourself confronted with some confusing choices. Your objective is to head for Waialua. The better way is to take Highway 99 out of Wahiawa, and then take Highway 803 just past Schofield Barracks, where Highway 99 veers northeast. You coast northward through cane fields. Just outside Waialua town, at a traffic "triangle," you take Highway 930 northwest into Waialua. Follow Highway 930 (also called Farrington Highway) through the town to Dillingham Airfield (on the inland side). At the west end of Dillingham, there's a gate. Turn left through this gate and follow the paved road past the west end of the runways. Turn left again at the next junction and park in a rough-paved area from which a dirt road leads south toward the cliffs behind Dillingham, a little over ¹/3 mile from the gate and just under 44¹/2 miles from Waikiki.

TheBus routes: Not served by TheBus.

Permit/permission required: None.

Description. Take the old dirt road that heads generally south away toward the cliffs. Yes, you are going to climb them! But for now, the road angles into dry scrub, and you pass through a DLNR fence. The understory is very dense at times, and you may have trouble seeing where you're going. Non-native cherry tomatoes grow wild here.

Curve right and begin switchbacking up the cliff. Native dry-forest plants that deserve your attention here include a white-flowered plumbago with extremely cling-y seeds. Farther on, you'll see *aalii*, a native shrub with shiny, papery, four-part red fruits valued for leis. Look also for the soapberry, a tree whose black seeds you may see in the trail's tread. The pond far below is the water-filled remains of a quarry.

Near the top of the cliffs, the trail heads south through silk oak, swamp mahogany, Christmas berry, black wattle, ironwoods, and lemon-scented gums. You meet a 4WD road and follow it south to a junction (not on the topo) where you go ahead (south-southeast) through a gate. Continue uphill, curving left through ironwoods and past an old tank.

The road climbs moderately to steeply. Then, leveling out briefly, it traverses a flat area before making a very steep pull upward. You pass through a fence and emerge on a saddle overlooking Waialua and Haleiwa.

After enjoying the view, continue up the 4WD road. At the next saddle, climb steeply again, passing a ferny bank shaded by silk oaks.

At the next junction, a T-junction with the Keaau-Kalau-Mokuleia Road, turn left (generally east) onto that road—marked "Kuaokala Access Road" on at least one map—and continue uphill, curving around a little

The native shrub aalii *(*Dodonaea eriocarpa*) grows widely on dry slopes like those the Kealia Trail traverses*

meadow. Ignore a couple of 4WD roads that come in, one on either side. Continue ahead (south) to a eucalyptus-clad knob overlooking the head of Makua Valley and, clouds permitting, Mt. Kaala. To go farther, carefully descend the eroded track on the knob's steep valley-side slope to a narrow saddle, then climb very steeply up the other side. Follow the track a short way along the valley's north rim to a high point with sweeping views of the off-limits valley and the coast. (It's a military exercise area; you may find signs warning you not to touch any shells or other military hardware you might find. See Trip 37, Kuaokala Loop.)

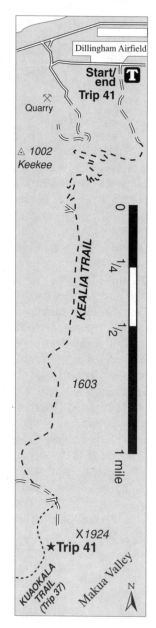

After taking in the views, retrace your steps with the help of the cues you memorized earlier.

Kaena's sea cliffs.... The cliffs that you're climbing on, or that you drove up to take Trip 37, or that formed the dramatic backdrop for your visit to Kaena Point (Trips 38–40) seem too far back from the ocean to be the result of wave erosion. Yet geologists judge they are indeed wave-cut. How can that be?

According to *A Nature Walk to Ka'ena Point*, the cliffs were formed some 400,000 years ago during a much warmer period on earth than we are living in now. The great glaciers far away had melted so much that the ocean stood about 95 feet higher than it does now! The cliffs you see were cut during that period. Now, with more water frozen in the glaciers, the ocean has retreated, and the cliffs are slowly crumbling into the piles of sandy-rocky rubble (called "talus fans") that you see at their feet.

Evidence of higher and lower stands of the sea abound in Hawaii, reminding you of the power that glaciers half a world away nevertheless possess to permanently change the face of the most remote archipelago on earth. Well, "permanently" until the ice melts once again. . . .

Trip 42. Wahiawa Botanical Garden Stroll

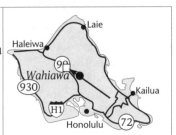

Distance: Up to you

Elevation gain: 50' if you descend into the gully; negligible otherwise

Hiking time: Up to you. Allow at least 1/2 hour

Topos: *Hauula*

Trail map: At the end of this trip.

Highlights: Wahiawa (locally pronounced "WAH-hee-wah") Botanical Garden is a shady retreat on the hot, dry Leilehua Plateau, between the Waianae and Koolau mountain ranges. Here, you'll find an attractive display of exotic trees and shrubs as well as a few native plants. Best of all is simply the opportunity to relax and stroll in this pretty setting. The garden is open from 9 AM to 4 PM daily except Christmas Day and New Year's Day; admission is free. It's one of the four botanical gardens run by the City and County of Honolulu; see also Trips 7, 11, and 33.

Driving instructions: From the intersection of McCully Street and Kapiolani Boulevard just outside Waikiki, continue northeast on McCully, crossing over the Lunalilo Freeway (H1) on a narrow bridge. Just across the bridge, follow the signs to get on H1 westbound (a quick left turn onto Metcalfe Street that leads to a westbound freeway on-ramp). Continue westbound on H1 to the junction with H2, which you take toward Wahiawa. The H2 freeway ends at Wahiawa, and you should bear right on Highway 80 (South Kamehameha) to California Avenue. Turn right onto California Avenue and follow it to Wahiawa Botanical Garden, on your left just before California curves right. Park in the lot at the southwest end of the garden, slightly more than 24 1/2 miles.

TheBus routes: Take Route 8, 19, 20, or 58 to the Ala Moana Shopping Center and transfer to Route 52 to Wahiawa Heights. There is a bus stop at the garden's parking lot; get off there.

Permit/permission required: None.

Description. You enter the garden by a gate on the right side of the parking lot (as you stand with your back to California Avenue) and walk past philodendron-draped ficuses and huge tree ferns to the office. Pick up the free brochure for the garden from the dispenser at the office and use it to guide your tour. (The map at the end of this trip is based on the map in that guide.) You can walk all the trails—as you see, you can make several loops through the garden. Or, if you prefer to avoid a climb, walk only those that aren't in the gully (they're shown on the right side of the map).

The trail that loops across the dry streambed, on the left side of the map and more or less on your left as you stand at the office, is an upside-down trip: you descend steeply into the cool, shady, palm-filled gully and then climb back out of it. Right by the office, growing tall out of the gully, is a huge jacaranda tree. When it's in bloom, its large, loose clusters of trumpet-shaped lavender-blue flowers are real show-stoppers. Don't be sorry if you can't have this beauty in your front yard. Better to enjoy it here! Jacarandas are messy trees, constantly dropping leaves, twigs, blobs of sap, and whatever the feature of the season is—blossoms or fruit pods. When it's damp, they have a slightly rotten smell. The lovely blossoms—also smelly—make a squishy little *pop!* sound when you step on them.

The trails that aren't in the gully, more or less on the right both on the map and as you stand by the office, are broader and fairly level. Interesting trees like the allspice, cinnamon, and camphor grow here.

As I strolled out of the gully and around the far end of the garden looking for the cinnamon tree, I noticed little groups of well-dressed people headed for a secluded corner of the garden. Some were giggling, like the little girl in her Sunday-best dress, skipping along beside her parents. Some looked solemn, like the handsome and nervous young man and his friends, all in uniform. Here came three pretty young women in party dresses, carrying flowers and chatting quietly. One was dressed in white—*wedding!* How lovely, a wedding in the garden! I hoped they wouldn't mind—and wouldn't notice me—as I watched them assemble on the lawn, taking their places on the folding chairs that had been set out. Just as everyone came together in the golden light that filtered through the overarching trees, the sprinklers came on. The wedding party exploded out of the way, flying in all directions to find a gardener to turn off the water. The gardener said, "Wedding? Oh, I forgot. Sorry!" I'll never forget that wedding. Fortunately, I remembered my manners and slipped away before the ceremony.

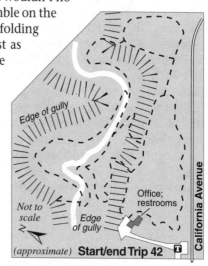

Edge of gully

Edge of gully

Office; restrooms

California Avenue

Not to scale

(approximate) **Start/end Trip 42**

Trip 43. Waimea Bay Loop

Distance: A little under 1 mile

V

Elevation gain: Negligible

Hiking time: Just under 1/2 hour

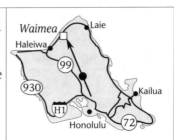

Topos: *Waimea*

Trail map (route approximated): Near the end of this trip.

Highlights: Kailua or Waimanalo may be the best *beach*, but Waimea has to be the loveliest *bay* on Oahu. Weather permitting, you can enjoy its scenery on this little loop hike, and then spend the rest of your day sunning and swimming there. *Note:* Waimea is notorious for its huge, dangerous storm surf. Don't turn your back on it!

Driving instructions: From the intersection of McCully Street and Kapiolani Boulevard just outside Waikiki, continue northeast on McCully, crossing over the Lunalilo Freeway (H1) on a narrow bridge. Just across the bridge, follow the signs to get on H1 westbound (a quick left turn onto Metcalfe Street that leads to a westbound freeway on-ramp). Continue westbound on H1 to the junction with H2, which you take toward Wahiawa. The H2 freeway ends at Wahiawa. When H2 ends, you can take either Highway 99, which veers west of Wahiawa, or Highway 80, which goes north and then northwest through Wahiawa. Either will do; they meet in the cane fields a little north of Wahiawa. (Note that if you take Highway 99, you must be sure to stay on Highway 99 when you come to the fork where Highway 803 branches left and Highway 99 branches right.) After the highways meet, they're known as Highway 99, the Kamehameha Highway. The road continues north and then northwest through cane fields to a traffic circle with the un-Hawaiian name of Weed Circle, just south of Haleiwa. Go toward Haleiwa as the highway becomes Highway 83 (but is still the Kamehameha Highway). (Confused? You should be!) You cruise through charming Haleiwa, crossing a pretty little bridge over the Anahulu River, and then curve north-northeast along Oahu's famous North Shore to Waimea Beach Park. Turn left (seaward) onto the park's access road just before you'd cross the Waimea River, a little over 38 3/4 miles.

TheBus routes: Take Route 8, 19, 20, or 58 to the Ala Moana Shopping Center and transfer to Route 52 to Turtle Bay ("Circle Island"). Get off at Waimea Bay and walk to the start of this hike.

Permit/permission required: None.

Description. Start your hike at the memorial to Eddie Aikau (see below), just seaward of the parking lot, and pay your respects. Bear left (southwest) from the plaque, along the paved path through a grassy picnic area. You stroll briefly under Christmas berry, *milo*, and *koa haole*. The paved path ends abruptly at a steep drop, so you bear a little to the right to step rather than tumble down to the beach. Mosey along the beach below some low, dark, crumbling cliffs and toward a huge rock. The rock extends out into the ocean, and some people are daring (or careless) enough to climb up the beach side of the rock and jump off its top into the ocean. The sea may have thrown up some treasures along the high tide line here, such as tiny, translucent scallop shells. Along the high tide line, you also find the burrows of the shy ghost crabs. Beyond the rock there's a little cove that may be swamped at high tide or that may offer more of those fragile sea-treasures at low tide.

Turn around here and walk along the beach, generally northeast. If there's a sandbar—a bay-mouth bar—across the mouth of the Waimea River, you won't have to wade across it. Alas, the lagoon it forms looks murky and is too polluted for swimming. The seaward views are lovely, and the views inland, upriver beyond the highway bridge, are lush, romantic, and idyllic—everything you hoped for in the tropics.

You reach the bluff below the highway and walk up a few feet to

Beautiful Waimea Bay, seen from the cliffs above it

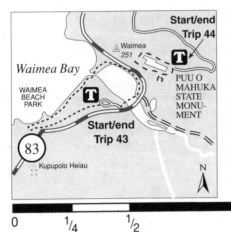

the highway shoulder. Follow a trail-of- use along the highway shoulder on the safe side of the highway barrier, past *hau, koa haole, milo,* air plants, sisal, and ficuses. Where the barrier ends, curve into a NO PARKING AT ANY TIME area, pick up a stub of paved road, pass the bus stop, and then pick up the pedestrian path that leads to a wood footbridge next to the highway bridge. Cross the Waimea River and follow the paved path past Java plum, *milo, koa haole,* the yellow-flowered be-still, and Christmas berry to the park's entrance.

Close the loop at Eddie Aikau's monument and head for your beach towel and picnic basket.

"Eddie would go"....That's what a bumper sticker on Rabbit Kekai's van says. "What does that mean?" I asked a friend. She explained: Eddie Aikau (1946–1978) was a lifeguard at Waimea Bay for many years. He saved thousands of lives there, braving the dangerous surf with no thought for his own safety, intent only on saving a life—probably of someone he'd never seen before. Eddie would go to help when no one else would have dared. He was famous for surfing the huge North Shore waves, too—another thing few dared.

On the night of March 17, 1978, the Polynesian Voyaging Society's double hulled canoe, the *Hokule'a,* a modern replica of the ancient Polynesian long-distance canoes, capsized in heavy seas about 20 miles off Oahu's shores. Eddie was on board along with several other people. He had his surfboard with him. It must have been second nature to him to get onto it and to paddle away alone into the darkness to get help. Neither he nor his surfboard were ever seen again. Mercifully, the rest survived that hellish night. As the plaque on the boulder at Waimea Beach Park says:

> Eddie Aikau is gone, but his name will live in the annals of heroism in Hawaii. His spirit will live, too, wherever the *Hokule'a* sails and on the beach at Waimea Bay. . . .This was a great man, a great Hawaiian, and he will live in our hearts forever.

See Trip 32 for more about Rabbit Kekai.

Trip 44. Puu o Mahuka *Heiau* State Monument

G **V** 👞 〰〰〰	**Distance:** A little over ¼ mile **Elevation gain:** Negligible **Hiking time:** 8–9 minutes	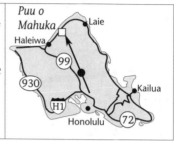

Topos: *Waimea*

Trail map (route approximated): Near the end of Trip 43.

Highlights: This large *heiau* is interesting and easy to visit as you tour the spectacular North Shore. The view over Waimea Bay (Trip 43) and along the northwest coast of Oahu from the *heiau's* precincts is excellent.

Driving instructions: Follow the driving instructions of Trip 43 but don't turn off at Waimea Bay. Instead, continue northeast on Highway 83 into Waimea town. Look on the inland side of the road for a little shopping center with a supermarket. The street that runs inland just before this shopping center is Pupukea Homestead Road. Turn right (inland) onto Pupukea Homestead Road and follow it as it twists up the cliffs behind Waimea town. Just beyond the point where Pupukea Homestead Road tops the cliffs, you turn right onto a very narrow road to Puu o Mahuka (the turnoff is marked for the monument). Follow it to its end in a speed-bump-filled parking lot, a little over 41 miles.

TheBus routes: Not served by TheBus.

Permit/permission required: None.

Description. A path encircles the *heiau*, running just outside the remaining rocks that define the *heiau* site, which is built in two levels—higher at the inland east end, lower at the seaward west end. A park service marker names the site but says little else about it. According to one source, this was a *heiau* of human sacrifice—a solemn note on this open, sunny, view-filled plateau—built, legend had it, by Hawaii's "little people," the Menehunes, in a single night. From the marker, turn either way to circle the *heiau*. By going right from the marker, you pass a side path into the *heiau*. It's obvious that the heiau is far from being a dried-up old relic. No more human sacrifices occur here, but an altar just outside the upper part of the *heiau* is laden with fresh offerings: fruit, flowers, and stones and bundles wrapped in *ti* leaves. Please respect the *heiau* and its offerings as you would respect any place of worship. Please do *not* disturb the *heiau* area, even to take or add a stone for an offering. To do so interferes with the archaeological record.

Continuing around the *heiau*, you pass Christmas berry, guava, and Java plum trees where the white-rumped shama perches to pour out its wonderful songs. The path curves around the seaward end of the *heiau*, passing stiff, spiky sisal plants and *koa haole*. At the edge of the plateau, there are breathtaking views over Waimea Bay and all the way down Oahu's north coast as far as Kaena Point—sea-haze permitting. Why not pause here, find a place to sit, and enjoy the view for a while? But presently you go on, passing a heap of boulders shaded by Java plum trees, around which a beaten path makes a little loop. Kids like to climb over these boulders and perch on them.

Follow the path around the inland end of the *heiau*, between the *heiau* walls and a fence behind which guava trees grow in deep weeds, and then turn back to the parking lot to close your loop.

The old gods.... Had you realized before this visit that the old Hawaiian religion was still alive though much changed, in spite of the many

religions imported from Europe and Asia? The overthrow of the *kapu* changed the way in which the old gods and goddesses were honored, but many kept traditional beliefs even as they adopted the new religions. That is not to say that the new beliefs are not deeply cherished; they are. But the old ones are part of the earth, of the sea, of the air one breathes, of one's family—inseparable from the land and the lives lived on it.

Hikers enjoy the view over Waimea Bay from Puu o Mahuka

Trip 45. Kaunala Loop

Distance: Just over 4¹/2 miles

Elevation gain: 940'

Hiking time: 2¹/2 hours

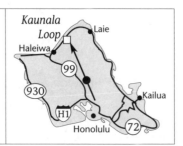

Topos: *Waimea, Kahuku*

Trail map (route partly approximated): At the end of this trip.

Highlights: This wonderful hike has forested valleys, ridges with far-ranging views, and scenic back roads. It's one of my three favorites on Oahu (Trips 22 and 36 are the other two). The 4WD segment is suitable for mountain bikes. Use trails have made the footpath hard to follow in places, but the main trail is generally broader and makes switchbacks, instead of plunging straight up or down the slope.

Note: You may hike this loop only on weekends and on state and national holidays.

Driving instructions: Follow the driving instructions of Trip 43 but then continue north-northeast on Highway 83. Following the driving instructions of Trip 44, turn right onto Pupukea Road. However, don't turn off Pupukea Road toward the *heiau* as described in Trip 44 Instead, continue inland on Pupukea Road to its end at Camp Pupukea, a Boy Scout camp. You are permitted to park just inside the fence of Camp Pupukea (or park off the road), a little over 41¹/2 miles.

TheBus routes: Not served by TheBus.

Permit/permission required: None, but note the restriction to weekends and holidays (above).

Description. Head southeast on the dirt road just outside Camp Pupukea's fence. The road leads onto a military installation, and a gate bars your way. (If there's no convenient hikers' pass-through, you may have to circumvent it by going inside Camp Pupukea's fence, parallel to the road, and around some tanks not shown on the map.) Sign in at the hunter's check station on the left just past the tanks.

The road is lined with swamp mahogany trees that provide shade along with a spicy eucalyptus scent. You pass a ruined gate, a corral, and a side road to an antenna tower on your right. Continue ahead and descend slightly past *koa, kukui,* and rose apple trees. You have glimpses of the valleys on either side—you're hiking on a ridge! Silk

oaks, strawberry guava, and *uluhe* and *palapalai* ferns grow thickly on
the road embankments. Stick to the road; the land on your right is
private property; a sign on the gate that guards the access road (to your
right) announces:

PUPUKEA RANGE—PRIVATE PROPERTY
NO HUNTING • NO BIKE'S
NO MOTORCYCLE'S • NO HIKING
UNAUTHORIZED PERSON'S WILL BE "PROSCUTED"
PROPERTY OF BISHOP CORP.

Just beyond that sign and ahead on the main road, there's a knoll
forested with paperbark eucalyptus; look for a signed junction at the
knoll's base. There are three forks: the right one is the main road curving right around the knoll; the middle one is a dirt road climbing the
knoll; and the left one is a footpath curving left around the knoll. The
loop part of this trip begins here; take the left fork (the footpath); you'll
return on the main road.

Go hard left here on the foot trail, west-northwest through tall
paperbark eucalyptuses, initially climbing a little. Ignore a steep use
trail that shortly darts left and downhill to a saddle; instead, go right to
stay on the main trail. With stunning views over the adjacent valley,
you twine down over paperbark roots, down into the forest to an unmarked fork. Go left here, contouring around a little ridge and passing
a clump of *ti*. Ignoring the confusing trails-of-use around here, you
make a switchback turn. Where small, shiny, purplish-black fruits on
the trail betray the presence of Java plum trees, you angle into a muddy
gully where the air is still, thick, and wet. It's a relief to climb to a spot
where *ohia* trees grow and where you may catch a breeze. *Ti* has become more abundant as the trail has grown damper, and tree ferns
burst through the tangled understory now.

The trail descends again, crosses a streambed, and then climbs
moderately to steeply out of the gully under the shade of swamp mahogany, octopus trees, and paperbarks. The ground here and the roots
that protrude from it are dotted with hummocks of a pale green, velvety moss. More *ti* as well as *ieie* grace the trail now.

The trail presently curls over the nose of a paperbark-clad ridge,
passing over a saddle and below an *uluhe*-covered knob to the northwest. Down in the gully to your left, you can see the light green crowns
of *kukui* trees and the glimmer of a flowing stream. The trail degenerates
into a steep slot worn into sticky brown clay as you descend to the stream.
Cross the stream and ascend the other side into strawberry guava and *ti*.
You dip into another damp gully, cross another stream, and ascend to
an open slope with a view over the gully. A little farther on, beautiful
views of the countryside and over the ocean spread out below as you

stand on the next ridge nose. Pause and listen for the white-rumped shama around here, and don't be surprised if a skinny, flattish, dusty-brown mongoose streaks across the trail. Now you curve inland into the forest, contour around a side gulch, and, almost at the head of the gulch, switchback steeply up to meet a 4WD road.

Turn right (south-southeast) onto the 4WD road and continue climbing, sometimes very steeply! (Ignore the trail-of-use across the road from the point where you emerged from the gulch.) Up you go through paperbarks to a saddle with a fine view of the Waianae Range to the southwest and of the ocean to the west. Continue climbing from here past *koa, ohia, ieie,* and even a few mountain *naupaka* shrubs as well as rigidly symmetrical Norfolk pines. There are lots of purple Philippine orchids and wiry *uluhe* ferns here, too. At the top of the climb you are rewarded with magnificent views, including flat-topped Mt. Kaala, Oahu's highest point, to the southwest. Resuming the hike, you pass a road cut that's left the terrain mottled with wonderful volcanic-soil colors: soft brown, of course, and purplish red, ochre, soft orange, and dusty-rose pink. The road drops very steeply downhill toward some Norfolk pines, and you circumvent a gate.

In a few steps, you reach a T-junction and turn right (west) through a deep, ferny road cut. The descent becomes more gradual now, leveling out or climbing a little, and there are ridgetop views as well as the broken shade of a variety of trees: silk oak, paperbark, ironwood, swamp mahogany, *ohia,* and *kukui.* Be alert for dirt bikes on this stretch! You pass a picnic shelter on the right side of the road. Nearing the end of the loop, the road makes a short climb to a small, flat area and closes the loop at the junction by the paperbark-forested knoll.

Retrace your steps on the 4WD road back to Camp Pupukea.

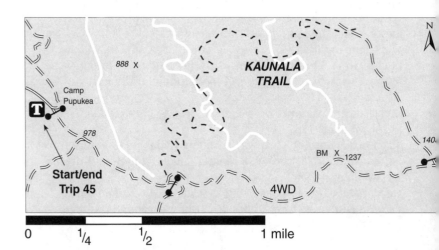

Bibliography

Beckwith, Martha. *Hawaiian Mythology.* New Haven: Yale University Press (for the Folklore Foundation of Vassar College), 1940. Reprint. Honolulu: University of Hawaii Press, 1970, 1976.

Bisignani, J.D. *Hawaii Handbook.* 3rd ed. Chico, California: Moon Publications, Inc., 1991.

Carlquist, Sherwin. *Hawaii, A Natural History.* 2nd ed., 2nd printing. Lawai, Kauai: National [formerly Pacific] Tropical Botanical Garden, 1980, 1985.

Chisholm, Craig. *Hawaiian Hiking Trails.* 3rd ed. Lake Oswego, Oregon: The Fernglen Press, 1989.

Clark, John. *Hawaii's Secret Beaches, A Guide to Twenty-Four Hawaiian Beaches.* Honolulu: Tongg Publishing.

Day, A. Grove, and Carl Stroven, Eds. *A Hawaiian Reader.* Appleton-Century-Crofts, 1959. Reprint. Honolulu: Mutual Publishing Company, 1984.

Day, A. Grove. *Hawaii and Its People.* New York: Duell, Sloan and Pearce, 1955.

Epidemiology Branch, State Department of Health, State of Hawaii. "Leptospirosis in Hawaii." October 1, 1987.

Hargreaves, Dorothy, and Bob Hargreaves. *Hawaii Blossoms.* Japan: Dorothy and Bob Hargreaves, 1958. Reprint. Lahaina: Ross-Hargreaves.

——. *Tropical Trees of Hawaii.* Kailua: Hargreaves Company.

Haselwood, E.L., and G.G. Motter, Eds. *Handbook of Hawaiian Weeds.* 2nd ed., rev. and exp., ed. Robert T. Hirano. Honolulu: University of Hawaii Press, 1983.

Hawai'i Audubon Society. *Hawaii's Birds.* 4th ed. Honolulu: Hawai'i Audubon Society, 1989.

Joesting, Edward. *Hawaii, An Uncommon History.* New York: W.W. Norton & Company Inc., 1972.

Kirch, Patrick Vinton. *Feathered Gods and Fishhooks: An Introduction to Hawaiian Archaeology and Prehistory.* Honolulu: University of Hawaii Press, 1985.

Levi, Herbert W., and Lorna R. Levi. *Spiders and their Kin.* New York: Golden Press, 1987.

Macdonald, Gordon A., Agatin T. Abbott, and Frank L. Peterson. *Volcanoes in the Sea, the Geology of Hawaii.* 2nd ed. Honolulu: University of Hawaii Press, 1986.

Macdonald, Gordon A., and Will Kyselka. *Anatomy of an Island: A Geological History of Oahu.* Honolulu: Bishop Museum Press, 1967.

Malo, David. *Hawaiian Antiquities (Moolelo Hawaii)*. Translated by Dr. Nathaniel B. Emerson. 2nd ed. Honolulu: Bishop Museum, 1951.

> David Malo (1793(?)–1853), a native Hawaiian, was born and raised under the *kapu* system. He won the favor of the *alii* for his ability to memorize and recite their complicated genealogies. In his middle years, he became one of Hawaii's first outstanding native scholars by European criteria. He wrote this work some time around 1840.

Merlin, Mark David. *Hawaiian Coastal Plants and Scenic Shorelines*. 3rd printing. Honolulu: Oriental Publishing Co., 1986.

——. *Hawaiian Forest Plants*. 3rd ed. Honolulu: The Oriental Publishing Co., 1980.

Neal, Marie C. *In Gardens of Hawaii*. Rev. ed. Honolulu: Bishop Museum Press, 1965.

Pukui, Mary Kawena, Samuel H. Elbert, and Esther T. Mookini. *The Pocket Hawaiian Dictionary*. Honolulu: University of Hawaii Press, 1975.

——. *Place Names of Hawaii*. 2nd ed. 1974. Reprint. Honolulu: University of Hawaii Press, 1976.

Richardson, Jim, Ed. *The Honolulu Advertiser's Wildlife of Hawaii*. Honolulu: The Honolulu Advertiser, 1986.

Sohmer, S.H., and R. Gustafson. *Plants and Flowers of Hawai'i*. Honolulu: University of Hawaii Press, 1987.

Timmons, Grady. *Waikiki Beachboy*. Honolulu: Editions Limited, 1989.

Westervelt, W.D. *Myths and Legends of Hawaii*. (Selected and edited by A. Grove Day.) Honolulu: Mutual Publishing Company, 1987.

Woolliams, Keith. *A Guide to Hawaii's Popular Trees*. 2nd ed. Aiea, Hawaii: Island Heritage Publishing, 1988.

Appendix A. Camping and Other Accommodations on Oahu

For the visitor, camping on Oahu is for all practical purposes limited to car camping. A variety of state and county parks provide car camping opportunities. However, not all of them offer desirable camping because of their proximity to big cities and/or busy roads. Camping at such places is unsafe. Other parks are, as one authority put it, "extended outdoor homes for local residents where transient campers are not particularly welcome." Thefts and disturbances may be a problem. There are lots of people competing for Oahu's limited recreational resources! The campgrounds listed in this section are those that are deemed reasonably safe—*no guarantees.*

Car camping at the state parks is by permit only and for a maximum of 5 consecutive nights in any 30-day period. Permits are free. They are issued Monday through Friday, 8 A.M. to 4 P.M., at the Division of State Parks office in Honolulu. The person appearing to apply for the permit must provide proper identification for each person in the party who is 18 years old or older. "Proper identification" means a driver's license or a passport. You may also apply by mail *not less than seven days, but no more than thirty days,* in advance of your proposed trip by writing to the Division of State Parks. When applying by mail, include a copy of the proper identification for each person in the party who is 18 years old or older. Trailers and RVs are not permitted in Hawaii's state parks. For the state parks, except for Malaekahana State Recreation Area (below), write or call them at the address in "Getting Permits or Permission," pages 24–25.

State park car-camping day and time restrictions. On Oahu, state park campgrounds are *open only from Friday through Tuesday.* As of this writing, all state parks that allow camping are gated and have hours during which their gates are open: *7 a.m. to 7:45 p.m. from April 1 to Labor Day and from 7 a.m. to 6:45 p.m. from the day after Labor Day to March 31.* These hours apply whether or not the campground is open. The gates are closed at other times, and you cannot get in or out.

State park campground amenities generally include tables, barbecue grills, piped water, toilets, dressing rooms, and cold showers.

Malaekahana State Recreation Area. There is a housekeeping cabin at Malaekahana State Recreation Area in addition to the campground. Call 808-293-1736 to make reservations for the cabin or for a campsite there.

Car camping on Division of Forestry and Wildlife lands. At present, there are no car campgrounds in areas managed by the Division of Forestry and Wildlife. There is some camping along certain trails, and there are some trail shelters in hunting areas. With all due respect, the camping possibilities I saw did not strike me as being worth a *visitor's* trouble. Contact the Division of Forestry and Wildlife for information at the address in "Getting Permits or Permission," pages 24–25.

Car camping at county parks. Permits are required for the county's car campgrounds. You can get information about and permits for the county parks from:

Department of Parks and Recreation, City and County of Honolulu
650 South King Street
Honolulu, HI 96813
808-523-4523 (recreation information number)

They prefer that you come in in person for information and permits. The building is near South King and Alapai streets, and the county parks office is on the ground floor near the elevators.

Car-camping summary table. The following table summarizes the better car-camping opportunities on Oahu, according to one source. I haven't car-camped on Oahu myself.

Name	Type	Nearest Town	Amenities; Restrictions
Kaiaka	State	Haleiwa	See above. Beach
Keaiwa *Heiau*	State	Aiea, Honolulu	See above. Low-mountain area with possible rain, cold nights. Fine loop trail (Trip 34)
Malaekahana	State	Kahuku	See above. Beach
Sand Island	State	Honolulu	See above. Beach
Waimanalo Bay	State	Waimanalo	See above. Beach
Bellows Field	County	Waimanalo	Beach
Kahana Bay	County	Kaaawa, Punaluu	Beach. Near Trips 5 and 6
Kualoa	County	Kaneohe	Beach
Makapuu	County	Waimanalo	Beach
Mokuleia	County	Waialua	Beach. Near Trips 39–41

Other non-hotel accommodations. Bed-and-breakfast accommodations are widely available throughout the islands; they're my choice when I'm not backpacking. Try agencies like Bed and Breakfast Hawaii (800-733-1632) and Bed and Breakfast Honolulu (800-288-4666); both have rooms statewide. Military personnel will find vacation cottages at Bellows Air Force Base on Oahu and should inquire about similar units at other military installations.

Appendix B.
Hikes You Won't Find Here and Why

You may have read articles on the following hikes, seen them mentioned in other books, or noticed them on maps. Some of them are in this book but under different names. Some of these routes are closed because landowners no longer give permission to hike them. Development has interfered with access to some routes. Other trails have become unsafe; I firmly believe that a vacation is not enhanced by a trip to the emergency room that you could have missed by avoiding a dangerous route. I have deliberately excluded routes that require rappels. Finally, I judge that some are just too remote *and* too boring to be worth your time.

Getting permission may be another obstacle. You'll be able to get permits from agencies and landowners that maintain regular offices and office hours. If you have to telephone to set up some kind of appointment, or just to find out where to go to get the permit, you may wind up playing telephone-tag. Your vacation time on Hawaii is too precious for you to hang around the telephone for hours or days, hoping to intercept the return call. I suggest you not bother with trips that require multiple permits or permits you can't get by going to a place of business. Trip 37 is an exception: you turn the first permit in for another on the spot, and that's reasonable.

Check with organized hiking groups (see Appendix C) for a possible opportunity to visit one of these trails with people who are familiar with the area and its difficulties and who can get the necessary landowner permission for you. I've listed some hiking groups in Appendix C.

Trails in the Koolaus in general. You'll see on your maps many more trails in the Koolaus than are included in this book. There's a reason for that. Many of the once-well-trod trails in the Koolaus are closed because they've become unsafe (budget cuts have reduced trail maintenance), or because access has been cut off by development, or because land ownership has changed. For example:

- *Manana Trail.* The first part is *very* overused and crisscrossed by use trails. Motorized dirt bikes illegally use the first part of the trail. The rest of the trail is in poor condition as far as I went. It marches along a muddy ridgetop, up one steep knob, down to a little saddle, up another steep knob....One knob is so steep and its trail segment so eroded that you must rappel up/down one side of it! After hiking this trail, I understood why our friend and Oahu native Ken Luke said of trails in the Koolaus, "Ugh! All I remember about hiking in the Koolaus is going up and down and up and down forever." The nearby Waimano Trail (Trips 35 and 36) is a far better choice as of this writing.

• *Lanipo (Mauumae) Trail*. This well-known trail was once thought to be on public land. A recent investigation revealed that it is partly on public land and partly on private land—the boundary apparently runs up the middle of the trail! Neither party is taking responsibility for the trail, I'm told, so it has deteriorated considerably. You are technically trespassing if you hike it.

• *Wiliwilinui Trail*. Public access has been cut off by recent development. The Division of Forestry and Wildlife hopes to be able to provide a new public access some day, but it hasn't happened yet.

• *Maunawili Ditch Trail*. I've chosen not to include this pleasant but unremarkable trail for now. It's on the western outskirts of Waimanalo and is accessed from the Waimanalo end of the new Maunawili Demonstration Trail (see Trip 29). Briefly, it doodles through the rainforest behind Waimanalo, beginning from a point about 1/4 mile up the Maunawili Demonstration Trail from Waikupanaha Street. The Maunawili Ditch Trail rejoins the Waimanalo street system near the end of Mahiku Place in 2 1/4 miles. From there, hikers can close a loop by walking 3/4 mile, up Mahiku Place to its junction with Waikupanaha Street and then turning right a short distance to the Waimanalo trailhead, for a moderate hike, 3 1/4 miles and 200 feet of elevation gain, on the *Koko Head* topo (trail not shown on topo).

• *Kolowalu Trail*. No parking provided. Boring and buggy. The excruciatingly steep second half is almost like climbing a ladder. You ought

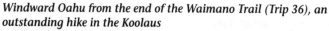

Windward Oahu from the end of the Waimano Trail (Trip 36), an outstanding hike in the Koolaus

to at least have some views to enjoy as you struggle upward, but the vegetation is so dense you can't see much. Try the lovely Puu Pia Trail (Trip 13), which starts from the same trailhead. Or try the scenic Waahila Ridge Trail (Trip 12), just one ridge over and a lot more fun.

• *East Honolulu-Kuliouou*. Three relatively new trails have been opened in the East Honolulu-Kuliouou area, between Diamond Head and Haunama Bay. They are the Hawaiiloa Ridge, Kuliouou Valley, and Kuliouou Ridge trails. Alas, I can't recommend them to visitors from the mainland. They're hard to get to and very hard to find: road construction in the area has had the area's roads torn up for years, and the confusion and traffic are nightmarish. Also, they're unrewarding: you struggle uphill to ridgetops only to find that dense, non-native vegetation hides the views you'd expected to find.

Hanauma Bay. This is a state underwater park. Its gate opens at 7 A.M. except on Wednesdays; Hanauma Bay is closed Wednesday mornings. That's a concession to the fact that Hanauma Bay is an ecosystem in crisis. Why? Overuse. Commercial and ecological concerns clash here. By midday, its once crystal-clear waters are murky with sand tossed up by hundreds of feet and with soggy crumbs of fish food. Dust kicked up by cars in the parking lot and urine also foul the water. So I can't recommend that you contribute to Hanauma's problems by *hiking* there, too. Also, I judge that the wave-cut shelves along the edge of the bay (and adjacent areas) are too dangerous to hike on. Such shelves are slippery and sharp, and a big wave could wash you off and sweep you into a dangerous situation. Visit Hanauma Bay as early as possible in the morning in order to enjoy the snorkeling before the crowds overwhelm the bay. Or seek out other snorkeling opportunities; there are many on windward Oahu. Other considerations:

• *Halona Blowhole*. You can easily see the Halona Blowhole from a well-designed roadside turnout a little north of Hanauma Bay.

• *Toilet Bowl*. Interesting to see, but I can't recommend jumping into it. The Toilet Bowl is a natural hole in the stony shelf edging a tiny "sub-cove" a little southeast of the main part of Hanauma Bay. Water surges into the hole and fills it, then drains out leaving the water level inside the hole well below its rim. Swimmers in the Toilet Bowl can get out only when the surge fills the hole. You can get to the Toilet Bowl by walking seaward on some old 4WD roads from the highest overview point provided by the walkways around the Hanauma Bay parking lot. Where the roads peel off left and right, bear to your left toward a gully, rather than to your right toward Hanauma Bay. As you near the edge of the gully, you'll spot a trail-of-use below you. Pick it up by contouring around to the end of the gully and follow it seaward to the Toilet Bowl.

Koko Head. Koko Head is off-limits now. The FAA equipment that guides your plane safely in and out of Honolulu Airport sits atop Koko Head. Try the superb views from Diamond Head (Trip 30) and from Makapuu State Wayside (Trip 10) instead.

Koko Crater. You can enjoy the botanical garden on Trip 11. The job corps center no longer allows hikers to pass through their property, which cuts off access to the rim of the crater.

Puu Piei. Reportedly requires the use of cables. Who needs it? Enjoy the area as described in Trips 5 and 6 instead.

Laie. Not worth the trouble. Permit required; hard to obtain. The dirt road to the trailhead is in such terrible condition that 4WD vehicles may be able to go partway, but some segments demand a dirt bike—or the Ankle Express. So you must walk the 2 or so miles to the trailhead now, which would be okay if the trail itself weren't in appalling condition: extremely narrow and overgrown, with steep dropoffs on one side and a steep upslope on the other. If you're in the area and want to hike, Trips 1, 2, and 3 are far more enjoyable, and you don't need a permit for them.

Poamoho Ridge, Valley. Poamoho Ridge requires permission from a sugar company, a fruit canner, and the Army—which wants you to apply three weeks in advance. The sugar company and the fruit canner want only 24 hours notice. It's enough to make a hiker feel unwanted! Poamoho Valley is no longer listed by the Division of Wildlife and Forestry as a possible hike. Reportedly trailless, I wouldn't recommend it anyway.

Dupont Trail (Mt. Kaala). Too much trouble for a bad trail. Lots of people are intrigued by Mt. Kaala because it's the highest point on Oahu. The bad news is that the current public route to Mt. Kaala is reported to be one of the most dangerous "trail" routes in Hawaii . Avoid it unless you take it as an organized trip with an experienced, reputable guide. It requires permission from a sugar company and a ranch. You may have to play phone-tag with the ranch. Both want 24 hours' notice. The good news is that trail organizations are negotiating with the military for public access to Mt. Kaala by a much safer route. The negotiations are said to be going well. I think it's worth waiting for.

Waimea Falls Park, Waimea Arboretum. I remember when this area was undeveloped and free. Now it's been developed into a commercial attraction, and the entrance fee is quite hefty. I find the change unfortunate—taking a beautiful, free, natural feature and turning it into a tourist attraction—so I can't recommend this place, though some readers tell me they have enjoyed it very much and the arboretum is excellent. I'll stick to the public botanical gardens, thank you, and to reasonably-priced attractions like the Waikiki Aquarium and the Honolulu Zoo, all of which may be enjoyed for a total cost that's probably close to the price of one ticket into the commercial park/arboretum.

Appendix C.
Groups Offering Organized Hikes

Here are some groups you may want to hike with. Write well in advance to find out what hikes they will be offering when you are on Oahu and whether visitors may join a particular hike. I have included only the street address or post office box and the zip code, because all addresses' city and state data are the same: Honolulu, HI. You may need to reserve a place on the hike you're interested in.

Group Number	Street or P.O. Box	Zip Code	Telephone
Friends of Foster Garden (see Trip 33)	50 N. Vineyard Blvd.	96817	808-537-1708
Hawaii Nature Center (see Trip 18)	2131 Makiki Heights Dr.	96822	808-955-0100
Hawaiian Trail and Mountain Club	P.O. Box 2238	96804	—
Lyon Arboretum Association (see Trips 14 and 15)	3860 Manoa Rd.	96822	808-988-7378
Sierra Club, Honolulu Group	P.O. Box 2577	96803	—
Waikiki Aquarium	2777 Kalakaua Ave.	96815	808-923-9741

Appendix D. One Visitor's Suggestions About Driving in Honolulu

I found getting into, out of, and around in Honolulu so frustrating that I'm adding some hard-learned driving suggestions for you right here. Review these suggestions with a good Honolulu street map in front of you (they won't mean a thing otherwise):

Getting out of Waikiki ("basic escape route from Waikiki"). From wherever your hotel may be, find your way to Ala Wai Boulevard, which is one-way going *northwest* (toward downtown Honolulu). Keep to the right, looking for McCully Street. McCully is fairly easy to spot, as it's your first opportunity to cross the Ala Wai Canal as you're going northwest on Ala Wai Boulevard. Turn right at McCully Street, crossing the Ala Wai Canal. You are now technically out of Waikiki and headed roughly northeast toward intersections with Kapiolani Boulevard (which comes up almost immediately) and more importantly with:

• ***South King Street*** *for trailheads east of Waikiki along the Kalanianaole Highway (Highway 72).* Turn right at South King Street, which soon becomes the *eastbound* Lunalilo Freeway (H1) and then shortly becomes the *eastbound* Kalanianaole Highway. ("Kalanianaole" is pronounced "ka-la-ni-a-na-O-le.")

• ***Westbound Lunalilo Freeway (H1)*** *for most trailheads north and west of Honolulu (such as Pearl City, trailheads off the Pali and Kamehameha highways, and Kaena Point; also for the airport).* As you continue northeast on McCully, watch the lane you're in so you don't get scooped off to the left or right before you cross *over* the freeway. Cross the freeway on a narrow bridge. At the foot of the bridge over the freeway, follow signs for a quick left on Metcalfe that leads to a westbound freeway on-ramp.

• ***Dole Street*** *for Waahila Ridge.* Just after you cross Metcalfe Street, make a right turn onto Dole Street.

• ***Wilder Avenue*** *for trailheads in Manoa Valley and for the Roundtop-Tantalus area* (such as Makiki Valley and Manoa Cliffs). The next intersection after Dole/Metcalfe as you continue up McCully is Wilder. Turn left on Wilder.

Getting back into Waikiki. Here are some routes I used with fair success—and one disaster:

• *An Excellent Route from the freeway eastbound but west of the Punahou Street offramp (airport; most trailheads north and west of Honolulu).* From the west or north, get on the Lunalilo Freeway (H1) *eastbound.* Get off at Punahou Street and get ready to make a wide right turn at the next intersection, Beretania Street. After your wide right onto Beretania, scoot quickly over into one of the leftmost two lanes in preparation for a left turn onto Kalakaua Avenue. Turn left onto Kalakaua. Follow Kalakaua into Waikiki.

• *From Wilder Street eastbound but west of Punahou Street-Manoa Road (Tantalus-Roundtop area, Manoa Valley, etc.).* Wilder Street eastbound intersects Punahou Street about where it changes to Manoa Road. Turn right on Punahou-Manoa and follow the directions to Kalakaua Avenue given in the paragraph above.

• *From the Kalanianaole Highway westbound.* I never found a satisfactory route. One not-very-satisfactory route is to get off southbound on Kilauea Avenue, following it as it swings west and becomes a small residential street. Turn left on 18th Street and follow it to Diamond Head Road. Turn right on Diamond Head Road and follow it around the north side of Diamond Head, past the entrance into Diamond Head State Monument. Diamond Head Road merges with Monsarrat Avenue on the northwest side of the cone. Monsarrat becomes one-way the wrong way at Paki Avenue, so turn right on Paki and follow it north-northwest as it crosses Kapahulu Avenue and merges with Ala Wai Boulevard (one-way northwest). Grope your way back to your hotel from Ala Wai Boulevard.

• *Don't try to get back into Waikiki from the east by way of Kapiolani Boulevard!* My experience was that Kapiolani became one-way eastbound—the wrong way—at just the wrong time, leaving me to wander through back streets.

Appendix E. How I Got Distances, Elevations, Times, and Trail Maps

I estimated distances primarily by time, knowing that I hike 2 miles/hour. I compared the distances I got by time with distance values supplied by the agencies in charge of the trails. In a few cases, I also had distance data from plots I'd made from the topos. When those distances were close, I felt satisfied with the distance I'd estimated by time. I rounded the distances off to the nearest 1/4 or 1/3 mile.

I got many driving distances by rental-car odometer. When I had not started from Waikiki, I added or subtracted the distance from my starting point to Waikiki. I found that in a number of cases, particularly the longer drives, I did not get consistent odometer data: when there were multiple routes between my starting point and the trailhead—for example, between Waikiki and Hauula—I managed unintentionally to take almost all of them on repeated drives. In those cases, I used data from the University of Hawaii Press map of Hawaii or calculated the mileage from the topos.

I determined elevation from topos and with an altimeter. Where I had altimeter data, I looked for close correspondence between those values, topo values, and any values supplied by the agency in charge of the trail.

Trail times are based on the time I actually spent in motion on the trail.

I made the original trail maps by first scanning relevant pieces of the applicable map(s)—usually the USGS topos—into a computer. I put the resulting digitized topo information that applied to a trip or a set of trips into the bottom layer of a multiple-layer electronic drawing. I then traced selected topo information from the bottom layer onto a transparent electronic top layer. I left out the elevation contours because they make these gray-scale maps far too cluttered and they would have taken me too long to draw. I added, deleted, or modified topo information that I knew had changed. My choices of conventions for trails, roads, boundaries, etc., primarily reflect the software's capabilities. For this second edition, I updated the trail maps with newer, more capable software.

Some trails on Oahu do not appear at all on the topos or in usable form on any official agency map. For them, I approximated the route based on field notes and sketches and any agency or landowner information I could find.

Acknowledgements

My husband Ed Schwartz has supported me in word, in deed, and in bank account as I abandoned an aerospace career for the hiking trail.

For sending useful information to and answering questions from a total stranger, I thank the people at the Division of Forestry and Wildlife, Oahu District; the Division of State Parks, Oahu District; and the Hawaii Visitors Bureau, Los Angeles office.

Thanks to Tom Bionde and Jeannine Poling of Laie for dinners, showers, and shared laughter. Thanks also to Lance Amero of Pearl City, whom I met on Mauna Kea on the Big Island, and to his family; they shared one of their favorite hikes with Ed and me. My hostess in Kailua, Vicki Patterson, recommended the Keolu Hills hike (Trip 9). Special thanks also to Mrs. Joanne Flannery, another one of my hostesses in Kailua, for her advice and comments.

Ken Luke and Wellington Kao, both Oahu natives now "exiled" to California, shared their memories of Oahu and of their favorite hiking trails and childhood haunts. Dan Masaki, born on Kauai and another "exile" on the mainland, shared many stories of Hawaii, including the story of Benny Kanahele (Trip 30).

I'm grateful to Dave Hill and his fellow staff members at the Hawaii Nature Center in Makiki Valley on Oahu. Dave answered a number of questions, and I took advantage of the Hawaii Nature Center's program of scheduled and very enjoyable hikes.

Thanks to Rabbit Kekai, who shared his anecdotes about and insights on Waikiki with my friend and me (Trip 32). Waikiki has been transformed almost beyond recognition, but Rabbit remains a beachboy in the best sense: to paraphrase Grady Timmons, not a professional but one who lives "for the ocean and for a lifestyle centered on the beach."

Thanks to an inspiring group of men and women—"We're just a bunch of retirees who get together for a couple of hikes on Wednesdays"—whom I happened to meet on the trail, and especially to one of their members, Billie, who identified a number of plants for me.

I am very much indebted to Jerry Schad. His use of icons to help summarize hikes in his outstanding *Afoot and Afield. . .* series of guides for Southern California (available from Wilderness Press) inspired me to create and use icons in this book and in its predecessors, *Kauai Trails, Maui Trails*, and *Hawaii Trails*.

The quotation on page 18 from *Leaving Home* by Garrison Keillor, copyright © 1987 by Garrison Keillor, is used by permission of Viking Penguin, a division of Penguin Books USA Inc.

I hope I have accurately and adequately reflected the information these people, and many others, provided directly or indirectly. Any misunderstanding or errors are my responsibility.

—*K.M.*

Index